Annual Recipes 2019

Better Homes & Gardens®

Meredith. Consumer Marketing
Des Moines, Iowa

MARBLED CARAMEL
APPLES
Recipe on page 232

from the editor

At *Better Homes & Gardens®* magazine our goal is to help you solve the daily dilemma of making delicious, healthful food for your family—and staying inspired and engaged while you're at it.

What's for dinner? It's the perennial question we get asked (or ask ourselves) every day. When we talk to you about how you address that issue in your own homes, the answer is most often, "Whatever my family will eat." Accordingly, many of you have developed a rotating cast of guaranteed hits: baked or grilled chicken, spaghetti, tacos, meat loaf, burgers, pizza. There aren't really any surprises there. And I agree: Don't mess with success, right? Then again, don't we sometimes get a little bored? If so, see "Dinner in America" on page 121. We took tried-and-true recipes and refreshed them with spins on traditional flavors, creative cooking techniques, and a handful of new ingredients.

When I was a kid, my mom's favorite dishes included chicken and dumplings, beef stew, steak fingers (ask a Texan), and pot roast. During the summer, Saturdays were special because my parents invited guests over for a barbecue and homemade ice cream, but weeknights we mostly ate from a roster of tried-and-trues. Mom read magazines like *Better Homes & Gardens*, I think, partly as an escape from the demands of running a household of six, but also for new recipe ideas.

This book—a collection of all of the recipes that have appeared in *Better Homes & Gardens* magazine throughout the year—gives you the same thing my mom was looking for. We're sure that as you page through it, something will catch your eye and draw you to the kitchen—whether it's something entirely unfamiliar or an intriguing new take on an old favorite.

Stephen Orr, Editor in Chief
Better Homes & Gardens. magazine

Better Homes & Gardens

Annual Recipes 2019

Our seal assures you that every recipe in *Better Homes & Gardens. Annual Recipes 2019* has been tested in the Better Homes & Gardens. Test Kitchen. This means that each recipe is practical and reliable, and it meets our high standards of taste appeal. We guarantee your satisfaction with this book for as long as you own it.

All of us at Meredith Consumer Marketing are dedicated to providing you with information and ideas to enhance your home. We welcome your comments and suggestions. Write to us at: Meredith Consumer Marketing, 1716 Locust St., Des Moines, IA 50309-3023.

Pictured on front cover:
Apricot Skillet Pie, recipe on page 191.

MEREDITH CONSUMER MARKETING
Consumer Marketing Product Director: Daniel Fagan
Consumer Marketing Product Manager: Max Daily
Consumer Products Marketing Manager: Kylie Dazzo

WATERBURY PUBLICATIONS, INC.
Editorial Director: Lisa Kingsley
Associate Editor: Tricia Bergman
Creative Director: Ken Carlson
Associate Design Director: Doug Samuelson
Production Assistant: Mindy Samuelson
Contributing Copy Editors: Terri Fredrickson, Peg Smith
Contributing Indexer: Mary Williams

BETTER HOMES & GARDENS® MAGAZINE
Editor in Chief: Stephen Orr
Food Editor: Jan Miller

MEREDITH CORPORATION
Chairman: Stephen M. Lacy
Vice Chairman: Mell Meredith Frazier

In Memoriam: E.T. Meredith III (1933–2003)

**CHICKEN-APPLE
BURGERS**
Recipe on page 236

CHEF'S SALAD
Recipe on page 81

ANTICIPATION: *The act of looking forward or the visualization of a future state or event.*

We live in the age when waiting is avoided, prevented even. However, there is much to gain from anticipation—especially when it's about food. In spring we eagerly watch for slender asparagus stalks; in late summer we yearn for the first juicy ripe peaches; in autumn, crisp apples and pumpkins. We latch on to recipes that spark our appetites, then await that first taste—the reward for making something delicious.

In *Better Homes & Gardens Annual Recipes 2019* you'll find many delicious recipes, featuring fresh ingredients, familiar tastes as well as adventurous international flavors, comfort foods, updated standbys, and hearty plant-based dishes. We hope this vast collection provides you with much to anticipate.

LOOK FOR

MONTHLY FEATURES Sometimes you just need a nudge to get out of your culinary rut, and we're happy to help. Every month cookbook authors, popular bloggers, and *BH&G* food specialists share recipes that we hope not only become family favorites but also serve as a springboard for your own creativity: warming veg-centric soups from author Lindsay Maitland; updated Seder dishes from three next-gen foodies; and beautiful recipes showcasing rhubarb—both sweet and savory—from the *Better Homes & Gardens* Test Kitchen. Entertaining takes a turn with Super Bowl and Kentucky Derby Day nibbles, blogger Kate Ramos goes modern with Mexican fare, and cookbook author Julia Turshen shares her relaxed approach to hosting a party. These features and more will inspire you to seek new-to-you foods and flavors.

HOW TO COOK A little cooking knowledge can go a long way. *BH&G* food specialists and other food pros teach the hows and whys of a variety of techniques. In February, a lesson on braising: Take the time and turn short ribs, pork shoulder, chicken thighs, and root vegetables into tender and flavorful dishes. Master the Easter ham in April, then enjoy recipes using the plentiful leftovers. In July, cooking class moves outdoors—smoking on your backyard grill is the lesson, and

the recipes make it easy. October brings a step-by-step class in pan-searing, a technique that adds dimension—deeply caramelized crust, juicy interior, and a velvety sauce.

GREAT STARTS Breakfast—to break the fast of the night before—is the favorite meal of the day for many, and can be simple or lavish, sweet or savory. One thing it should always be is delicious, and this new feature showcases reimagined favorites, like Steak and Eggs Breakfast Pizza, on-the-go Fruit and Nut Freezer Oatmeal Cups, tender Honey-Lemon Cottage Cheese Pancakes, and revamped Cheesy Grits Bowl with hearty topping options.

FAST & FRESH Weeknight dinners need to be equally easy and scrumptious, with a healthy dose of fresh. This tasty collection of recipes combines lean proteins, hearty grains, and fresh fruits and vegetables with quick-to-the-table cooking techniques. Tempt your family with Meyer Lemon and Rosemary Chicken Salad, Grilled Moroccan Beef Kabobs with Yogurt Sauce, and Sausage with Skillet Potatoes and Buttered Cabbage. If you're not familiar with cooking food en papillote, a cooking lesson awaits with Parchment-Baked Halibut with Thyme and Olives. Cook with confidence—these tested recipes work every time.

JAM-FILLED HAND PIES
Recipe on page 33

contents

98

144

265

HIBISCUS PUNCH
Recipe on page 212

MEDITERRANEAN
THREE-BEAN
SALAD
Recipe on page 184

**POZOLE WITH
PINTO BEANS AND
QUESO FRESCO**
Recipe on page 24

january

The new year beckons healthful eating—plus comfort foods. These veg-forward soups and fresh entrées offer both. An added attraction: confidently building cheese boards for easy entertaining.

15

16

21

great starts

SECRET INGREDIENT

Cottage cheese in the batter results in a tender texture and a protein boost for lightly lemony pancakes.

HONEY-LEMON COTTAGE CHEESE PANCAKES

Added moisture equals delicate texture. Pour small amounts of batter on a hot griddle and use a gentle hand to flip them—only once.

TOTAL TIME 30 min.

6	eggs, lightly beaten
1	16-oz. carton small curd cottage cheese
2	Tbsp. honey
2	Tbsp. unsalted butter, melted
2	tsp. vanilla
1	tsp. lemon zest
1½	cups all-purpose flour
1	tsp. baking powder
1	tsp. baking soda
½	tsp. salt
	Butter, maple syrup, and/or berries

1. In a large bowl stir to combine eggs, cottage cheese, honey, butter, vanilla, and zest. Add flour, baking powder, baking soda, and salt. Stir just until moistened. (Batter will be slightly lumpy.)
2. Pour about ¼ cup batter onto a hot, lightly greased griddle or heavy skillet. Cook over medium heat 2 minutes; turn over when top is bubbly and edges are slightly dry. Cook an additional 2 minutes or until both sides are brown. Keep warm in a 200°F oven while cooking remaining pancakes. Serve warm with butter, maple syrup, and/or berries. Makes 4 servings.
PER SERVING *341 cal, 11 g fat, 205 mg chol, 792 mg sodium, 43 g carb, 1 g fiber, 17 g sugars, 17 g pro.*

A STACK OF PUFFY PANCAKES, WITH CRISP EDGES AND TENDER CENTERS, WILL CONVINCE YOU THAT COTTAGE CHEESE IS THE IDEAL STAND-IN FOR TYPICAL MILK.

entertaining
BUILD A BOARD

Eager to serve a cheese tray—yet staggered by choosing from the vast variety of cheeses? With three major milks used to make cheese (cow, sheep, and goat) and from literally hundreds of cheeses produced—intimidation is understandable. Here's help, by way of narrowing selections to one of three themes: Classic, Pickled, or Antipasto.

CLASSIC BOARD

This collection covers some main categories of cheese, including a variety of milk sources and flavors. Pairing additions are kept simple.

1 Parmesan Hard aged cheese with dense, crystalline texture and fruit-forward nutty flavor. Parmigiano-Reggiano and Grana Padano are good alternatives.

2 Chèvre (goat cheese) Tart and mellow with spreadable texture. Look for a fresh chèvre log or a mild, soft-ripened option.

3 Rustic-Style Blue This mild blue has smooth, crumbly texture and almost sweet flavor. Try Point Reyes.

4 Havarti Semisoft cow's milk cheese with smooth texture and buttery finish.

5 Brie Soft-ripened cow's milk cheese with thin rind, fruity flavor, and butterlike texture.

6 Aged Cheddar Crumbly with sharp, salty flavor. Kerrygold is our go-to brand.

PAIR WITH Fresh and/or dried fruit, marcona almonds, fruit preserves, crackers, and toasted baguette slices.

LET CHEESE STAND AT ROOM TEMP ABOUT AN HOUR BEFORE SERVING. COLD CHEESE HAS MUTED FLAVORS.

PICKLED BOARD

For a board that includes pickles and olives, choose a few mild cheeses and one or two aged cheeses with strong flavors to play off the piquant tang of the condiments.

1 Sharp Cheddar This salty-sweet semihard cheese has full flavor.

2 Fresh Mozzarella A tender cow's milk cheese with mild dairy-forward flavor.

3 Triple-Creme Brie Added cream gives this mild, spreadable cheese rich texture.

4 American Blue Strong blue-veined cheese with crumbly texture and notes of lemon.

5 Comté Dense, slightly grainy cheese with toasted flavor.

PAIR WITH Pickles and pickled vegetables, such as asparagus, carrots, peppers, beets; sauerkraut; kimchi; marinated olives; and Italian breadsticks.

ANTIPASTO BOARD

Half cheese, half cured meat, this board easily does double duty as light dinner. Choose bold cheeses that stand up to salty charcuterie.

1 Ash-Ripened Goat Cheese Edible vegetable ash adds smoky, herbal flavor to this goat's milk cheese, which has a dual texture of smooth soft-ripened edges with fresh, slightly chalky core.

2 Stilton English-style cow's milk blue with semisoft texture and strong, almost spiced flavor.

3 Manchego Spanish sheep's milk cheese with grassy, nutty flavor and firm, buttery texture.

4 White Cheddar Aged cow's milk cheese that can range from mild to sharp. The longer the aging, the sharper the cheddar.

PAIR WITH Cured meats (prosciutto, soppressata, Calabrese, and capocollo), marinated vegetables and artichokes, whole grain mustard, toasted baguette slices, flatbreads, and crackers.

FAST & FRESH

Easy, delicious recipes for a better dinner tonight.

SPICED-BEEF SLOPPY JOES

Garam masala—a popular Indian spice blend—usually includes cinnamon, cardamom, cloves, cumin, coriander, nutmeg, and peppercorns, although blends vary by region. This blend is equally delicious with ground lamb, which can be swapped for the beef.

TOTAL TIME 30 min.

- 1¼ lb. ground beef
- 1 cup onion, chopped
- 2 cloves garlic, minced
- 1 Tbsp. fresh ginger, grated
- 1½ tsp. garam masala
- ½ tsp. ground cumin
- ¼ tsp. salt
- 3 tomatoes, chopped
- ½ cup frozen peas
- 2 limes, halved
- 3 Tbsp. tomato paste
- ¼ cup chopped fresh cilantro
- 4 sesame buns, split and toasted

1. In a large skillet cook beef, onion, and garlic over medium heat until meat is browned; drain fat. Add ginger, garam masala, cumin, and salt. Cook and stir 1 minute. Add tomatoes. Cook and stir 5 minutes or until tomatoes break down. Add frozen peas. Cook and stir 1 minute. Squeeze juice from limes (about 3 Tbsp.) into beef. Add tomato paste and cilantro; stir to combine. Heat through.
2. Serve Sloppy Joes in buns with additional cilantro. Makes 4 servings.
PER SERVING *593 cal, 30 g fat, 97 mg chol, 921 mg sodium, 47 g carb, 5 g fiber, 11 g sugars, 33 g pro.*

**ROASTED FISH
AND FENNEL WITH
GRAPEFRUIT SALSA**

ROASTED FISH AND FENNEL WITH GRAPEFRUIT SALSA

The mild anise flavor of fennel fronds adds dimension to the quick-to-make salsa. Store as you would any fresh herb: Wrap in a lightly damp paper towel and place in a resealable plastic bag in the refrigerator up to 3 days.

TOTAL TIME 30 min.

2 medium fennel bulbs, halved, cored, and cut into thin wedges, plus 2 Tbsp. chopped fronds
3 Tbsp. olive oil
  Salt
4 1-inch-thick firm whitefish fillets, such as cod, grouper, or hake
  Black pepper
1 large pink grapefruit, peeled and sectioned
2 Tbsp. coarsely chopped flat-leaf parsley
2 Tbsp. finely chopped shallot
1 Tbsp. white wine vinegar

1. Preheat oven to 425°F. Line a shallow baking pan with foil. Add fennel wedges. Toss with 1 Tbsp. oil; season with salt. Arrange in a single layer. Roast 12 to 15 minutes or until starting to brown.
2. Turn fennel and move to one side of pan. Add fish. Drizzle with 1 Tbsp. oil. Season with salt and black pepper. Bake 10 to 12 minutes or until fish flakes easily.
3. Meanwhile, in a small bowl combine chopped fennel fronds, grapefruit, parsley, shallot, vinegar, and remaining 1 Tbsp. oil; season with salt and black pepper. Serve fish with roasted fennel and salsa. Makes 4 servings.
PER SERVING *321 cal, 13 g fat, 83 mg chol, 319 mg sodium, 18 g carb, 5 g fiber, 11 g sugars, 34 g pro.*

SAUSAGE WITH SKILLET POTATOES AND BUTTERED CABBAGE

SAUSAGE WITH SKILLET POTATOES AND BUTTERED CABBAGE

Savoy cabbage is favored for its thin leaves and delicate texture. Napa or green cabbage are good substitutes.

TOTAL TIME 35 min.

4 Tbsp. vegetable oil
12 oz. cooked chicken-apple sausage links
3 Tbsp. butter
1½ lb. Yukon gold potatoes, cut into ¾-inch cubes
1 lb. savoy cabbage head, roughly chopped
½ cup mixed fresh herbs, such as dill, parsley, and/or chives, coarsely chopped
¼ tsp. salt
¼ tsp. black pepper
3 Tbsp. cider vinegar
1 Tbsp. coarse ground mustard

1. In a 12-inch skillet heat 1 Tbsp. oil over medium-high heat. Add sausage. Cook 7 to 10 minutes or until heated through, stirring occasionally. Transfer sausage to a platter; cover to keep warm. Add 1 Tbsp. butter to drippings; add potatoes. Reduce heat to medium. Cook, without stirring, 5 minutes or until golden brown on bottom. Stir. Cook 10 to 15 minutes or until tender and browned, stirring occasionally. Transfer to platter; cover to keep warm.
2. Heat remaining 2 Tbsp. butter in skillet. Add cabbage. Cook and stir 3 to 5 minutes or until tender yet still bright green. Transfer to platter; sprinkle with herbs, salt, and pepper.
3. In a small bowl whisk together remaining 3 Tbsp. oil, vinegar, and mustard. Pour over sausage, potatoes, and cabbage. Makes 4 servings.
PER SERVING *525 cal, 30 g fat, 83 mg chol, 678 mg sodium, 48 g carb, 5 g fiber, 14 g sugars, 19 g pro.*

CURRIED SWEET
POTATO SOUP

SOUP SEASON

The veg-centric soups in Lindsay Maitland Hunt's cookbook, *Healthyish,* bridge the gap between light meals to reset during the holidays and the comfort foods craved during winter.

CURRIED SWEET POTATO SOUP

Pumpkin seed oil, toasted seeds, and cilantro add flavor, crunch, and appeal.

HANDS-ON TIME 25 min.
TOTAL TIME 45 min.

¼ cup olive oil
2 onions, chopped (about 2 cups)
1½ tsp. kosher salt
1 tsp. freshly ground black pepper
4 cloves garlic, chopped
2 tsp. curry powder
1 tsp. ground coriander
8 cups stock from Whole Poached Chicken with Bonus Stock, page 27; purchased chicken stock, or vegetable broth
3 large sweet potatoes (3 lb.), peeled and cut into ¾-inch pieces
2 large carrots, peeled and chopped
1 Tbsp. fresh lime juice
Toppings, such as fresh cilantro leaves, toasted pumpkin seeds, and/or pumpkin seed oil or olive oil

1. Heat oil in a 6-qt. stock pot or Dutch oven over medium heat. Add onions, 1 tsp. salt, and pepper. Cook, stirring often, until onions are translucent and soft, 10 to 12 minutes. Stir in garlic, curry powder, and coriander; cook until garlic is fragrant, about 1 minute more.
2. Add stock, sweet potatoes, and carrots. Cook, covered, over high heat until boiling. Reduce heat. Simmer, stirring occasionally, until sweet potatoes are fork-tender, 20 to 25 minutes.
3. Puree soup in batches in a blender or with an immersion blender. Stir in lime juice and remaining ½ tsp. salt.
4. Serve with cilantro, pumpkin seeds, and/or pumpkin seed oil. Makes 6 servings.
PER SERVING *477 cal, 18 g fat, 10 mg chol, 886 mg sodium, 67 g carb, 9 g fiber, 18 g sugars, 14 g pro.*

THE SWEET SIDE OF SWEET POTATOES OFTEN OVERPOWERS OTHER FLAVORS IN A DISH. TO PUSH THIS VELVETY POTATO AND CARROT SOUP SQUARELY INTO SAVORY TERRITORY, LINDSAY ADDS CARAMELIZED ONIONS, LOTS OF GARLIC, ALONG WITH HITS OF CURRY POWDER AND CITRUSY GROUND CORIANDER.

POZOLE IS A MEXICAN SOUP TRADITIONALLY MADE WITH PORK AND HOMINY—CORN THAT'S DRIED AND SOAKED IN AN ALKALINE SOLUTION TO REMOVE THE HULL AND PUFF THE KERNELS.

POZOLE WITH PINTO BEANS AND QUESO FRESCO

One of Lindsay's tweaks to traditional pozole is a puree of roasted poblanos, onion, and tomatillos (palm-size green fruits with papery husks in the tomato family). Choose firm tomatillos and avoid those with loose husks. Refrigerate in an open paper bag for up to 1 month. The color of pozole may vary based on tomatillos' ripeness.

HANDS-ON TIME 20 min.
TOTAL TIME 40 min.

2   Tbsp. vegetable or canola oil
2   tsp. chili powder
3   tsp. kosher salt
1¼ tsp. freshly ground black pepper
1   lb. tomatillos (6 medium or 8 small), husked, washed, and halved
3   poblano peppers (12 oz. total), quartered, stemmed, and seeded
1   medium yellow onion, quartered and pieces separated
4   cloves garlic, peeled
8   cups chicken stock from Whole Poached Chicken with Bonus Stock, page 27, or purchased chicken stock
4   cups shredded chicken
1   29-oz. can hominy, rinsed and drained
1   15- to 16-oz. can pinto beans, rinsed and drained
1   lime (juice half, cut half in wedges for serving)
1   tsp. sugar
     Toppings, such as crumbled queso fresco, sliced radishes, fresh cilantro leaves, and/or Quick-Pickled Red Onions (recipe, right)

1. Set an oven rack 3 to 4 inches from heat source. Preheat broiler to high.
2. In a small bowl stir together oil, chili powder, 2 tsp. salt, and 1 tsp. black pepper. Put tomatillos, poblano peppers, onion, and garlic on a foil-lined baking sheet; rub all over with oil-chili powder mixture. Broil, tossing once, until vegetables are golden brown and can be easily pierced with a fork, 13 to 15 minutes (vegetables might get a bit charred.)
3. Transfer contents of baking sheet to a blender. Cover and puree until completely smooth. Pour into a 5- to 6-qt. stock pot or Dutch oven; add stock. Cover; bring to boiling over high heat. Reduce heat. Add shredded chicken, hominy, and beans. Simmer, covered, until heated through, 5 to 7 minutes. Stir in lime juice, sugar, remaining 1 tsp. salt, and remaining ¼ tsp. black pepper.
4. Serve with lime wedges, queso fresco, radishes, cilantro, and/or Quick-Pickled Red Onions. Makes 8 servings.
PER SERVING *443 cal, 15 g fat, 72 mg chol, 967 mg sodium, 44 g carb, 5 g fiber, 11 g sugars, 33 g pro.*

QUICK-PICKLED RED ONIONS

These onion slices have subtly sweet and tangy flavor after marinating for 15 minutes—an hour maximizes their bright piquancy.

TOTAL TIME 20 min.

1   large red onion (12 to 14 oz.), halved and thinly sliced (about 2 cups)
¼   cup red wine vinegar
2   tsp. kosher salt

1. Place onion in a screw-top jar; add vinegar and salt. Cover; shake vigorously to coat.
2. Let stand, shaking occasionally, until onion is softened, at least 15 minutes. (Or combine onion, vinegar, and salt in a bowl; stir frequently.) Refrigerate up to 2 weeks. Makes 2 cups.

POZOLE WITH
PINTO BEANS AND
QUESO FRESCO

SAUSAGE, POTATO,
WHITE BEAN, AND
KALE SOUP

SEARING A SMALL AMOUNT OF ITALIAN SAUSAGE IN A BIT OF OLIVE OIL—ALLOWING THE SAUSAGE TO CARAMELIZE AND CRISP—BUILDS DEEP FLAVOR.

SAUSAGE, POTATO, WHITE BEAN, AND KALE SOUP

TOTAL TIME 35 min.

- 2 Tbsp. olive oil
- 8 oz. bulk Italian sausage
- 2 onions, chopped (about 2 cups)
- 1 tsp. dried oregano, crushed
- 1 tsp. fennel seeds
- 1 tsp. kosher salt
- 1 tsp. freshly ground black pepper
- 2 Yukon gold potatoes (1 lb.), cut into 1-inch pieces
- 8 cups chicken stock from Whole Poached Chicken with Bonus Stock, right), or purchased chicken stock
- 1 bay leaf (optional)
- 1 15- to 16-oz. can cannellini beans, rinsed and drained
- 1 large bunch kale, stemmed and leaves torn (10 to 12 cups)
- 2 Tbsp. red wine vinegar
  Freshly grated Parmesan cheese

1. Heat oil in an 8-qt. stock pot or Dutch oven over medium-high heat. Add sausage; use a wooden spoon to break up sausage into bite-size pieces. Cook, without stirring, until brown on the bottom, 2 to 3 minutes. Use tongs to turn sausage. Cook until cooked through and golden brown, 2 to 3 minutes more.
2. Use a slotted spoon to transfer sausage to a paper towel-lined plate. Cover with foil to keep warm.
3. Return pot to medium heat; add onions, oregano, fennel seeds, salt, and pepper to sausage drippings. Cook, stirring often, until onions are translucent and soft, 10 to 12 minutes. Add potatoes, stock, and, if desired, bay leaf. Cover and bring to boiling over high heat; reduce heat. Simmer until potatoes are fork-tender, 8 to 10 minutes.

4. Stir in beans, kale, and reserved sausage. Cook until beans are heated through. Remove bay leaf. Stir in vinegar; season with additional salt and pepper.
5. Top servings with Parmesan cheese. Makes 6 servings.
PER SERVING *457 cal, 18 g fat, 36 mg chol, 1,048 mg sodium, 50 g carb, 9 g fiber, 10 g sugars, 24 g pro.*

WHOLE POACHED CHICKEN WITH BONUS STOCK

Poaching a whole chicken with veggies, herbs, and garlic also yields stock. The flavor and body of homemade stock is incomparable, but making it is a time commitment. Purchased chicken stock or vegetable broth is a good stand-in.

HANDS-ON TIME 30 min.
TOTAL TIME 2 hr.

- 1 4- to 5-lb. whole chicken, patted dry and giblets removed
- 2 carrots, scrubbed and quartered
- 2 celery stalks, quartered
- 1 medium onion, quartered
- 1 head garlic, halved horizontally
- 10 sprigs fresh thyme
- 10 stems flat-leaf parsley
- 15 black peppercorns
- 2 bay leaves
- 1 Tbsp. kosher salt

1. To poach chicken: Place chicken in an 8- to 10-qt. stock pot or Dutch oven. Add remaining ingredients. Fill pot with water to within 1 inch of rim. Cover; bring to boiling over high heat. Reduce heat until broth gently bubbles. Cook, covered, until chicken is done (thigh registers 175°F), about 50 minutes. Use tongs to transfer chicken to a large bowl, retaining liquid in pot. Cool chicken until comfortable to handle. Remove skin and return it to pot. Remove meat from bones, return bones to pot.
2. Shred meat. Refrigerate cooled meat in an airtight container up to 3 days.
3. To make stock: Add water to reach 1 inch below rim of pot. Bring to boiling, reduce heat. Simmer 20 minutes or up to 2 hours for more flavorful stock. Cool completely. Set a fine-mesh strainer over a large bowl and strain stock into bowl. Discard solids.
4. Refrigerate stock in airtight containers up to 1 week or freeze up to 3 months. Makes 4½ cups chicken and 10 to 12 cups stock.

PEAS ADD SWEETNESS AND CREAMY
STARCHINESS. TOASTED CARAWAY SEEDS
CONTRIBUTE NUTTY, ALMOST MALTLIKE FLAVOR,
AND PARMESAN RIND CREATES DEEP UMAMI.

FRICO

A lacy cheese wafer looks
intriguing on soup, and it adds
crunch and richness.

Preheat oven to 400°F. Coarsely
shred 6 oz. Parmesan cheese. Line
a baking sheet with nonstick foil or
parchment paper. For each crisp,
place about 1 Tbsp. shredded cheese
on prepared sheet; pat into a 2-inch
circle, allowing 2 inches between
circles. Bake 7 to 8 minutes or until
bubbly and light golden. Let stand
on baking sheet 1 to 2 minutes or until
cooled but still pliable. Carefully peel
crisps off foil or paper. Cool on a
wire rack.

CHEESY BROCCOLI AND PEA SOUP

Save the rinds from Parmesan and
other hard cheeses to add flavor to
sauces, soups, and braises. Tightly
wrap individual rinds in plastic wrap,
store in a freezer bag, and freeze up to
6 months. For a vegetarian version,
substitute vegetable broth.

TOTAL TIME 35 min.

3   Tbsp. olive oil
2   onions, chopped (about 2 cups)
1   tsp. caraway seeds, crushed
2   tsp. kosher salt
½   tsp. freshly ground black pepper
3   10-oz. pkg. frozen broccoli florets
    or two 16-oz. pkg. frozen broccoli
    florets
6   cups chicken stock from Whole
    Poached Chicken with Bonus Stock,
    page 27, purchased chicken stock,
    or vegetable broth
2   oz. Parmesan cheese, finely grated
    (about ½ cup packed), plus rind
1   10-oz. pkg. frozen peas
2   to 3 Tbsp. lemon juice
6   slices buttered toast

1. Heat oil in a 6-qt. stock pot or Dutch
oven over medium-high heat. Add
onions, caraway seeds, 1 tsp. salt, and
½ tsp. pepper. Cook, stirring often, until
onions are golden and translucent, 10 to
12 minutes.
2. Add broccoli, stock, Parmesan, and
Parmesan rind. Stir to submerge broccoli.
Cover; bring to boiling. Reduce heat;
simmer until broccoli is fork-tender, 9 to
12 minutes. Add peas; cook until heated
through, about 1 minute more.
3. Remove cheese rind. Puree soup in
batches in a blender or with a handheld
immersion blender. Stir in lemon juice
and remaining 1 tsp. salt.
4. Top soup with grated Parmesan,
additional black pepper, and toast.
Makes 6 servings.
PER SERVING *383 cal, 18 g fat, 26 mg*
chol, 939 mg sodium, 41 g carb, 8 g fiber,
12 g sugars, 18 g pro.

CHEESY BROCCOLI
AND PEA SOUP

HEART COOKIES
Recipe on page 40

february

Show love to your Valentines with cake, cookies, and personalized hand pies. Score a win with cheesy artichoke dips and learn how to slow braise for beautiful, tender results.

PASTRY LOVE NOTES

For Valentine's Day, hand out pastries instead of cards.

JAM-FILLED HAND PIES

Trade scissors for cookie cutters and color pencils for sugar glaze. Seal a spoonful of your sweetheart's favorite jam or chocolate-hazelnut spread inside a golden flaky pastry. Then decorate to your heart's content with mini cutouts, tinted glaze, and sanding sugar. Sweet, indeed.

HANDS-ON TIME 25 min.
TOTAL TIME 50 min.

1¾ cups all-purpose flour
1 Tbsp. sugar
½ tsp. salt
¾ cup butter
1 egg, lightly beaten
2 to 4 Tbsp. milk
6 Tbsp. jam or chocolate-hazelnut spread
½ recipe Cookie Glaze

1. In a large bowl stir together flour, sugar, and salt. Using a pastry blender, cut in butter until mixture resembles fine crumbs. Stir in egg. Sprinkle 1 Tbsp. milk at a time over part of flour mixture; gently toss with a fork. Push moistened pastry to side of bowl. Repeat, adding only enough milk until pastry begins to come together. Gather into a ball, kneading gently just until it holds together. (Or combine all ingredients except milk in a food processor. Pulse; add milk 1 Tbsp. at a time until pastry comes together.) Divide pastry in half; form two balls. If desired, cover with plastic wrap and chill until ready to use.

2. Preheat oven to 375°F. On a lightly floured surface, slightly flatten one pastry ball. Roll into a 9×8-inch rectangle. Cut in half lengthwise to form two 9×4-inch rectangles; cut each in thirds crosswise to form six 3×4-inch rectangles. Repeat with remaining pastry ball.*

3. Spread 1 Tbsp. jam each onto six rectangles. Moisten edges with additional milk; top with remaining pastry rectangles; press edges with a fork to seal. Using a floured spatula, transfer filled pastries to a baking sheet. Brush tops with additional milk.

4. Bake 17 to 20 minutes or until golden. Remove; let cool on a wire rack 5 minutes. Drizzle with Cookie Glaze. Serve warm. Makes 6 pastries.

*Note For pastries with heart cutouts: Using ½- to 1½-inch heart-shape cookie cutters, cut shapes from half the rectangles. Discard hearts or brush with milk and press onto rectangle tops. Continue as above. For heart-shape pastries: Roll pastry to ⅛-inch thickness. Cut out shapes using a 3-inch cookie cutter, rerolling scraps. Spread 1 tsp. jam onto half the hearts; add tops. Continue as above. Makes 16 hearts.

Cookie Glaze In a bowl whisk together 4 cups powdered sugar, ¼ cup corn syrup, 5 Tbsp. milk, 1 tsp. vanilla, ½ tsp. almond extract (if desired), and a pinch salt until smooth. Add paste food coloring to tint.

PER PASTRY 414 cal, 24 g fat, 92 mg chol, 398 mg sodium, 44 g carb, 1 g fiber, 12 g sugars, 5 g pro.

score a party touchdown with
ARTICHOKE DIP

The most super thing about the big game (other than the commercials, of course) is diving into a bowl of cheesy, tangy goodness.

ITALIAN SAUSAGE ARTICHOKE DIP

HANDS-ON TIME 20 min.
TOTAL TIME 1 hr.

2   14-oz. cans artichoke hearts, rinsed and drained
4   oz. bulk hot Italian sausage
1   8-oz. carton sour cream
2   Tbsp. all-purpose flour
½   cup mayonnaise
¾   cup finely shredded Parmesan cheese
¼   cup pitted Kalamata olives, coarsely chopped
½   cup roasted cherry tomatoes
2   Tbsp. capers, drained and patted dry

1. Preheat oven to 350°F. Place artichoke hearts in a fine-mesh sieve or colander set over a bowl. Firmly press with paper towels to remove excess liquid. Chop artichoke hearts; discard liquid.
2. In a large skillet cook sausage over medium-high heat until browned, stirring to break up meat as it cooks. Use a slotted spoon to transfer sausage to a paper towel-lined plate.
3. In a large bowl stir together sour cream and flour. Stir in mayonnaise, ½ cup cheese, olives, artichokes, and sausage. Transfer to a 9-inch pie plate. Sprinkle with remaining cheese.
4. Bake, uncovered, 30 minutes or until bubbly in center and edges are lightly browned. Cool 15 minutes. Top with roasted cherry tomatoes and capers. Makes 16 servings.
PER SERVING *141 cal, 13 g fat, 19 g chol, 332 mg sodium, 4 g carb, 1 g fiber, 1 g sugars, 3 g pro.*

CHORIZO-POBLANO ARTICHOKE DIP

HANDS-ON TIME 30 min.
TOTAL TIME 1 hr. 25 min.

2   fresh poblano peppers
2   14-oz. cans artichoke hearts, rinsed and drained
4   oz. bulk uncooked chorizo sausage
1   8-oz. carton sour cream
2   Tbsp. all-purpose flour
½   cup mayonnaise
¾   cup finely shredded Parmesan cheese
¼   cup sliced green onions
¼   cup chopped fresh cilantro

1. Preheat oven to 425°F. Halve peppers lengthwise; remove stems, seeds, and membranes. Place pepper halves, cut sides down, on a foil-lined baking sheet. Roast 25 minutes or until peppers are charred and tender. Enclose in foil; let stand 15 minutes or until cool enough to handle. Use a sharp knife to gently pull off and discard skins in strips. Chop roasted peppers. Reduce oven temperature to 350°F.
2. Meanwhile, place artichoke hearts in a fine-mesh sieve or colander set over a bowl. Firmly press with paper towels to remove excess liquid. Chop artichoke hearts; discard liquid.
3. In a large skillet cook chorizo over medium-high heat until browned, stirring to break up meat as it cooks. Use a slotted spoon to transfer to a paper towel-lined plate.
4. In a large bowl stir together sour cream and flour until combined. Stir in mayonnaise, ½ cup of the cheese, roasted peppers, artichokes, chorizo, green onions, and cilantro. Transfer to a 9-inch pie plate. Sprinkle with remaining ¼ cup cheese.
5. Bake, uncovered, 30 minutes or until bubbly and edges are lightly browned. Cool 15 minutes. Top with additional sliced green onions and cilantro leaves. Makes 16 servings.
PER SERVING *140 cal, 12 g fat, 20 mg chol, 293 mg sodium, 5 g carb, 1 g fiber, 1 g sugars, 4 g pro.*

SERVE DIPS WITH AN ASSORTMENT OF CHIPS, TOASTS, AND CRISP VEGETABLES.

ITALIAN
SAUSAGE
ARTICHOKE
DIP

CHORIZO-
POBLANO
ARTICHOKE DIP

BROWN BUTTER
CAULIFLOWER
ARTICHOKE DIP

SPICY ROASTED
RED PEPPER
ARTICHOKE DIP

THE RICH NUTTY FLAVOR OF BROWN BUTTER (AKA BEURRE NOISETTE) ENHANCES THE FLAVOR OF JUST ABOUT ANY DISH—SWEET OR SAVORY.

BROWN BUTTER CAULIFLOWER ARTICHOKE DIP

HANDS-ON TIME 25 min.
TOTAL TIME 1 hr. 10 min.

- 2   14-oz. cans artichoke hearts, rinsed and drained
- ¼   cup butter
- 2   cups small cauliflower florets
- 1   clove garlic, minced
- 1   8-oz. carton sour cream
- 2   Tbsp. all-purpose flour
- ½   cup mayonnaise
- ¾   cup finely shredded Parmesan cheese
- ¼   cup hazelnuts, toasted and coarsely chopped
- 2   Tbsp. fresh sage leaves; 1 Tbsp. chopped

1. Preheat oven to 350°F. Place artichoke hearts in a fine-mesh sieve or colander set over a bowl. Firmly press with paper towels to remove excess liquid. Chop artichoke hearts; discard liquid.
2. In a large skillet melt butter over medium-high heat. Continue cooking 1 to 2 minutes or just until butter starts to brown. Add cauliflower and garlic. Cook and stir 4 minutes or until cauliflower is golden brown. Remove from heat; cool slightly. Set aside ½ cup mixture.
3. In a large bowl stir together sour cream and flour until combined. Stir in mayonnaise, ½ cup cheese, artichokes, remaining cauliflower mixture, 2 Tbsp. hazelnuts and 1 Tbsp. chopped sage. Transfer to a 9-inch pie plate. Sprinkle with remaining ¼ cup cheese and reserved cauliflower.
4. Bake, uncovered, 30 minutes or until bubbly and edges are lightly browned. Cool 15 minutes. Top with remaining hazelnuts and sage leaves. Makes 16 servings.
PER SERVING *141 cal, 13 g fat, 22 mg chol, 231 mg sodium, 4 g carb, 1 g fiber, 1 g sugars, 3 g pro.*

SPICY ROASTED RED PEPPER ARTICHOKE DIP

HANDS-ON TIME 15 min.
TOTAL TIME 1 hr.

- 2   14-oz. cans artichoke hearts, rinsed and drained
- 1   8-oz. carton sour cream
- 2   Tbsp. all-purpose flour
- 1   Tbsp. harissa paste
- ¾   cup finely shredded Parmesan cheese
- ½   cup mayonnaise
- ½   cup bottled drained and chopped roasted red bell peppers or home-roasted red bell peppers*
- ¼   cup almonds, toasted** and coarsely chopped
     Fresh mint leaves

1. Preheat oven to 350°F. Place artichoke hearts in a fine-mesh sieve or colander set over a bowl. Firmly press with paper towels to remove excess liquid. Chop artichoke hearts; discard liquid.
2. In a large bowl stir together sour cream, flour, and harissa paste until combined. Stir in ½ cup cheese, the mayonnaise, roasted peppers, and artichokes. Transfer to a 9-inch pie plate. Sprinkle with remaining ¼ cup cheese.
3. Bake, uncovered, 30 minutes or until bubbly and edges are lightly browned. Cool 15 minutes. Top with almonds and mint leaves. Makes 14 servings.
*Tip To roast red peppers, preheat oven to 425°F. Halve one red bell pepper lengthwise; remove stems, seeds, and membranes. Place pepper halves, cut sides down, on a foil-lined baking sheet. Roast 20 to 25 minutes or until pepper is charred and tender. Enclose pepper in foil; let stand 20 minutes or until cool enough to handle. Use a sharp knife to gently pull off and discard skins in strips. Chop into bite size pieces.
**Tip Toast small amounts of nuts or seeds in a dry skillet over medium heat 3 to 5 minutes, stirring frequently. For larger amounts, preheat oven to 350°F. Spread nuts or seeds in a shallow baking pan. Bake 5 to 10 minutes or until light brown, shaking pan once or twice.
PER SERVING *134 cal, 11 g fat, 16 mg chol, 267 mg sodium, 5 g carb, 1 g fiber, 2 g sugars, 3 g pro.*

WE HEART CAKE

For Molly Yeh, nothing else says love like cake. Every February, the blogger and Food Network star designs a whimsical new look for a much-loved family recipe.

Molly Yeh grew up in a family that was lax about holiday traditions—barring one. "Our Valentine's Day cake was the one recipe we made once a year, every single year," says the author, blogger (mynameisyeh.com), and host of Food Network's *Girl Meets Farm*. Molly has continued the annual bake since moving away from home (first to New York City, then to her husband's family farm in North Dakota). Although the almond-flavor sponge cake and whipped cream frosting are nonnegotiable, Molly decorates the cake differently every year. "My mom would do a simple dusting of powdered sugar and a dollop of whipped cream, but I go all out on decorations."

We love this sweet tradition so much, we made it our own with this design inspired by Molly.

VALENTINE'S CAKE

HANDS-ON TIME 40 min.
TOTAL TIME 2 hr.

- ¾ cup all-purpose flour
- 1½ tsp. baking powder
- 9 eggs, separated
- 1 tsp. kosher salt
- ¾ cup sugar
- 8 oz. almond paste, crumbled
- 1½ tsp. vanilla
- ¾ tsp. almond extract
- 1 cup strawberry-rhubarb jam
  Whipped Cream Frosting

1. Preheat oven to 350°F. Grease and line bottom of three 8-inch round cake pans with parchment paper.* Grease paper; set pans aside.
2. In a small bowl whisk together flour and baking powder. In a large bowl beat egg whites and salt with a mixer on medium until soft peaks form. Beat in sugar 1 Tbsp. at a time. Continue beating until stiff peaks form; set aside.

3. In another large bowl combine almond paste and egg yolks; beat on high 2 minutes until pale and fluffy (allow some almond paste chunks to remain intact), scraping down sides of bowl as needed. Mix in vanilla and almond extract. Gently fold whites into yolk mixture; fold in flour mixture. Pour batter into prepared pans. Bake 20 to 25 minutes or until a toothpick inserted in centers comes out clean.
4. Cool in pans on wire racks 10 minutes. Remove from pans; remove paper. Let cool completely on racks. Spread ½ cup each jam and Whipped Cream Frosting between layers. Frost cake with remaining Whipped Cream Frosting. Decorate as desired. Chill, covered, up to 24 hours. Makes 12 servings.
Whipped Cream Frosting In a bowl beat 2 cups heavy cream, ⅔ cup powdered sugar, and 1 tsp. almond extract until stiff peaks form.
***Tip** For a two-layer cake, use 9-inch round cake pans; reduce jam to ½ cup.
PER SERVING *479 cal, 24 g fat, 185 mg chol, 229 mg sodium, 54 g carb, 1 g fiber, 42 g sugars, 8 g pro.*

IN ADDITION TO VARYING DECORATIONS ON HER CAKE YEAR TO YEAR, MOLLY PLAYS WITH FILLING FLAVORS. THIS ONE HAS WHIPPED CREAM FROSTING AND STRAWBERRY-RHUBARB JAM BETWEEN THE LAYERS.

HEART COOKIES

HANDS-ON TIME 45 min.
TOTAL TIME 1 hr. 25 min.

3   cups all-purpose flour
½   tsp. baking soda
¾   tsp. baking powder
¾   tsp. kosher salt
1   cup unsalted butter, softened
1   cup granulated sugar
1½   tsp. vanilla
½   tsp. almond extract
1   large egg
      Powdered sugar
1   recipe Cookie Glaze
      Assorted sprinkles

1. Preheat oven to 350°F. Line two baking sheets with parchment paper; set aside.
2. In a medium bowl whisk together flour, baking soda, baking powder, and salt. In a large bowl beat together butter and granulated sugar with a mixer on medium-high 3 to 4 minutes until pale and fluffy.
3. Reduce speed to medium. Add vanilla, almond extract, and egg; mix to combine. Reduce speed to low. Gradually add dry ingredients; mix until combined. Transfer dough to a work surface. Knead to form a ball. Divide dough in half. If desired, cover with plastic wrap and chill until ready to use.
4. Dust work surface and a rolling pin with powdered sugar. Roll dough to ¼-inch thickness. Using 1¼- to 3-inch heart-shape cutters, cut out shapes. Place 1 inch apart on baking sheet. Reroll scraps; repeat. Bake 8 to 10 minutes until bottoms are lightly browned. Let cool 5 minutes. Transfer to a rack to cool. Decorate with Cookie Glaze and sprinkles. Makes about sixty-six 1¼- to 3-inch cookies.
Cookie Glaze In a bowl whisk together 4 cups powdered sugar, ¼ cup corn syrup, 5 Tbsp. milk, 1 tsp. vanilla, ½ tsp. almond extract (if desired), and a pinch salt until smooth. Add paste food coloring to tint.
PER COOKIE *59 cal, 3 g fat, 10 mg chol, 29 mg sodium, 8 g carb, 3 g sugars, 1 g pro.*

COOKIE TIPS

Glazed cookie pops add sweetness to Molly's Valentine cake.

1 Molly's sugar cookie dough holds its shape as cookies bake. Cutters in various sizes add interest.

2 Outline cooled cookies with cookie glaze before flooding with glaze. Molly's method: Dip the tops in glaze, letting excess run off before decorating.

3 Add sprinkles while glaze is wet, gently pressing large sprinkles and nonpareils to stay put. Some of Molly's go-to sprinkle brands are India Tree, Wilton, Fancy Sprinkles, and Sweetapolita.

FAST & FRESH

Easy, delicious recipes for a better dinner tonight.

MEYER LEMON AND ROSEMARY CHICKEN SALAD

Meyer lemons are sweeter than others and have thin, edible rinds.

TOTAL TIME 30 min.

- 2   Meyer lemons
- 1   finely chopped shallot
       Pinch salt
- 3   Tbsp. olive oil
       Freshly ground black pepper
- 2   8- to 10-oz. chicken breasts, halved horizontally
- 1   Tbsp. finely chopped fresh rosemary
- 1   head escarole, trimmed and chopped (4 cups)
- 1   head Belgian endive, trimmed and chopped
- 4   to 5 radishes, thinly sliced

1. For dressing: Juice 1 lemon into a small bowl; stir in shallot and a pinch of salt. Drizzle in 3 Tbsp. oil, whisking constantly until emulsified. Season with pepper.

2. Preheat a grill pan or large skillet over medium-high; brush with additional oil. Season chicken with salt and pepper. Sprinkle with rosemary. Rub lightly with additional oil. Grill 5 minutes or until golden brown on one side. Turn; cook 5 to 6 minutes more or until done (165°F).

3. Thinly slice and quarter remaining lemon; transfer to a large bowl. Add escarole, endive, and radishes. Toss with dressing. Serve chicken with dressed greens. Sprinkle with additional black pepper. Makes 4 servings.

PER SERVING *156 cal, 3 g fat, 83 mg chol, 196 mg sodium, 5 g carb, 2 g fiber, 1 g sugars, 27 g pro.*

SHEET-PAN
GREENS AND FETA
FRITTATA

SHEET-PAN GREENS AND FETA FRITTATA

Have leftover frittata? Turn it into breakfast sandwiches. Spread halved ciabatta rolls with basil or dried tomato pesto then add a wedge of frittata. Wrap in foil and warm in a 350°F oven.

HANDS-ON TIME 10 min.
TOTAL TIME 50 min.

Nonstick cooking spray
2 Tbsp. olive oil
1 16-oz. bunch rainbow chard
1 cup cherry tomatoes, halved
1 shallot, thinly sliced
¼ tsp. salt
12 eggs
1 cup milk
4 oz. feta cheese, crumbled
¼ tsp. black pepper
¼ cup grated Parmesan cheese
¼ cup fresh herbs, such as basil, oregano, and/or flat-leaf parsley
1 cup cherry tomatoes (optional)

1. Preheat oven to 375°F. Coat a 15×10-inch baking pan with nonstick cooking spray. Add 1 Tbsp. oil to pan. Place in hot oven 5 minutes. Meanwhile, remove chard leaves from stems. Chop leaves (about 8 cups). Thinly slice stems (about 2½ cups). Add stems to baking pan. Roast 5 minutes. Add leaves, 1 cup tomatoes, shallot, remaining 1 Tbsp. oil, and salt. Toss to coat. Roast 10 minutes or until chard is wilted and tomatoes soften, stirring once.
2. Meanwhile, in a large bowl whisk eggs, milk, feta, and pepper. Pour evenly over vegetables. Sprinkle with Parmesan.
3. Bake 20 minutes or until set. If desired, roast 1 cup cherry tomatoes, drizzled with olive oil, on a separate baking pan 10 minutes or until tomatoes soften, stirring once. Remove frittata from oven; let stand 10 minutes. Top with fresh herbs and, if using, roasted tomatoes. Makes 6 servings.

PER SERVING *291 cal, 20 g fat, 395 mg chol, 635 mg sodium, 9 g carb, 2 g fiber, 5 g sugars, 19 g pro.*

PARCHMENT-BAKED HALIBUT WITH THYME AND OLIVES

PARCHMENT-BAKED HALIBUT WITH THYME AND OLIVES

In the oven parchment packets puff with steam to gently cook fish and potatoes. This method yields flaky, tender fish and cleanup is a snap.

HANDS-ON TIME 20 min.
TOTAL TIME 35 min.

1 lb. fingerling potatoes, halved
¼ cup olive oil
4 small halibut fillets or other whitefish (cod or hake), skinned
   Salt and black pepper
8 to 12 sprigs fresh thyme
½ cup olives pitted (optional)
   Lemons (optional)

1. Preheat oven to 425°F. Place potatoes in a large microwave-safe bowl with 1 Tbsp. water; cover. Microwave on high 5 minutes or until almost tender. Cool slightly.
2. Cut four sheets of parchment paper 15 inches long. Fold each in half; unfold. For each packet, spoon about ½ tsp. oil in center of one side. Arrange potatoes on oil. Place fish on potatoes. Season lightly with salt and pepper. Drizzle with remaining oil (about 1 Tbsp.). Top with thyme sprigs and olives.
3. Fold opposite half of parchment over fish. Beginning at one corner of fold, tightly fold both layers of parchment toward center. Continue folding and pleating around edge to enclose packet. Tuck final corner underneath. Transfer packets to a baking sheet.
4. Bake 10 to 12 minutes or until paper has puffed and fish is opaque. If desired, serve with lemon wedges. Makes 4 servings.

PER SERVING *449 cal, 24 g fat, 69 mg chol, 429 mg sodium, 33 g carb, 6 g fiber, 2 g sugars, 29 g pro.*

COCONUT-CURRY
SHORT RIBS

LOVE ME TENDER

Braising, you're the answer to our cold-weather cooking dreams. All you ask for is a little time and, in return, you give us the juiciest, most comforting dishes.

COCONUT-CURRY SHORT RIBS

Lemongrass can be found near fresh herbs at many grocery stores or Asian supermarkets. To prepare: Remove the root end. Cut the stalk lengthwise and peel off tough layers. Finely chop the pale inner core.

HANDS-ON TIME 30 min.
TOTAL TIME 2 hr. 30 min.

3   lb. bone-in beef short ribs, cut into 2- to 3-rib portions*
½   tsp. salt
1   Tbsp. coconut oil or vegetable oil
1   shallot, finely chopped
1   Tbsp. grated fresh ginger
2   tsp. minced fresh lemongrass
2   cloves garlic, minced
3   Tbsp. Thai red curry paste
1   Tbsp. packed brown sugar
1   14-oz. can unsweetened coconut milk
1   Tbsp. fish sauce
4   heads baby bok choy, halved lengthwise
    Mint leaves
    Lime wedges

1. Season meat with ½ tsp. salt. Preheat oven to 325°F. In a 5- to 6-qt. Dutch oven heat oil over medium-high heat. Cook ribs in batches 3 to 5 minutes on each side until deep brown. Transfer to plate.
2. Reduce heat to medium. Add shallot, ginger, lemongrass, and garlic; cook 1 minute. Stir in curry paste and brown sugar; cook 1 minute. Stir in coconut milk and fish sauce; bring to a simmer. Return ribs and juices to pot, meat sides down. Cover; braise in oven 2 to 2½ hours or until meat is fork-tender.
3. Transfer meat to a platter; keep warm. Skim fat from braising liquid. Bring liquid to a simmer over medium-high heat. Add bok choy; simmer 2 to 3 minutes or just until tender, turning once. Transfer bok choy to platter with meat. Pour liquid over. Serve with mint and limes. Makes 4 to 6 servings.
*Tip Ask a butcher to cut beef short ribs into 2- to 3-rib portions.
PER SERVING *808 cal, 52 g fat, 242 mg chol, 1,459 mg sodium, 12 g carb, 3 g fiber, 6 g sugars, 70 g pro.*

THE COMBINATION OF COCONUT MILK, GINGER, AND LEMONGRASS INFUSES SHORT RIBS WITH LUSCIOUS FLAVOR. WHILE THE MEAT RESTS, COOK BABY BOK CHOY IN THE LIQUID FOR A FEW MINUTES. THE CRISP, DELICATE TASTE OF BOK CHOY TEMPERS THE RICHNESS OF THE RIBS.

BRAISING ELEVATES AN INEXPENSIVE CUT LIKE PORK SHOULDER TO TENDER, SUCCULENT GOODNESS. SHRED IT WHILE IT IS IN THE POT SO IT CONTINUES TO SOAK UP ALL THOSE FLAVORFUL JUICES.

CHIPOTLE PORK TACOS

Pork, shredded in braising liquid, is tender and moist. Double the tortillas for each taco for easier eating.

HANDS-ON TIME 35 min.
TOTAL TIME 2 hr. 35 min.

1	2- to 2½-lb. boneless pork shoulder, trimmed and cut into 2-inch pieces
1	tsp. salt
2	Tbsp. vegetable oil
1	orange, cut into 6 wedges
1	cup sliced onion
2	cloves garlic, minced
1	tsp. ground cumin
1	tsp. dried oregano, crushed
1	12-oz. bottle dark lager beer or 1½ cups beef broth
¾	cup orange juice
2	to 3 canned chipotle peppers in adobo sauce, finely chopped, plus 1 Tbsp. adobo sauce
24	6-inch corn tortillas, warmed
2	cups finely shredded red cabbage
¾	cup crumbled queso fresco or feta cheese

1. Preheat oven to 325°F. Season meat with salt. In a 5- to 6-qt. Dutch oven heat 1 Tbsp. oil over medium-high heat. Cook meat in batches 3 to 5 minutes on each side or until deep brown. Transfer to a plate.

2. Reduce heat to medium. Add remaining 1 Tbsp. oil. Place orange wedges cut sides down in pot; cook 2 minutes each side until deep brown. Remove from pot; set aside. Add onion to pot. Cook 3 minutes or until lightly browned. Stir in garlic, cumin, and oregano; cook 1 minute. Add beer, orange juice, chipotle peppers, and adobo sauce. Bring to a simmer, scraping pan bottom. Return meat and juices to pot; return to a simmer. Cover.

3. Transfer pot to oven. Bake 2 to 2½ hours or until meat is fork-tender. Use two forks to shred meat in pot. For excess cooking liquid, simmer over medium heat to reduce and thicken slightly.

4. Serve pork in doubled tortillas with cabbage and cheese. Serve with seared orange wedges. Makes 6 servings.

PER SERVING *408 cal, 18 g fat, 89 mg chol, 594 mg sodium, 26 g carb, 3 g fiber, 7 g sugars, 31 g pro.*

SLOW COOKING CARROTS, CELERY, AND PARSNIPS RESULTS IN A VELVETY TEXTURE. THE MAGICAL TASTE BEGINS WITH THE SAUCE—IT'S THICKENED WITH LEEKS COOKED SLOWLY IN BUTTER UNTIL NEARLY DISAPPEARING.

BRAISED VEGETABLES AND CARAMELIZED LEEKS

HANDS-ON TIME 15 min.
TOTAL TIME 1 hr. 20 min.

3	Tbsp. olive oil
3	cups thinly sliced leeks
1	tsp. salt
2½	cups reduced-sodium vegetable or chicken broth
6	stalks celery, trimmed to fit pan, strings removed*
1	lb. carrots, peeled or scrubbed, cut in half lengthwise if thick
1	lb. parsnips, peeled or scrubbed, cut in half lengthwise if thick
5	Tbsp. butter
1	lemon (2 tsp. zest; 3 Tbsp. juice)
3	sprigs fresh thyme
1	bay leaf
⅓	cup panko
3	Tbsp. chopped almonds
1	Tbsp. minced garlic
¼	cup chopped flat-leaf parsley

1. Preheat oven to 325°F. In a deep oven-going skillet or 5-qt. Dutch oven heat 2 Tbsp. oil over medium-low. Stir in leeks and ½ tsp. salt. Cover; cook 6 to 8 minutes or until leeks are tender but not browned. Uncover; stir in 1 Tbsp. broth. Cook until caramelized and starting to break into small bits, 20 to 25 minutes, stirring in 1 Tbsp. broth every 6 to 8 minutes (¼ cup total)

2. Stir in remaining 2¼ cups broth, the celery, carrots, parsnips, butter, lemon juice, thyme, and bay leaf. Bring to a simmer, scraping pan bottom to loosen browned bits. Cover. Transfer pot to oven. Bake 45 to 55 minutes or until vegetables are fork-tender.

3. Meanwhile, heat a small skillet over medium. Add panko, almonds, garlic, and remaining 1 Tbsp. oil; cook and stir 2 to 3 minutes or until toasted. Remove from heat. Stir in parsley and lemon zest.

4. Transfer vegetables to a platter. Discard thyme and bay leaf. Pour braising liquid over vegetables. Top with panko mixture and remaining ½ tsp. salt. Makes 4 to 6 servings.

*Tip Remove strings from celery by peeling off outer ridges with a vegetable peeler.

PER SERVING *461 cal, 28 g fat, 38 mg chol, 905 mg sodium, 50 g carb, 12 g fiber, 16 g sugars, 6 g pro.*

HOW TO CLEAN LEEKS

Cut off the root end and dark green top, leaving the white and light green. Cut in half lengthwise then into thin slices. Place slices in a bowl of water and swish them around to release dirt. Transfer to paper towels to soak up water.

WHEN IT COMES TO BRAISING CHICKEN, OPT FOR BONE-IN SKIN-ON THIGHS. THEY'RE NEARLY IMPOSSIBLE TO OVERCOOK, AND BOTH THE BONES AND THE FAT FROM THE SKIN IMPART FLAVOR.

HOW TO BRAISE ANYTHING

What is braising, really? At its most basic, it is gently cooking tough cuts of meat in liquid at low temperatures. The process breaks down the collagen that holds the meat together. (You can apply the same technique to hearty vegetables, too.) You'll need a large heavy pot with a tight-fitting lid. Then follow these simple steps.

1. BROWN ALL OVER This step isn't about cooking the meat through; it's about searing all the sides to develop a dark golden brown crust. During the process, caramel flavors transfer to the cooking fat.

2. BUILD DEPTH Once the meat is browned, remove it to make room for any combination of vegetables, aromatics, herbs, and spices. As they sizzle in the fat, flavors amplify and build complexity.

3. DEGLAZE THE POT At this point there will be lots of browned bits at the bottom of the pot. This is braising gold. Pour in liquid (broth, wine, beer, etc.) and use a wooden spoon to scrape up the tasty stuck-on bits.

4. COOK LOW AND SLOW It's time to return the meat to the pot, cover, and pop it in the oven. Now your work is pretty much done. As the meat cooks in this moist environment, the tough connective tissues melt away to yield fall-from-the-bone tenderness.

ZA'ATAR CHICKEN AND LENTILS

Za'atar—a Middle Eastern spice blend—gives this dish decidedly aromatic flavor. To make your own, combine 1 Tbsp. each ground sumac and ground dried thyme with 1 tsp. each sesame seeds, salt, and black pepper.

HANDS-ON TIME 10 min.
TOTAL TIME 1 hr. 5 min.

6   bone-in, skin-on chicken thighs, excess fat trimmed
3   Tbsp. za'atar
2   Tbsp. olive oil
1   cup coarsely chopped onion
1   cup carrot matchsticks
2   cloves garlic, minced
3½ cups reduced-sodium chicken broth
1   cup French green lentils*
2   Tbsp. tomato paste
1   cup pitted green olives, such as Castelvetrano, whole or halved
    Lemon peel or zest
    Fresh thyme sprigs

1. Preheat oven to 325°F. Season chicken with za'atar. In a deep oven-going skillet or 5-qt. Dutch oven heat oil over medium-high heat. Add chicken; cook 3 to 4 minutes on each side or until browned. Transfer to a plate.

2. Reduce heat to medium. Add onion and carrot to pot; cook 4 to 5 minutes or until lightly browned. Stir in garlic; cook 1 minute. Stir in broth, lentils, and tomato paste. Return chicken and juices to pot. Bring to a simmer. Cover. Transfer pot to oven. Bake 45 to 55 minutes or until chicken is fork-tender (175°F).

3. Transfer chicken to a platter; cover to keep warm. Strain remaining mixture, reserving liquid. Add lentils and vegetables to chicken on platter; cover. Return liquid to pot. Boil over medium-high heat 10 to 15 minutes or until reduced by half. Return chicken, lentils, and vegetables to pot. Top with olives, lemon peel, and thyme. Makes 6 servings.

*Tip French green lentils have a firm texture that holds up to longer cooking methods better than most other varieties.

PER SERVING *587 cal, 24 g fat, 130 mg chol, 941 mg sodium, 53 g carb, 13 g fiber, 5 g sugars, 42 g pro.*

PORTOBELLO POT ROAST
Recipe on page 64

march

Learn what's new in the food world with recipes that showcase the earthy flavor of mushrooms and spice blends that enliven everyday dishes. Plus, discover fresh takes on familiar recipes.

55

56

59

ZAP AND GO: POP IN A BOWL, MICROWAVE FOR A COUPLE MINUTES, AND BREAKFAST IS DONE.

great starts
A NEW WAY TO OATMEAL

Healthy and convenient? That's a breakfast win-win. Freezing oatmeal and your favorite fruit and nuts in muffin cups means a homemade, good-for-you start any day.

FRUIT AND NUT FREEZER OATMEAL CUPS

HANDS-ON TIME 15 min.
TOTAL TIME 6 hr. 25 min., includes freezing

5	cups water
½	tsp. salt
2	cups regular rolled oats
⅓	cup packed brown sugar
1	Tbsp. butter
1	tsp. ground cinnamon
½	cup dried fruit
1	cup fresh berries
½	cup chopped toasted nuts (tip, page 37)
	Milk (optional)

1. In a medium saucepan bring water and salt to boiling; stir in oats. Cook 5 minutes, stirring occasionally. (Mixture thickens as it cools.) Remove from heat. Stir in brown sugar, butter, and cinnamon. Transfer to a bowl. Cover and refrigerate until cool. Stir in dried fruit.
2. Grease twelve 2½-inch muffin cups. Scoop about ½ cup oatmeal into each prepared muffin cup. Sprinkle with berries and nuts; press lightly. Cover; freeze 6 hours. Let stand at room temperature 5 minutes. Transfer frozen oatmeal cups to freezer bags or airtight containers. Freeze up to 3 months.
3. To serve, place one frozen oatmeal cup in a bowl microwave-safe bowl. Microwave, covered, 2 minutes or until heated through, stirring once. Stir again before serving and add milk if desired. Makes 12 servings.
PER SERVING 132 cal, 4 g fat, 3 mg chol, 110 mg sodium, 22 g carb, 3 g fiber, 11 g sugars, 3 g pro.

TOPPINGS & STIR-INS

DRIED FRUIT Cranberries, tart cherries, raisins, and/or snipped apricots or pitted dates.

BERRIES Blueberries, blackberries, raspberries, and/or chopped strawberries.

NUTS Almonds, walnuts, pecans, and/or hazelnuts.

SHAKE IT UP

Inspired by our favorite seasonal milkshake and one of the most buzzed-about ingredients of late, this modern mash-up is perfect for St. Patrick's Day.

MATCHA-MINT SHAKE

Antioxidant-rich matcha powder (dried, ground green tea leaves), mint-chocolate chip ice cream, and fresh mint blend together for an herbal, floral, sweet, better-for-you minty treat. For a festive top, cut a shamrock shape from cardstock, hold over shakes, and dust with matcha.

In a small bowl whisk together 1 Tbsp. matcha powder and ½ cup milk or almond milk until smooth. In a blender combine matcha mixture, 1 pt. slightly softened mint-chocolate chip ice cream, and 3 Tbsp. chopped fresh mint. Cover and blend until combined. Top with whipped cream. If desired, dust with additional matcha powder. Makes 4 milkshakes.

FAST & FRESH

Easy, delicious recipes for a better dinner tonight.

SKILLET CHICKEN AND GREEN BEANS WITH LEMON-TAHINI SAUCE

Tahini is a key ingredient in Middle Eastern cuisine. Keep a jar on hand to add nutty flavor to dips, marinades, dressings, even baked goods.

TOTAL TIME 30 min.

- 8   skinless, boneless chicken thighs
       Salt and black pepper
- 1   Tbsp. ground cumin
- 2   tsp. dried thyme, crushed
- 2   tsp. paprika
- 2   Tbsp. olive oil
- 8   oz. green beans, trimmed
- 4   shallots, quartered
- 1¼   cups chicken broth
- 2   lemons
- ⅓   cup tahini

1. Season chicken with salt and black pepper. Sprinkle with cumin, thyme, and paprika; rub in with fingers. In a 12-inch skillet heat oil over medium-high heat. Add chicken. Cook 5 to 7 minutes or until well-browned, turning once. Transfer to a plate.

2. Return skillet to medium heat. Add beans, shallots, and ½ tsp. salt. Cook 3 minutes or until shallots are browned and beans soften, stirring occasionally. Return chicken and juices to skillet. Add 1 cup broth. Bring to boiling. Simmer, uncovered, 6 to 8 minutes or until chicken is done (170°F).

3. Using a slotted spoon, transfer chicken and vegetables to a plate. Remove zest and ¼ cup juice from one lemon. Whisk tahini, remaining ¼ cup broth, and lemon juice into liquid in skillet. Season with salt and pepper. Return chicken and vegetables to skillet; heat through. Cut remaining lemon into wedges. Sprinkle with lemon zest and serve with lemon wedges. Makes 4 servings.

PER SERVING *497 cal, 27 g fat, 214 mg chol, 738 mg sodium, 15 g carb, 4 g fiber, 4 g sugars, 50 g pro.*

LIME-COCONUT
SHRIMP AND RICE

LIME-COCONUT
SHRIMP AND RICE

*Chewy black rice has more fiber than
brown rice and a nutty taste. Find it
at health markets and large grocery
stores. In a pinch, substitute long grain
white rice.*

HANDS-ON TIME 15 min.
TOTAL TIME 45 min.

- 1½ cups black rice
- 1 cup unsweetened coconut milk
- ¾ tsp. salt
- 2 Tbsp. vegetable oil
- 1 Tbsp. finely chopped serrano chile
  pepper*
- 2 tsp. grated fresh ginger
- 8 oz. asparagus cut into 1-inch pieces
- 1 lb. shrimp, peeled and deveined
- ¼ cup lime juice
- 2 green onions, chopped
  Coconut shards, toasted**
  (optional)
  Crushed red pepper (optional)

1. In a medium saucepan combine rice,
1½ cups water, coconut milk, and salt.
Bring to boiling; stir. Reduce heat; cover.
Simmer 25 to 30 minutes or until tender.
Remove from heat. Let stand 10 minutes.
2. Meanwhile, in a large skillet heat
1 Tbsp. oil over medium heat. Add
serrano chile and ginger. Cook
30 seconds. Add asparagus. Increase
heat to medium-high. Cook and stir
4 minutes or until tender. Transfer to a
large platter.
3. Add remaining 1 Tbsp. oil to skillet.
Add shrimp in a single layer. Cook 3 to
4 minutes or until opaque, turning once.
4. Fluff rice with a fork; transfer to platter
with asparagus. Drizzle with lime juice.
Top with shrimp and green onions. If
desired, sprinkle with toasted coconut
and/or crushed red pepper. Makes
4 servings.
***Tip** Chile peppers contain oils that can
irritate skin and eyes. Wear plastic or
rubber gloves when working with them.
****Tip** To toast coconut, preheat oven
to 350°F. Spread in a shallow baking
pan. Bake 5 to 6 minutes or until lightly
browned, shaking pan once or twice.
PER SERVING *481 cal, 20 g fat, 159 mg
chol, 362 mg sodium, 52 g carb, 4 g fiber,
2 g sugars, 27 g pro.*

MOROCCAN RED
LENTIL SOUP

*Aleppo pepper is a dried coarsely
ground chile with undertones of
cumin and fruit. If you like a mild
kick, sprinkle it on almost anything:
eggs, roasted veggies, even peanut
butter toast.*

HANDS-ON TIME 15 min.
TOTAL TIME 40 min.

- 2 Tbsp. olive oil
- 1 medium yellow onion, finely
  chopped (1 cup)
- 2 Tbsp. finely chopped fresh ginger
- 2 garlic cloves, minced
- 1 tsp. ras el hanout
- ½ tsp. Aleppo pepper
- 3 roma tomatoes, chopped
- 2 cups dried red lentils, rinsed and
  drained
- 6 cups vegetable broth
  Salt and black pepper
  Plain yogurt
  Fresh cilantro

1. In a 5- to 6-qt. pot heat oil over
medium heat. Add onion, ginger, and
garlic. Cook 8 minutes or until softened,
stirring occasionally. Stir in ras el hanout
and Aleppo pepper. Cook 1 minute or
until fragrant. Add tomatoes, lentils,
broth, and 2 cups water.
2. Bring to boiling; reduce heat. Cover;
simmer 25 minutes or until lentils are
tender, stirring occasionally. Season to
taste with salt and black pepper. Top
each serving with yogurt, additional
pepper flakes, and cilantro. Makes
8 servings.
PER SERVING *425 cal, 6 g fat, 1 mg chol,
515 mg sodium, 67 g carb, 17 g fiber, 6 g
sugars, 25 g pro.*

MUSHROOM
SALAD WITH SOY
VINAIGRETTE

THE MIGHTY MUSHROOM

Versatile, packed with nutrition, and available in a crazy number of varieties, mushrooms make plant-based eating more interesting and delicious than ever.

MUSHROOM SALAD WITH SOY VINAIGRETTE

If the sad slices at the salad bar have turned you off from eating uncooked mushrooms, this salad will make you rethink raw. Here, tender cremini and slightly crunchy enoki are paired with watercress and radishes for a combo that's a little woodsy, a little spicy, and a whole lot of yummy texture. If you like, substitute button for the cremini or toss in some stemmed shiitakes for a smokier flavor.

TOTAL TIME 15 min.

1   large fresh red Thai chile (tip, page 59)
¼   cup fresh lemon juice
1   small shallot, minced
3   Tbsp. canola oil
2   Tbsp. soy sauce
1   Tbsp. toasted sesame oil
    Pinch salt and black pepper
1   lb. fresh cremini mushrooms, sliced, and/or enoki mushrooms, trimmed and broken into small clusters
4   cups watercress and/or baby arugula
2   radishes, thinly sliced
1   tsp. sesame seeds

1. Mince 1 tsp. chile from the whole chile; slice remaining. In a large bowl whisk together lemon juice, minced chile, shallot, canola oil, soy sauce, sesame oil, and a pinch each salt and black pepper. Gently fold in mushrooms to coat.
2. Divide greens and radishes among serving plates. Spoon mushroom mixture over greens. Sprinkle with sesame seeds and sliced chile. Makes 4 servings.
PER SERVING *166 cal, 14 g fat, 535 mg sodium, 8 g carb, 1 g fiber, 3 g sugars, 5 g pro.*

MANCHEGO-STUFFED MUSHROOMS

Photo on page 62.

Spanish tapas favorites—briny olives, ham, and nutty Manchego cheese—fill button mushrooms for enticing one-bite appetizers. Top these Spanish-inspired mushrooms with Jamón Ibérico, a specialty dry-cured ham unique to the Iberian Peninsula. Prosciutto or thinly sliced serrano ham would be delicious too.

HANDS-ON TIME 20 min.
TOTAL TIME 1 hr.

½   cup panko
2   oz. Manchego or Parmesan cheese, finely shredded
6   Tbsp. extra virgin olive oil
2   Tbsp. chopped flat-leaf parsley
2   cloves garlic, minced
½   tsp. smoked paprika
¼   tsp. salt
1   lb. 2- to 2½-inch button mushrooms (12 to 14), stemmed
¼   cup chopped pitted Castelvetrano olives
3   thin slices Jamón Ibérico, cut into narrow strips

1. Preheat oven to 400°F. Line a 15×10-inch baking pan with parchment paper.
2. In a small bowl stir together panko, cheese, 2 Tbsp. oil, the parsley, garlic, paprika, and salt. Spoon filling into mushroom caps, pressing and mounding very full caps. Arrange in prepared pan. Drizzle remaining 4 Tbsp. oil over mushrooms. Bake 25 minutes or until mushrooms are tender and filling is golden. Cool slightly.
3. To serve, top with olives and ham. Makes 12 to 14 servings.
PER SERVING *105 cal, 9 g fat, 145 mg sodium, 3 g carb, 1 g fiber, 1 g sugars, 3 g pro.*

WILD MUSHROOMS

It has become popular to label mushrooms as wild. But because of advances in cultivation practices, most mushrooms sold in the market are commercially grown in a highly controlled environment—even uncommon varieties marketed as wild. Only foraged mushrooms are truly wild, and we recommend eating only those foraged by an expert.

MANCHEGO-
STUFFED
MUSHROOMS
Recipe on page 61

PORTOBELLO POT ROAST
Recipe on page 64

THE SECRET TO SAUTÉING MUSHROOMS: START WITH A DRY SKILLET THEN BROWN (WITHOUT STIRRING) TO BUILD DEEP FLAVOR BEFORE ADDING BUTTER, OIL, OR OTHER FLAVORING.

MUSHROOMS TIPS

HOW TO STORE Store, unwashed, in the fridge up to two days in a paper bag or the original packaging. Avoid storing mushrooms in a plastic bag (they need to breathe). Clean immediately before using.

HOW TO CLEAN Using a damp towel or soft brush, wipe each mushroom to remove any dirt. It's also OK to lightly rinse with cool water and pat dry, but do not soak. Mushrooms absorb water like sponges and won't brown if full of water.

PORTOBELLO POT ROAST

Photo on page 52 and 63.

It's not necessary to remove portobello gills, but you might want to. Gills can trap dirt and they have an inky quality that can potentially turn other ingredients black. To remove, cut or twist off the stem (save to use in stuffed mushrooms or stock). Hold the mushroom cap in one hand and use a spoon to gently scrape out the gills.

HANDS-ON TIME 15 min.
TOTAL TIME 1 hr.

- 12 oz. baby yellow potatoes, halved if large
- 8 4-inch portobello mushrooms, stems and gills removed
- 1 Vidalia onion, cut into 8 wedges
- 12 oz. baby carrots with ½-inch tops, scrubbed
- 3 cloves garlic, sliced
- ½ cup dry white wine
- 1 Tbsp. chopped fresh oregano
- 2 Tbsp. extra virgin olive oil
- 1 tsp. salt
- ½ tsp. black pepper
  Grated fresh horseradish

1. Preheat oven to 375°F. In a 6-qt. Dutch oven layer potatoes, mushrooms, onion, carrots, and garlic. Add white wine. Sprinkle with oregano. Drizzle with oil; sprinkle with salt and pepper. Bake, covered, 45 to 60 minutes or until vegetables are tender, stirring once.
2. Carefully transfer Dutch oven to stove top. Use a slotted spoon to transfer vegetables to a serving platter. Bring cooking liquid to boiling. Boil gently, uncovered, 5 minutes or until reduced by half. Pour liquid over vegetables on platter; sprinkle with horseradish. Season with additional salt and pepper. Makes 4 to 6 servings.

PER SERVING *278 cal, 8 g fat, 405 mg sodium, 43 g carb, 8 g fiber, 15 g sugars, 8 g pro.*

SAUTÉED MUSHROOM MEDLEY

Bourbon has caramel notes that amplify those in browned mushrooms. The combination results in a savory rustic side dish.

TOTAL TIME 35 min.

- 1 lb. fresh mushrooms, such as button, cremini, maitake, chanterelle, shiitake, and/or beech
- 8 oz. fresh asparagus, trimmed and cut into 1- to 2-inch pieces
- ¼ cup finely chopped shallots
- 2 Tbsp. extra virgin olive oil
- 2 Tbsp. butter
- 4 sprigs fresh sage
- ¼ cup bourbon or vegetable broth
- ½ tsp. salt
  Black pepper

1. Heat a large skillet over medium-high heat. Add one-fourth of the mushrooms in a single layer to dry skillet. Cook 4 to 5 minutes, turning once, until deep golden brown. Transfer to a bowl. Repeat with remaining mushrooms.
2. Return all mushrooms to skillet. Add asparagus, shallots, olive oil, butter, and sage. Cook and stir 3 minutes or until asparagus is crisp-tender. Remove skillet from heat. Carefully add bourbon and salt. Return to heat. Bring to a simmer. Cook 1 minute or until almost all liquid has evaporated, stirring often. Remove and discard sage. Season with black pepper. Top with additional fresh sage. Makes 4 to 6 servings.
PER SERVING *196 cal, 13 g fat, 193 mg sodium, 11 g carb, 5 g fiber, 3 g sugars, 3 g pro.*

SAUTÉED
MUSHROOM
MEDLEY

ADD DRIED GROUND PORCINI TO THE BISCUIT MIX
TO LEND CONCENTRATED MUSHROOM FLAVOR
WITHOUT SACRIFICING TENDER, FLUFFY TEXTURE.
AN ASSORTMENT OF FRESH MUSHROOMS ALSO
STARS IN A GRAVY THAT'S CREAMY BUT LESS HEAVY
THAN THE TRADITIONAL SAUSAGE VERSION.

PORCINI BISCUITS AND MUSHROOM GRAVY

A popular ingredient in Tuscany, porcini powder is made by grinding dried porcini mushrooms. Grind it yourself or buy at specialty spice shops. The powder enhances baked goods without changing the texture, and is delicious whirled into a sauce or added to a rub for roast chicken or grilled steak.

HANDS-ON TIME 25 min.
TOTAL TIME 40 min.

Porcini Biscuits

2   cups all-purpose flour
1   Tbsp. Porcini Powder (recipe, right)
1   Tbsp. sugar
4   tsp. baking powder
1   tsp. salt
½   cup cold unsalted butter, cubed
⅔   cup whole milk

Mushroom Gravy

2   Tbsp. unsalted butter
1   cup finely chopped onion
4   large cloves garlic, minced
½   tsp. salt
1   lb. fresh mushrooms, such as button, cremini, maitake, chanterelle, shiitake, and/or beech
½   cup dry white wine
1   Tbsp. all-purpose flour
2   cups whole milk
1   oz. Parmesan cheese, finely shredded
8   Fried Eggs (recipe, right)
    Chopped fresh chives

1. For Porcini Biscuits: Preheat oven to 425°F. Line a baking sheet with parchment paper.
2. In a large bowl stir together flour, porcini powder, sugar, baking powder, and salt. Cut butter into flour mixture with a pastry blender until mixture resembles coarse meal. Add milk. Stir with a fork until dry ingredients are evenly moistened.
3. Gently gather into a ball; turn out onto a lightly floured surface. Gently knead five or six times. Pat or roll dough to ½-inch thickness. Use a lightly floured 2½-inch round cutter to cut dough; transfer to prepared baking sheet, spacing 1 inch apart. Gather scraps, knead once or twice, reroll dough, and cut out rounds (8 total). Bake 12 to 15 minutes or until golden brown.
4. Meanwhile, for Mushroom Gravy: In a 12-inch skillet heat butter over medium heat. Add onion, garlic, and salt. Cook 5 minutes or until onion is tender, stirring occasionally. Add mushrooms; increase heat to medium-high. Cook 8 to 10 minutes, stirring occasionally, until liquid is evaporated and mushrooms begin to brown.

5. Carefully add wine. Cook 2 minutes or until almost all liquid is evaporated. Stir in flour to coat mushrooms. Add milk all at once. Cook and stir until thickened and bubbly. Cook and stir 1 minute more. Remove from heat; stir in Parmesan.
6. Use a fork to split biscuits open. Serve open-faced topped with eggs and gravy. Sprinkle with chives. Makes 8 servings.

Porcini Powder In a spice grinder or small food processor grind or pulse ½ oz. dried porcini to a fine powder. Keeps 1 month. Makes 3 Tbsp.

Fried Eggs In a 10-inch skillet melt 2 tsp. butter over medium heat or coat skillet with nonstick cooking spray. Break 4 eggs into skillet; sprinkle with salt and black pepper. Reduce heat to medium-low. Cook eggs 3 to 4 minutes or until whites are almost completely set and yolks begin to thicken. Repeat to cook 4 more eggs.

PER SERVING *444 cal, 25 g fat, 652 mg sodium, 37 g carb, 2 g fiber, 8 g sugars, 15 g pro.*

MUSHROOMS, HEARTY AND FILLING YET LOW IN CALORIES, ARE GOOD SOURCES OF VITAMIN D, POTASSIUM, AND THE ANTIOXIDANTS SELENIUM AND ERGOTHIONEINE.

MAKE ROOM FOR MUSHROOMS

Experiment with these popular varieties from grocery stores and farmers markets.

ENOKI Clumps of stems look like spaghetti; the mushrooms have appealing crunchy texture and almost fruity taste.

OYSTER Prized for subtle seafood flavor and velvety texture. Stems are a bit chewy.

CREMINI Also known as baby bellas, these dark brown all-purpose mushrooms have meatier flavor than buttons.

PORTOBELLO Large round cap with meatlike texture and flavor—popular alternatives for vegetarians.

BUTTON Most common grocery store variety, with mild earthiness for most versatility.

CHANTERELLE Funnel-shape fungi tastes as complex as fine French wine with notes of black pepper and apricot.

MAITAKE Golden, frilly showstopper has semi-firm texture and rich woodsy flavor.

SHIITAKE A distinct cap—like an umbrella—tops this Asian cooking staple that has slightly smoky flavor.

BEECH Named because it commonly grows on beech trees, this petite variety (white or brown) is sweet and nutty with crisp texture.

ROASTED MAITAKE-GOAT CHEESE TART

Roasting flowerlike clusters of maitake mushrooms (also known as hen of the woods) in a hot oven browns and crisps the frilly edges to look especially artful on this savory tart. The creamy filling of goat cheese, crème fraîche, and lemon balances the richness of the mushrooms.

HANDS-ON TIME 20 min.
TOTAL TIME 2 hr. 15 min.

Nonstick cooking spray
1¼ cups all-purpose flour
½ cup cold unsalted butter, cubed
½ tsp. kosher salt
2 Tbsp. ice water
3 whole heads maitake mushrooms (12 to 15 oz. total) or two 8-oz. pkg. fresh sliced button mushrooms
3 Tbsp. extra virgin olive oil
   Salt and black pepper
3 Tbsp. cold unsalted butter, cubed
4 oz. goat cheese, crumbled
¼ cup crème fraîche
1 egg
1½ tsp. chopped fresh thyme
½ cup coarsely chopped flat-leaf parsley
   Zest of 1 lemon

1. For crust: Lightly coat a 9-inch square or round tart pan with removable bottom with nonstick cooking spray.
2. In a food processor pulse flour, ½ cup butter, and salt until fine crumbs form. Add water; pulse until crumbly pieces form and mixture holds together when pinched, scraping bowl as needed. Transfer dough to prepared tart pan. Press evenly on bottom and up sides. Cover; freeze 10 minutes or until firm.

3. Meanwhile, for filling: Preheat oven to 425°F. Line a shallow baking pan with foil. Break maitakes into smaller pieces. Place in prepared pan. Drizzle with oil; season generously with salt and black pepper. Dot tops with 3 Tbsp. butter. Roast 25 to 30 minutes or until crisp and tops are brown.
4. Lightly coat a piece of foil with nonstick cooking spray. Line tart shell with foil, coated side down. Fill with pie weights or dried beans. Place on a baking sheet. Bake 25 minutes in oven with maitakes. Remove weights and foil (crust may crack slightly.) Bake 5 minutes more or until center is set. Cool.
5. For filling: In a small bowl stir together goat cheese, crème fraîche, egg, thyme, ½ tsp. salt, and ¼ tsp. black pepper until nearly smooth. Evenly spread filling on baked crust. Arrange roasted mushrooms on filling.
6. Bake 10 to 15 minutes or until filling edges are puffed and center is set. Cool in pan on a wire rack 30 minutes. Remove sides of pan; transfer to a serving plate. Sprinkle with parsley and lemon zest. Makes 9 servings.
PER SERVING *313 cal, 25 g fat, 74 mg chol, 254 mg sodium, 17 g carb, 2 g fiber, 1 g sugars, 6 g pro.*

MUSHROOM
MISO SOUP

JAPANESE MISO, A FERMENTED SOYBEAN PASTE, GIVES SAVORY FLAVOR TO SOUPS, SAUCES, MARINADES, AND SALAD DRESSINGS.

MUSHROOM MISO SOUP

Find Japanese miso in Asian markets or in the refrigerator section at health food stores and large grocery stores.

TOTAL TIME 20 min.

6   oz. thin rice noodles
2   cloves garlic, thinly sliced
½   tsp. salt
¼   cup white miso paste
1   lb. white button mushrooms, thinly sliced
4   green onions, thinly bias-sliced
     Juice of 1 lime
     Crushed red pepper
     Sesame seeds
     Soy sauce (optional)

1. Cook noodles according to package directions; drain.
2. Meanwhile, in a 4- to 5-qt. pot bring 6 cups water, garlic, and salt to boiling. In a small heatproof bowl whisk together miso and ½ cup water mixture until smooth. Stir into pot. Add mushrooms and green onions. Return to boiling; reduce heat to medium. Cook 2 minutes. Stir in noodles and lime juice; heat through.
3. Ladle into soup bowls. Sprinkle with crushed red pepper, sesame seeds, and additional chopped green onions. If desired, serve with soy sauce. Makes 8 servings.
PER SERVING *111 cal, 1 g fat, 509 mg sodium, 22 g carb, 2 g fiber, 2 g sugars, 4 g pro.*

"CREAM" OF MUSHROOM SOUP

This soup gets rich flavor from deeply browned mushrooms and sherry, and it has amazingly velvety texture.

TOTAL TIME 30 min.

3   Tbsp. extra virgin olive oil, plus more as needed
1   lb. white button mushrooms, halved
1   cup chopped yellow onion
4   fresh thyme sprigs
½   tsp. salt
4   cups vegetable stock
¼   cup dry sherry
     Black pepper
¼   cup pine nuts, lightly toasted (tip, page 37)
2   Tbsp. sliced fresh chives

1. In a 6-qt. Dutch oven heat 2 Tbsp. oil over medium-high heat. Add half the mushrooms cut sides down. Cook, without stirring, 4 to 5 minutes or until cut sides are dark golden brown. Transfer to a bowl. Repeat with remaining oil and mushrooms. Return all mushrooms to pot. Add onion, thyme, and ¼ tsp. salt. Reduce heat to medium-low. Cook, uncovered, 10 minutes, stirring occasionally.
2. Add ½ cup stock. Bring to boiling. Cook, uncovered, 3 minutes or until liquid is almost evaporated, stirring occasionally. Carefully add sherry. Cook, uncovered, 2 to 3 minutes or until almost evaporated, stirring occasionally. Add remaining stock. Bring to boiling; reduce heat to medium-low. Simmer, uncovered, 5 minutes. Stir in remaining ¼ tsp. salt. Remove from heat. Cool slightly.
3. Remove thyme sprigs. Use an immersion blender to puree soup until smooth. Season to taste with additional salt and black pepper. Ladle into serving bowls; sprinkle with pine nuts and chives. Makes 4 to 6 servings.
PER SERVING *223 cal, 17 g fat, 821 mg sodium, 13 g carb, 2 g fiber, 6 g sugars, 6 g pro.*

"CREAM" OF MUSHROOM SOUP

SPICE BLENDS

Inhale the fragrance—then add a pinch of global flavor.

BERBERE

Ethiopia's hot-sweet blend brings warm citrus notes to beef stews, lentils, and roasted vegetables.

Combine 2 Tbsp. New Mexico or Ancho ground chile pepper; 2 tsp. cayenne pepper; 1 tsp. each paprika, onion powder, and ground ginger; and ½ tsp. each ground cinnamon, ground cardamom, garlic powder, ground coriander, and salt. Makes about 5 Tbsp.

DUKKAH

The savory Egyptian nut-and-spice blend has coarse texture that makes a wonderful crust for meat and a crunchy addition to grains or pasta dishes.

In a small skillet toast ½ cup coarsely chopped hazelnuts over medium-high heat 3 minutes or until fragrant. Transfer to a bowl. In hot skillet combine 1 Tbsp. each coriander and sesame seeds and 1½ tsp. anise seeds. Toast 2 minutes or until fragrant. Let cool. Using a spice grinder, grind seeds and hazelnuts just until coarsely ground. Transfer to a bowl. Stir in ½ tsp. salt and ¼ tsp. black pepper. Makes about ¾ cup.

RAS EL HANOUT

The name of this North African blend means top shelf, reflecting spice sellers' practice of creating it from their best spices. Rub on chicken, mix into lamb or beef meatballs, or stir into couscous.

Combine 1 tsp. each ground cumin, ground ginger, and salt; ½ tsp. each ground allspice, black pepper, cinnamon, cayenne pepper, and turmeric; and ¼ tsp. ground cloves. Makes about 2 Tbsp.

ZA'ATAR

Sprinkle this traditional Middle Eastern blend on grilled vegetables or whirl into yogurt dip and hummus.

Combine 1 Tbsp. each ground sumac and dried thyme; 2 tsp. dried oregano; and 1 tsp. each toasted sesame seeds, salt, and ground black pepper. Makes about 4 Tbsp.

BERBERE IS A COMBO OF CINNAMON, CAYENNE PEPPER, CARDAMOM, GINGER, PAPRIKA, AND MORE.

DUKKAH INCLUDES ANISE, CORIANDER, AND SESAME SEEDS, PLUS HAZELNUTS OR ALMONDS.

RAS EL HANOUT VARIES BUT OFTEN CONTAINS CINNAMON, CUMIN, BLACK AND RED PEPPERS, AND TURMERIC.

ZA'ATAR TENDS TO MIX THYME, TOASTED SESAME SEEDS, OREGANO, AND SUMAC.

CHECK YOUR SPICE COLLECTION. YOU MAY ALREADY HAVE THE INGREDIENTS TO MAKE THESE EXOTIC-NAMED SPICE BLENDS.

RHUBARB TART
Recipe on page 87

april

Celebrate spring. Serve rhubarb in sweet and savory dishes, gather around Seder dinners that honor tradition, and find fresh ideas for Easter, plus quick-to-the table weeknight meals.

79

82

95

EASTER BASKET CAKE

A basket-weave piping tip makes easy work of creating this impressive cake.

EASTER BASKET CAKE

HANDS-ON TIME 30 min.
TOTAL TIME 2 hr.

        Butter
2   cups all-purpose flour
1   tsp. baking powder
½   tsp. baking soda
½   tsp. salt
½   cup shortening
1¾   cups sugar
1   tsp. vanilla
4   egg whites, room temperature
1⅓   cups buttermilk
¼   cup miniature semisweet chocolate
     pieces
½   tsp. coconut extract
⅓   cup plus 3 Tbsp. unsweetened
     cocoa powder
     Brown Butter Frosting
1   cup toasted coconut flakes
     (tip, page 59)
     Egg Sugar Cookies (recipe, right)

1. Preheat oven to 350°F. Butter and lightly flour a 13×9-inch baking pan. In a medium bowl stir together flour, baking powder, baking soda, and salt.
2. In a large bowl beat shortening with a mixer on medium 30 seconds. Add sugar and vanilla; beat on medium 3 to 5 minutes or until light and fluffy. Add egg whites, one at a time, beating after each. Alternately add flour mixture and buttermilk, beating on low after each addition just until combined.
3. Divide batter in half. Stir chocolate pieces and coconut extract into half the batter and ⅓ cup of the cocoa powder into remaining half. Alternately spoon mounds of each batter into prepared pan. Using a table knife, swirl batters together.
4. Bake 30 minutes or until a toothpick inserted near center comes out clean. Cool in pan 10 minutes. Remove cake from pan; let cool on a wire rack.
5. Prepare Brown Butter Frosting. Set aside 2 cups of the frosting. Stir remaining 3 Tbsp. cocoa into the milk (1 to 2 tsp.) as needed to reach spreading consistency. Place cake on a serving platter. Frost entire cake with plain frosting. Place cocoa frosting in a pastry bag fitted with a basket-weave decorating tip. Pipe a basket pattern on lower half of cake (directions, right). Pipe on a basket handle. Sprinkle toasted coconut at top of basket and around

cake on platter. Add decorated Egg Sugar Cookies at top of basket. Makes 12 to 16 servings.
Brown Butter Frosting In a small saucepan heat ¾ cup butter over low heat until melted. Cook until light golden brown. Remove from heat; let cool. In a large bowl combine 6 cups powdered sugar, 4 Tbsp. milk, and 2 tsp. vanilla. Add brown butter. Beat with a mixer on low until combined. Beat on medium to high while adding additional milk 1 tsp. at a time to reach spreading consistency.
PER SERVING *753 cal, 29 g fat, 46 mg chol, 412 mg sodium, 122 g carb, 3 g fiber, 98 g sugars, 7 g pro.*

EGG SUGAR COOKIES

HANDS-ON TIME 20 min.
TOTAL TIME 3 hr.

1⅓   cups butter, softened
⅔   cup granulated sugar
1   tsp. baking powder
½   tsp. salt
2   eggs
2   tsp. vanilla
3   cups all-purpose flour
2   cups powdered sugar
2   Tbsp. milk
1   tsp. vanilla
     Gel food coloring
4   tsp. vanilla
1   Tbsp. unsweetened cocoa powder

1. In a large bowl beat butter with an electric mixer on medium 30 seconds. Add sugar, baking powder, and salt; beat until combined. Beat in eggs and 2 tsp. vanilla until combined. Beat in as much of the flour as you can; stir in remaining flour. Divide dough in half; wrap each half in plastic wrap. Chill 30 to 60 minutes or until easy to handle.
2. Preheat oven to 375°F. On a lightly floured surface, roll one dough portion to ¼-inch thickness. Using a 2½- to 3-inch egg-shape cutter, cut out dough. Arrange 2 inches apart on ungreased cookie sheets. Reroll scraps. Bake 7 minutes or until edges are firm. Remove; cool on a wire rack. Repeat with remaining dough.
3. For icing, in a medium bowl combine the powdered sugar, milk, and 1 tsp. vanilla. If necessary, add enough milk, 1 tsp. at a time, to make a glazing consistency. Divide icing among bowls. Tint each with food coloring. Dip tops

of cookies into glaze, allowing excess to drip off. Set on waxed paper. In a small bowl combine 4 tsp. vanilla and cocoa powder. Dip a small, clean food-safe brush into cocoa mixture and flick onto cookies to make spots (if cocoa mixture thickens, add a few drops of water at a time to desired consistency). Allow to stand until set. Makes 36 cookies.
PER COOKIE *146 cal, 7 g fat, 28 mg chol, 105 mg sodium, 19 g carb, 10 g sugar, 2 g pro.*

BASKET WEAVE

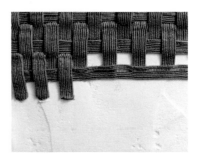

HORIZONTAL LINES For a dimensional basket-weave, use a decorating bag fitted with a basket-weave tip. Holding the bag with the serrated tip edge up, pipe a solid horizontal stripe.

VERTICAL LINES Using horizontal line as a guide, pipe short vertical lines over the horizontals, spacing each approximately the width of the decorating tip. Repeat horizontal and vertical lines, staggering vertical lines to cover.

how to cook
HAM IT UP

Easter—one holiday that supermarkets fill meat cases with hams of all types and sizes. Even if you have your plan down to a science, these recipes will inspire you.

STUFFED
SPIRAL HAM

STUFFED SPIRAL HAM

HANDS-ON TIME 20 minutes
TOTAL TIME 3 hours

1	8- to 10-lb. spiral-sliced ham
½	orange, thinly sliced
4	cloves garlic, slivered
6	sprigs fresh rosemary and/or thyme, chopped
	Glaze

1. Preheat oven to 325°F. Line a shallow roasting pan with foil. Between ham slices insert orange, garlic, rosemary, and/or thyme. Transfer ham, flat side down, to prepared pan. Cover with foil.
2. Bake 2 to 2½ hours or until browned and heated through (140°F). During last 45 minutes of cooking, uncover ham and spoon glaze over ham. Transfer to a platter using two large wide spatulas. Makes 16 servings.
PER SERVING 170 cal, 4 g fat, 98 mg chol, 1,978 mg sodium, 4 g carb, 3 g sugars, 32 g pro.
Spiced Pepper Glaze In a small bowl stir together ¾ cup red jalapeño pepper jelly and 1½ tsp. five-spice powder.
Cranberry-BBQ Glaze In a small bowl stir together ½ cup jellied cranberry sauce, ½ cup bottled barbecue sauce, and 2 Tbsp. honey.
Orange-Bourbon Glaze In a small bowl combine ½ cup orange marmalade or peach preserves, ½ cup stone ground mustard, and 2 Tbsp. bourbon.

FALL STUFFED HAM: OMIT ORANGE AND USE 1 APPLE AND 1 PEAR, EACH CORED, HALVED, AND THINLY SLICED.

HAM AND PEA TORTELLINI

HAM AND PEA TORTELLINI

HANDS-ON TIME 10 min.
TOTAL TIME 20 min.

1	9-oz. pkg. refrigerated cheese-filled tortellini
½	cup peas
1	Tbsp. butter
1	cup cubed ham
2	cups fresh arugula
½	cup half-and-half
¼	cup Parmesan cheese

1. Cook tortellini according to package directions, adding peas the last 2 minutes. Drain, reserving ½ cup cooking liquid.

2. In the same pot melt butter over medium heat. Add cubed ham; cook 2 minutes or until heated through. Stir in arugula until wilted. Stir in half-and-half; bring to boiling. Reduce heat; simmer 2 to 3 minutes or until thickened. Stir in Parmesan cheese and pasta mixture; heat through. Stir in reserved cooking liquid, if necessary. Makes 4 servings.
PER SERVING 309 cal, 12 g fat, 57 mg chol, 787 mg sodium, 35 g carb, 3 g fiber, 5 g sugars, 17 g pro.

CHEF'S SALAD

HANDS-ON TIME 15 min.
TOTAL TIME 45 min., includes marinating

⅓ cup olive oil
¼ cup malt or cider vinegar
1 Tbsp. chopped fresh dill
1 Tbsp. capers
¼ tsp. kosher salt
1 10-oz. container grape tomatoes, halved
6 cups torn iceberg lettuce
6 oz. cooked ham, cut into strips
1 cup shredded cooked chicken
4 oz. cubed cheddar cheese
4 hard-boiled eggs, halved
8 slices toasted* party rye bread

1. Whisk together oil, vinegar, dill, capers, and salt. Add tomatoes; let stand 15 minutes.
2. On a platter arrange lettuce, ham, chicken, cheese, eggs, and rye toasts. Spoon on tomatoes and dressing. Makes 4 servings.
*Tip Toast rye bread slices on a baking sheet under a broiler, 4 inches from the heat, about 3 minutes or until toasted, turning once.
PER SERVING *521 cal, 36 g fat, 271 mg chol, 1,214 mg sodium, 16 g carb, 3 g fiber, 6 g sugars, 32 g pro.*

OPEN-FACE CUBAN SANDWICH

TOTAL TIME 15 min.

4 ½-inch slices toasted country bread
2 Tbsp. yellow mustard
¼ cup dill pickle slices
8 oz. thinly sliced cooked ham
8 oz. thinly sliced deli roast beef
4 oz. Swiss cheese

On each toasted bread slice spread ½ Tbsp. mustard. Top with pickle slices, ham, roast beef, and Swiss cheese. Broil 1 to 2 minutes until cheese is melted. Makes 4 servings.
PER SERVING *299 cal, 13 g fat, 67 mg chol, 1,305 mg sodium, 19 g carb. 2 g fiber, 26 g pro.*

TEX-MEX HAM AND BEANS

TOTAL TIME 20 min.

2 slices bacon, chopped
1½ cups chopped ham
½ cup chopped onion
½ cup chopped green bell pepper
1 chopped jalapeño (tip, page 59) (optional)
2 cloves garlic, minced
3 medium tomatoes, chopped
1 15-oz. can pinto beans, rinsed and drained
Chopped fresh cilantro

In a large skillet cook bacon over medium heat until crisp. Add ham, onion, green bell pepper, jalapeño (if using), and garlic. Cook and stir 4 minutes until vegetables are tender. Stir in tomatoes and beans. Bring to boiling; reduce heat. Simmer, uncovered, 10 minutes, stirring occasionally. Top with cilantro. Makes 4 servings.
PER SERVING *225 cal, 6 g fat, 31 mg chol, 1,072 mg sodium, 23 g carb, 3 g fiber, 5 g sugar, 17 g pro.*

OPEN-FACE CUBAN SANDWICH

TEX-MEX HAM AND BEANS

great starts
CHIA

Mix chia seeds with Greek yogurt and a hint of sweetness, then top with fruit for an on-the-go pudding that's healthful enough to eat for breakfast.

BASIC CHIA PUDDING

Chia seeds are rich in fiber and a good source of omega-3 fats. Mixed with liquid, chia seeds swell into a gelled tapioca-like texture.

HANDS-ON TIME 10 min.
TOTAL TIME 2 hr. 10 min., includes chilling

1¾ cups milk or unsweetened
      nondairy milk
1   cup plain fat-free Greek yogurt
2   Tbsp. honey, maple syrup, or
      agave syrup
1   tsp. vanilla
¼   tsp. kosher salt
½   cup chia seeds
      Toppings, such as fruit, toasted nuts,
      granola, and/or toasted coconut

1. In a medium bowl whisk together milk, yogurt, honey, vanilla, and salt. Whisk in chia seeds.
2. Divide pudding among four half-pint jars or 6-oz. bowls or ramekins. Cover; chill at least 2 hours. Serve with toppings. Makes 4 servings.
PER SERVING *208 cal, 8 g fat, 9 mg chol, 145 mg sodium, 24 g carb, 6 g fiber, 16 g sugars, 12 g pro.*

Mexican Chocolate Chia Pudding Prepare Basic Chia Pudding, increasing honey to 3 Tbsp. and whisking 3 Tbsp. unsweetened cocoa powder and 1 tsp. ground cinnamon into pudding. Top with berries and/or chopped toasted hazelnuts.
Coconut and Tropical Fruit Chia Pudding Prepare Basic Chia Pudding, substituting unsweetened light coconut milk for the milk and coconut yogurt for plain yogurt. For toppings, in a small bowl combine ¼ cup each chopped fresh pineapple and mango with 1 tsp. lime zest. Top pudding with toasted unsweetened coconut flakes.

FAST & FRESH

Easy, delicious recipes for a better dinner tonight.

SPICED TURKEY PITAS WITH CUCUMBER, OLIVES, AND MINT

These turkey patties are inspired by kibbeh, a traditional Middle Eastern dish of ground meat (usually lamb), bulgur, onions, and spices which is often shaped into patties.

TOTAL TIME 35 min.

1	cup uncooked bulgur
3	Tbsp. olive oil
1	cup onion, finely chopped
1	lb. ground turkey
	Zest and juice of 1 lemon
¼	cup chopped fresh mint leaves
2	Tbsp. chopped flat-leaf parsley
1	tsp. za'atar seasoning
¾	tsp. salt
½	tsp. black pepper
2	cups chopped English cucumber
½	cup Kalamata olives, pitted and halved
6	pita bread rounds
¼	cup plain yogurt

1. In a small heatproof bowl place bulgur and enough boiling water to cover; let stand 10 minutes. Drain well.
2. Meanwhile, in a large skillet cook and stir onion in 1 Tbsp. hot oil 4 minutes or until tender. Transfer to a large bowl; cool slightly. Add turkey, bulgur, lemon zest, 1 Tbsp. mint, the parsley, za'atar, ½ tsp. salt, and ¼ tsp. pepper. Mix well. Shape into six 3½-inch patties. In the same skillet heat 1 Tbsp. olive oil over medium heat. Add patties. Cook 5 to 6 minutes on each side or until done (165°F). Add more oil if necessary to prevent sticking.
3. In a medium bowl whisk together lemon juice and remaining 1 Tbsp. oil. Add cucumber, olives, remaining 3 Tbsp. mint, and remaining ¼ tsp. each salt and pepper. Serve patties on pita bread with cucumber mixture, yogurt, and additional mint and/or parsley. If desired, drizzle with olive oil. Makes 6 servings.
PER SERVING *478 cal, 17 g fat, 53 mg chol, 744 mg sodium, 57 g carb, 5 g fiber, 3 g sugars, 25 g pro.*

CARROT AND
CHICKPEA SKILLET

LIME CHICKEN TORTILLA SOUP

CARROT AND CHICKPEA SKILLET

Briefly toasting the chickpeas crisps them and develops brown bits in the pan that flavor the dish. Chickpeas' starch also thickens the sauce.

TOTAL TIME 35 min.

- 3   Tbsp. olive oil
- 2   15-oz. cans chickpeas, rinsed and drained
- 1   lb. carrots, peeled and sliced ¼ inch thick
- 2   cups cauliflower florets
- 1   tsp. smoked paprika
- 1   tsp. ground cumin
- ½   tsp. salt
- 1   cup vegetable broth
- ½   cup orange juice
     Fresh mint leaves (optional)
     Cooked couscous, quinoa, or brown rice (optional)

1. In a 12-inch skillet heat 2 Tbsp. oil over medium-high heat. Add chickpeas; cook 4 minutes or until lightly browned, stirring occasionally. Remove chickpeas from skillet.
2. Add remaining 1 Tbsp. oil to skillet. Add carrots, cauliflower, paprika, cumin, and salt. Cook 5 minutes or just until carrots and cauliflower are tender, stirring occasionally. Add broth and orange juice. Bring to boiling; reduce heat. Boil gently, uncovered, 10 minutes. Stir in chickpeas; heat through. If desired, sprinkle with mint and serve with couscous, quinoa, or brown rice. Makes 4 servings.
PER SERVING *415 cal, 15 g fat, 771 mg sodium, 58 g carb, 14 g fiber, 14 g sugars, 14 g pro.*

LIME CHICKEN TORTILLA SOUP

Purchased rotisserie chicken works well here, or with extra time you can cook one. Poach 1 pound skinless, boneless chicken breasts or thighs in water or broth 15 minutes. Cool 5 minutes, then shred into bite-size pieces with two forks.

TOTAL TIME 30 min.

- 1   cup onion, chopped
- 1   fresh poblano chile pepper, stemmed, seeded, and chopped (tip, page 59)
- 1   Tbsp. olive oil
- 1   32-oz. container chicken broth
- 1½ cups chopped tomato
- 1   tsp. ground cumin
- ½   tsp. salt
- ¼   tsp. black pepper
- 4   6-inch corn tortillas, cut into ½-inch strips
- 2   cups shredded cooked chicken
- 1   cup frozen corn kernels
- 2   avocados, halved, seeded, peeled, and sliced
- 1   lime, juiced
     Fresh cilantro (optional)
     Thinly sliced radishes (optional)

1. Preheat oven to 375°F. In a 3-qt. saucepan cook onion and poblano in 1 Tbsp. hot oil over medium heat 4 to 5 minutes or until tender, stirring occasionally. Stir in broth, tomato, cumin, salt, and black pepper. Bring to boiling; reduce heat. Simmer, uncovered, 15 minutes, stirring occasionally.
2. Meanwhile, place tortilla strips in a single layer on a baking sheet. Bake 10 minutes or until crisp.
3. Stir chicken and corn into soup; heat through. Just before serving, stir in avocados and lime juice. Top each serving with tortilla strips and, if desired, cilantro and radish slices. Makes 6 servings.
PER SERVING *272 cal, 13 g fat, 42 mg chol, 596 mg sodium, 22 g carb, 5 g fiber, 4 g sugars, 19 g pro.*

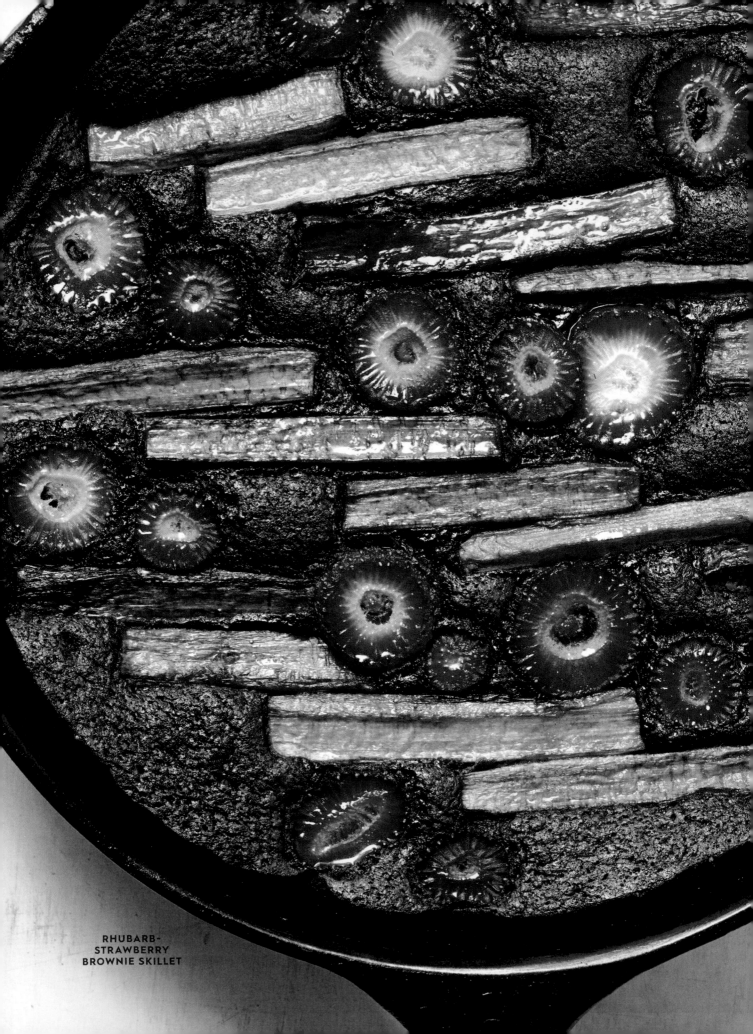

RHUBARB-
STRAWBERRY
BROWNIE SKILLET

SPRING FLING

Rhubarb—like strawberries—is a spring darling, and although famous for bright pink stalks they can also be light pink or pale green. Enjoy the tart stalks in these unexpectedly sweet and savory versions.

RHUBARB-STRAWBERRY BROWNIE SKILLET

Topping brownie batter with rhubarb and strawberries before baking yields rich, gooey treats.

HANDS-ON TIME 15 min.
TOTAL TIME 1 hr. 10 min.

- 2 Tbsp. butter, plus more for skillet
- 8 to 10 oz. fresh rhubarb, trimmed and cut into 4-inch pieces
- 1 cup plus 1 Tbsp. sugar
- ½ cup butter
- 3 oz. unsweetened chocolate, coarsely chopped
- 2 eggs
- 1 tsp. vanilla
- ⅔ cup all-purpose flour
- ¼ tsp. baking soda
- 1 cup sliced strawberries

1. Preheat oven to 350°F. In a 10-inch cast-iron skillet heat 2 Tbsp. butter over medium heat. Add rhubarb. Cook 5 minutes, gently stirring occasionally. Remove from skillet; sprinkle with 1 Tbsp. sugar. Let skillet cool then wipe out. Coat skillet with additional butter; set aside.
2. In a medium saucepan combine ½ cup butter and the unsweetened chocolate; stir over low heat until melted and smooth. Remove from heat. Stir in 1 cup sugar. Add eggs, one at a time, beating after each addition just until combined. Stir in vanilla. In a small bowl stir together flour and baking soda. Add flour mixture to chocolate mixture; stir just until combined. Spread in prepared skillet. Arrange rhubarb and strawberries on batter.
3. Bake 50 to 55 minutes or until edges are firm and center appears set. Makes 8 servings.
PER SERVING *368 cal, 21 g fat, 85 mg chol, 176 mg sodium, 41 g carb, 3 g fiber, 28 g sugars, 5 g pro.*

RHUBARB TART

Photo on page 74 and 88.

Simmering rhubarb in vanilla syrup yields crisp-tender stalks and tempers the puckery bite. Arrange in a graphic checkerboard pattern on mascarpone-filled shortbread crust and brush on syrup right before serving. Store leftover syrup to serve on pound cake, angel food cake, or yogurt.

HANDS-ON TIME 15 min.
TOTAL TIME 3 hr. 15 min., includes chilling

Crust
- ⅓ cup sugar
- 5 Tbsp. butter, softened
- 1 tsp. vanilla
- ¼ tsp. salt
- 1 cup all-purpose flour
- ½ cup almond flour

Filling and Topping
- ¾ cup heavy cream
- 1½ cups sugar
- ½ cup mascarpone cheese
- ½ tsp. vanilla
- ½ vanilla bean or 1 tsp. vanilla
- 1 lb. fresh rhubarb, trimmed and cut into 1½×½-inch pieces

1. For Crust: Preheat oven to 350°F. In a bowl beat sugar, butter, vanilla, and salt with a mixer on medium until combined. Add flours; beat until crumbly.
2. Press crumbs firmly and evenly into bottom and up sides of a 9-inch square tart pan with removable bottom. Bake 15 minutes or until edges are lightly browned. (Do not overbake.) Let cool.
3. For Filling and Topping: In a medium bowl beat heavy cream and ½ cup sugar with a mixer until soft peaks form. Add mascarpone and ½ tsp. vanilla; beat until stiff peaks form. Spread filling in baked tart shell; cover. Chill 2 hours.
4. Meanwhile, in a large skillet combine remaining 1 cup sugar and ½ cup water. Scrape out vanilla bean seeds with the tip of a knife and add to mixture. Bring to boiling, stirring to dissolve sugar. Add rhubarb; reduce heat. Simmer, uncovered, 6 minutes or until the tip of a knife easily pierces rhubarb. Remove rhubarb from syrup with a slotted spoon; cool to room temperature. Continue cooking syrup, uncovered, 3 minutes. Cool completely. (Syrup will thicken as it cools.)
5. Arrange rhubarb pieces on filling. Brush with some syrup. Serve with remaining syrup. Makes 9 servings.
Simplified Topping Rather than arrange rhubarb on filling, cut stalks into ½-inch slices; cook in syrup 4 minutes. Remove rhubarb with a slotted spoon. Spoon over tart just before serving.
PER SERVING *437 cal, 22 g fat, 57 mg chol, 130 mg sodium, 56 g carb, 2 g fiber, 42 g sugars, 4 g pro.*

WHAT GROWS TOGETHER GOES TOGETHER. BOTH STRAWBERRY AND RHUBARB PLANTS FLOURISH COME SPRINGTIME.

RHUBARB TART
Recipe on page 87

RHUBARB PULLED PORK
Recipe on page 90

TART RHUBARB STANDS UP TO THE SHARP TASTE OF FRESH GINGER AND GINGER ALE IN THIS BUBBLY MOCKTAIL. MAKE THE RASPBERRY-RHUBARB SYRUP AHEAD, THEN POUR IN GINGER ALE COME PARTY TIME.

RHUBARB PULLED PORK

Photo on page 89.

This seasonal riff on a BBQ favorite doubles up on rhubarb. First, rhubarb is cooked until tender in a sweet balsamic sauce that mellows the vegetable's tang and coats shredded slow-cooked pork. Second, raw rhubarb matchsticks added to cabbage slaw present a surprising note.

HANDS-ON TIME 40 min.
TOTAL TIME 5 hr. 40 min.

3   Tbsp. chopped fresh thyme
1   Tbsp. lemon zest
1   tsp. onion salt
1   tsp. garlic powder
1   2½- to 3-lb. boneless pork shoulder, trimmed
1   Tbsp. olive oil
⅓   cup plus ½ cup white balsamic vinegar
1   sweet onion, halved and sliced (1½ cups)
1   bulb fennel, trimmed, cored, and sliced (1 cup)
¼   tsp. salt
1   cup chicken broth
2   cups ½-inch slices fresh rhubarb
     Rhubarb Coleslaw (recipe, right) (optional)

1. In a bowl combine 2 Tbsp. thyme, the lemon zest, onion salt, and garlic powder. Rub pork with mixture. Wrap in plastic wrap; chill 2 to 24 hours.
2. Preheat oven to 325°F; position a rack in the lower third of oven. In a 4- to 5-qt. Dutch oven heat oil over medium-high heat. Add pork. Brown evenly on all sides, about 8 minutes. Remove pork. Add ⅓ cup vinegar to Dutch oven, scraping up any browned bits. Add onion, fennel, and ¼ tsp. salt. Cook 8 to 10 minutes or until browned, stirring occasionally.

3. Place pork on onion mixture. Add broth, ½ cup vinegar, and 1 Tbsp. thyme. Bring to boiling; cover. Transfer to oven. Bake 3 to 3½ hours or until pork is tender.
4. Transfer pork to a bowl; cover. For sauce: Add rhubarb to cooking liquid in Dutch oven. Bring to boiling; reduce heat. Cook, uncovered, 7 minutes or until rhubarb is softened and sauce is thickened, stirring occasionally. If sauce is too tart, add 1 tsp. brown sugar. Shred pork; add to sauce. Heat through. Serve on split hamburger buns with Rhubarb Coleslaw, if desired. Makes 8 servings.
PER SERVING *354 cal, 8 g fat, 70 mg chol, 576 mg sodium, 39 g carb, 2 g fiber, 17 g sugars, 30 g pro.*

RHUBARB COLESLAW

HANDS-ON TIME 10 min.
TOTAL TIME 2 hr. 20 min., includes chilling

1   cup julienned fresh rhubarb
¼   cup apple cider vinegar
2   tsp. sugar
½   cup mayonnaise
¼   tsp. salt
3   cups finely shredded green cabbage
1   cup finely shredded carrot

1. In a large bowl toss rhubarb with vinegar and sugar. Let stand 10 minutes.
2. Stir mayonnaise and salt into rhubarb mixture until combined. Add cabbage and carrot; stir to combine. Cover; chill 2 to 4 hours before serving. Makes 6 to 8 servings.
PER SERVING *147 cal, 14 g fat, 8 mg chol, 228 mg sodium, 5 g carb, 1 g fiber, 3 g sugars, 1 g pro.*

GINGER RHUBARB-RASPBERRY PUNCH

HANDS-ON TIME 20 min.
TOTAL TIME 2 hr. 40 min., includes chilling

1   cup sugar
3   cups ¼-inch slices fresh rhubarb
1   2-inch piece fresh ginger, peeled and sliced
1   6-oz. container fresh raspberries
¼   cup fresh lemon juice
1   2-liter bottle ginger ale, chilled
     Lemon slices and fresh raspberries
     Rhubarb stalks, trimmed

1. For rhubarb syrup: In a medium saucepan combine sugar, 1 cup water, the rhubarb slices, and ginger. Bring to boiling over medium-high heat, stirring to dissolve sugar. Reduce heat; cover. Simmer 10 minutes. Remove from heat; stir in raspberries. Let stand 10 minutes. Use a potato masher to mash mixture. Strain mixture through a fine-mesh sieve, pressing to remove all juices. Discard pulp. Add lemon juice to rhubarb syrup; cover. Chill 2 to 24 hours.
2. In a pitcher stir together ginger ale and rhubarb syrup. Add lemon slices and additional raspberries. Serve over ice; use rhubarb stalks as swizzle sticks. Makes 14 servings.
PER SERVING *125 cal, 13 mg sodium, 32 g carb, 2 g fiber, 29 g sugars, 1 g pro.*

GINGER RHUBARB-
RASPBERRY PUNCH

RHUBARB-BACON JAM

RHUBARB SMARTS

The stalks are long, but the season is short. From April to June you'll find an abundance of field-grown rhubarb at farmers markets. Those dark rosy stalks tend to have more flavor than hothouse rhubarb, which is what you'll often see in grocery stores from January through June. Those stalks may be lighter color and have tinges of green or pink speckles, but color doesn't indicate a significant variation in taste. For the most tender, sweetest stalks, look for firm young ones—less than 2 inches wide. Peak-season rhubarb does not need to be peeled, but by midsummer, stalks tend to be tough and fibrous. Remove and discard leaves right away because they contain oxalic acid, which is toxic. Store in the fridge in a plastic bag up to 3 days or freeze to enjoy year-round. To freeze, cut into 1-inch pieces, place on a baking pan lined with parchment paper, and freeze until firm. Transfer to freezer bags and store up to a year. It's easy to grow your own too. Plant in late fall or early spring where rhubarb will get at least a half day of sun and have room to spread 4 feet.

"RHU-BERRY" STREUSEL MUFFINS

ICED OATMEAL-RHUBARB COOKIES

RHUBARB-BACON JAM

There are endless ways to enjoy this smoky-sweet spread. Spoon on ricotta-topped toasts, layer it on a grilled cheese, spread it on grilled pork chops, or serve it on a cheese board.

TOTAL TIME 45 min.

- 3   to 5 slices bacon
- 2   cups finely chopped red onion
- 2   cups chopped fresh rhubarb
- ⅓   cup pure maple syrup
- 3   Tbsp. apple cider vinegar
- 1   lemon (1 tsp. zest; 1 Tbsp. juice)
     Crusty bread
     Whole milk ricotta cheese

1. Heat a large skillet over medium heat. Add bacon; cook 8 minutes or until brown and crisp. Remove, reserving 2 Tbsp. drippings in skillet; drain bacon on paper towels. Add onion to skillet, stirring to scrape up any browned bits.
2. Reduce heat to medium-low; cook 8 to 10 minutes or until onion is soft and slightly caramelized, stirring occasionally. Meanwhile, chop cooked bacon. Return to skillet. Stir in rhubarb, maple syrup, and vinegar. Continue to cook over medium-low heat 5 to 8 minutes or until rhubarb is soft, stirring occasionally. Stir in lemon zest and juice. Use a potato masher to slightly mash jam. Serve warm on bread spread with ricotta. Makes 14 servings.
PER SERVING *126 cal, 5 g fat, 12 mg chol, 127 mg sodium, 16 g carb, 1 g fiber, 6 g sugars, 4 g pro.*

RHU-BERRY STREUSEL MUFFINS

Blueberry muffins become less ordinary with fresh rhubarb in the batter, then some into the cardamom-spiced streusel topping. They reheat well, so freeze extras for a quick breakfast.

HANDS-ON TIME 20 min.
TOTAL TIME 1 hr.

     Nonstick cooking spray
- 2½ cups all-purpose flour
- ¼   cup packed brown sugar
- ¾   tsp. ground cardamom
     Salt
- ¼   cup cold butter, cut up
- ¼   cup finely chopped fresh rhubarb
- ½   cup granulated sugar
- 2½ tsp. baking powder
- 2   eggs
- ¾   cup plain Greek yogurt
- 6   Tbsp. butter, melted
- 1½ cups ½-inch pieces fresh rhubarb
- ½   cup fresh blueberries

1. Preheat oven to 375°F. Lightly coat fifteen 2½-inch muffin cups with nonstick cooking spray. Or line with paper bake cups and coat with cooking spray.
2. For streusel topping: In a small bowl combine ½ cup flour, the brown sugar, ¼ tsp. cardamom, and ⅛ tsp. salt. Cut in ¼ cup cold butter until mixture resembles coarse crumbs. Stir in ¼ cup finely chopped rhubarb.
3. In a medium bowl stir together 2 cups flour, granulated sugar, baking powder, ½ tsp. cardamom, and ¼ tsp. salt.
4. In a bowl whisk together eggs, yogurt, and melted butter; add all at once to dry mixture. Stir just until moistened. (Batter will be thick and lumpy.) Fold in 1½ cups rhubarb and the blueberries.
5. Spoon batter into prepared muffin cups, filling each about two-thirds full. Sprinkle with streusel topping. Bake 25 to 30 minutes or until golden and a toothpick inserted in center comes out clean. Cool in muffin cups on wire racks 10 minutes. Remove from cups. Cool slightly on wire racks. Serve warm. Makes 15 muffins.
PER MUFFIN *208 cal, 9 g fat, 46 mg chol, 216 mg sodium, 28 g carb, 1 g fiber, 11 g sugars, 4 g pro.*

ICED OATMEAL-RHUBARB COOKIES

Rhubarb replaces raisins in extra-buttery dough that spreads as it bakes to crisp cookies with lacy edges and chewy centers.

HANDS-ON TIME 20 min.
TOTAL TIME 1 hr.

- ¾   cup unsalted butter, softened
- 1   cup packed brown sugar
- 1   egg
- ½   tsp. vanilla
- 1   cup all-purpose flour
- ½   tsp. baking soda
- ½   tsp. ground cinnamon
- ¼   tsp. salt
- 1½ cups chopped fresh rhubarb
- 1½ cups regular rolled oats
- 1   cup powdered sugar
- 2   Tbsp. milk or lemon juice
- 1   drop liquid red food coloring (optional)

1. Preheat oven to 350°F. Line two cookie sheets with parchment paper.
2. In a large bowl beat butter, brown sugar, egg, and vanilla with a mixer on medium until smooth.
3. In a medium bowl combine flour, baking soda, cinnamon, and salt. Add rhubarb; toss to combine. Stir flour mixture and oats into butter mixture.
4. Drop ¼-cup mounds of dough 3 inches apart on prepared cookie sheets; press lightly with fingers.
5. Bake 15 to 18 minutes (rotate pan from front to back after 10 minutes) or until edges brown. Cool on cookie sheets 5 minutes. Transfer to a wire rack to cool. Repeat with remaining dough.
6. In a small bowl combine powdered sugar and milk; stir until smooth. If desired, add food coloring for a faint pink color. Spread icing on cooled cookies. Makes 16 cookies.
PER COOKIE *200 cal, 10 g fat, 35 mg chol, 85 mg sodium, 27 g carb, 1 g fiber, 15 g sugars, 2 g pro.*

new traditions
PASSOVER

For this generation of Jewish cooks and food writers, Seder dinners offer opportunities to honor tradition and innovation.

This month Jewish families and friends around the globe will gather for Passover Seder dinners, celebrating cherished traditions while creating original ones. As young cooks and food writers explore Jewish culinary heritage, they aim to preserve recipes and refresh and personalize them. Here, three next-gen foodies share updates on favorite holiday dishes. Their recipes are so delicious that you don't have to celebrate Passover to enjoy them.

LEAH KOENIG

"A Seder is basically an amazing dinner party with a lot of historical, religious, and cultural significance kind of layered on top," says Leah Koenig, author of *Little Book of Jewish Feasts*. Modernizing her family's traditions—using songs and puppets to tell the story of Passover, for instance—strengthens Leah's connection to the holiday. And her take on mina, a Sephardic dish commonly served during Passover, reinvents the traditional rustic meat pie as a vegetarian casserole bright with lemon zest and fresh oregano.

BALSAMIC AND BROWN SUGAR BRISKET

Onions browned in brown sugar and balsamic vinegar intensify the caramel flavors of braised brisket in cookbook author Leah Koenig's rendition of the Passover mainstay. To reheat brisket, transfer sliced meat and any juices to a baking dish and cover with foil. Heat in a 325°F oven 30 to 45 minutes.

HANDS-ON TIME 15 min.
TOTAL TIME 4 hr. 40 min.

1	4- to 5-lb. beef brisket
1	tsp. salt
1	tsp. black pepper
3	Tbsp. vegetable oil
3	large red onions, halved and thinly sliced (6 cups)
8	cloves garlic, thinly sliced
2	bay leaves
1½	cups beef or chicken stock
⅓	cup balsamic vinegar
1	Tbsp. red wine vinegar
⅓	cup packed brown sugar
2	tsp. onion powder
1	tsp. garlic powder

1. Preheat oven to 325°F. Season brisket with salt and black pepper.
2. Heat 2 Tbsp. oil in a Dutch oven or 12-inch skillet over medium-high heat. Add brisket. Cook 8 to 10 minutes or until browned on both sides. If brisket does not fit all at once in skillet, cut in half and sear in batches.
3. Remove brisket; set aside. Add remaining 1 Tbsp. oil to Dutch oven. Add onions, garlic, and bay leaves. Cook 5 to 10 minutes or until onions soften, stirring frequently.
4. Meanwhile, in a bowl whisk together stock, vinegars, brown sugar, onion powder, and garlic powder. Transfer onion mixture to a roasting pan; top with brisket. Pour balsamic mixture over. Cover tightly with foil; transfer to oven.
5. Bake 2 hours. Remove from oven. Uncover; carefully turn meat over. Cover with foil. Bake 2 to 2½ hours more or until meat is fork-tender.
6. Transfer meat to a cutting board. Cover loosely with foil; let rest 10 to 15 minutes. Slice meat against the grain. Using a slotted spoon, remove onions from pan; discard bay leaves. Arrange onions around brisket. Skim fat from pan juices. Spoon juices over brisket before serving. Refrigerate leftovers in an airtight container up to 4 days. Makes 8 servings.
PER SERVING *418 cal, 16 g fat, 137 mg chol, 471 mg sodium, 24 g carb, 2 g fiber, 16 g sugars, 46 g pro.*

REHEATED BRISKET IS EVEN BETTER THAN THE FIRST GO-ROUND: STANDING OVERNIGHT INTENSIFIES FLAVORS. IF YOU HAVE THE TIME, MAKE IT A DAY AHEAD.

WITH LAYERS OF MATZO (THIN, CRISP UNLEAVENED BREAD), VEGGIES, AND CHEESE, THIS MEATLESS MINA FALLS SOMEWHERE BETWEEN LASAGNA AND EGGY STRATA.

MINA (MATZO PIE WITH SPINACH AND LEEKS)

HANDS-ON TIME 20 min.
TOTAL TIME 1 hr. 30 min.

3   Tbsp. unsalted butter, plus more for dish
3   large leeks, white and light green parts thinly sliced (4½ cups)
2   medium shallots, finely chopped
    Salt
1   5- to 6-oz. pkg. baby spinach
4   cloves garlic, finely chopped
1   Tbsp. finely chopped fresh oregano
4   eggs
4   cups cottage cheese
1   cup crumbled feta cheese
¼   cup milk
½   tsp. lemon zest
    Black pepper
9   sheets matzo
    Fresh flat-leaf parsley

1. Preheat oven to 350°F. Butter bottom and sides of a 3-qt. rectangular baking dish; set aside. In a large skillet melt 3 Tbsp. butter over medium heat. Add leeks, shallots, and a pinch of salt. Cook 10 minutes or until softened, stirring occasionally. Add spinach, garlic, and oregano. Cook 2 to 3 minutes or until spinach is wilted. Remove from heat; cool slightly.

2. In a medium bowl whisk together three eggs, the cottage cheese, feta, milk, lemon zest, ½ tsp. salt, and a generous amount of black pepper.

3. Fill a shallow baking dish with warm water. Dip three sheets of matzo in water; let matzo soften 2 to 3 minutes. Shake off excess water. Arrange matzo sheets in bottom of prepared baking dish, breaking matzo to fit if necessary. Cover with half the cheese mixture then half the leek mixture. Repeat with three more softened matzo sheets and remaining cheese and leek mixtures.

4. Soften remaining three sheets of matzo; arrange on top. In a small bowl whisk remaining egg; brush over top.

5. Bake 45 minutes or until golden brown and bubbling. Let stand 10 minutes. Sprinkle with parsley. Serve warm. Refrigerate leftovers in an airtight container up to 4 days. Makes 8 servings.
PER SERVING *404 cal, 17 g fat, 142 mg chol, 689 mg sodium, 41 g carb, 3 g fiber, 7 g sugars, 22 g pro.*

THE TRADITIONS

Celebrated in early spring, Passover is an eight-day commemoration of the Jewish exodus from slavery in ancient Egypt. Though some of its roots are somber, Passover serves as a celebration of freedom and the arrival of spring. Following are a few basics.

SEDER SERVICE Includes the open invitation: "Let all those who are hungry come and eat." So it is no surprise that members of the Jewish community often see it as an opportunity to invite non-Jewish friends and family members to the dinner.

SEDER DINNERS Held the first night (or first two nights) of Passover, a Seder dinner includes wine and symbolic foods that help tell the story of Passover during a traditional ceremony and festive meal.

THE SEDER PLATE Typically contains six items—including bitter herbs, parsley or green onion, a roasted bone, and a hard-boiled egg—that symbolize parts of the Passover story and remind participants of Jewish history.

ANTHONY DRESSES GRILLED ASPARAGUS WITH TOUM, A CREAMY MIDDLE EASTERN SAUCE MADE OF BLENDED GARLIC, LEMON, AND OIL. HE TWEAKS THE TRADITIONAL COMBO WITH A BIT OF HONEY FOR SWEETNESS.

ANTHONY ROSE

On his Seder table and in his Toronto restaurants (Fat Pasha, Rose and Sons, and Schmaltz Appetizing), Anthony serves some updated family favorites. "When we were kids and my parents would go out for the night, my sister used to make super-buttery rice. It was one of the things she knew how to cook," the chef says. The version Anthony shares in his new cookbook, *The Last Schmaltz,* appeals to grown-up tastes for schmaltz (rendered chicken fat available at Jewish delis and specialty stores), spring sweet peas, sugar snap peas, pea shoots, and fresh herbs.

GRILLED ASPARAGUS WITH TOUM

TOTAL TIME 20 min.

1   head garlic, cloves separated and peeled
    Zest and juice of 1 lemon
1   Tbsp. kosher salt
1½   tsp. honey
1   cup canola oil
2   lb. asparagus

1. For toum: In a blender combine garlic and 3 Tbsp water; puree until blended. Add lemon juice, salt, and honey; process until well blended. With blender on low, slowly add oil. (Mixture should be thick and creamy.)
2. Preheat grill to medium-high. Prepare an ice bath. Bring a large pot of salted water to boiling; add asparagus. Cook 30 seconds; transfer immediately to ice bath. Grill asparagus 2 minutes each side. Serve with toum and sprinkle with lemon zest. Makes 6 servings.
PER SERVING *352 cal, 36 g fat, 563 mg sodium, 7 g carb, 1 g fiber, 3 g sugars, 3 g pro.*

BUTTERED SWEET PEA RICE

Anthony flavors rice with a homemade condiment he calls Chili Garlic Jazz, which adds flavor to grilled meats, grain bowls, and vinaigrettes. If you serve Seder dinner, keep in mind that some Jewish sects avoid rice and peas during Passover.

HANDS-ON TIME 15 min.
TOTAL TIME 40 min.

2   tsp. salt
1½   cups basmati rice
¼   cup slivered almonds
¼   cup butter,* schmaltz, or olive oil
1   Tbsp. Chili Garlic Jazz
1   cup shelled sweet peas or frozen baby sweet peas, thawed
1   cup sugar snap peas, sliced into ½-inch pieces
2   cups pea shoots or snow pea greens, plus more for garnish

1. Preheat oven to 375°F. In a small ovenproof saucepan with a lid bring 2 cups water and 1½ tsp. salt to boiling. Stir in rice; cover. Transfer to oven. Bake 20 minutes or until rice is tender and water is absorbed. Spread rice onto a baking sheet; cool completely.
2. Meanwhile, in a nonstick skillet toast almonds over medium-low heat 2 to 3 minutes or until starting to brown, stirring constantly. Transfer to a bowl.
3. Heat a large skillet over medium-high heat. Add ½ cup water, the butter, Chili Garlic Jazz, and remaining ½ tsp. salt. Bring to boiling. Add cooled rice to skillet. Cook 5 minutes or until hot. Add sweet and snap peas; stir to combine. Cook 30 seconds more or until heated through.
4. Remove from heat. Stir in pea shoots. Top with toasted almonds and additional pea shoots. Makes 8 servings.
***Tip** To make this recipe pareve (dairy- and meat-free), use the olive oil option.
Chili Garlic Jazz Preheat oven to 250°F. In a food processor combine 1 cup coarsely chopped garlic, ½ cup coarsely chopped red finger or Fresno chiles (tip, page 59), and ¼ cup canola oil. Process 2 to 3 minutes or a thick paste forms. Pour into a 1-qt. ovenproof pot. Add ½ to ⅔ cup canola oil to just cover the paste. Bake, covered, 45 to 60 minutes or until paste has a toasty aroma. Cool completely. Refrigerate in a screw-top jar up to 1 month.
PER SERVING *213 cal, 9 g fat, 15 mg chol, 328 mg sodium, 31 g carb, 3 g fiber, 1 g sugars, 5 g pro.*

GRILLED
ASPARAGUS
WITH TOUM

BUTTERED
SWEET
PEA RICE

COCONUT-HALVA
MACAROONS

TAHINI RAINBOW
COOKIES

TAHINI RAINBOW COOKIES

HANDS-ON TIME 35 min.
TOTAL TIME 1 hr. 50 min.

Butter or shortening
3½ cups almond flour
2 cups powdered sugar
1 tsp. kosher salt
1 cup unsalted butter or margarine
1 Tbsp. granulated sugar
8 eggs, separated
2 tsp. ground matcha
Green food coloring (optional)
2 tsp. ground dried hibiscus flowers
Purple or red food coloring (optional)
¾ cup tahini
2 Tbsp. honey
1 cup semisweet chocolate chips
1 Tbsp. coconut oil

1. Preheat oven to 350°F. Coat three 13×9-inch baking pans with butter or shortening; line bottoms with parchment paper. In a medium bowl whisk together almond flour, powdered sugar, and salt until combined.
2. In a large bowl beat butter and granulated sugar with a mixer on medium-high until fluffy. One at a time add egg yolks, mixing well after each addition. With mixer running, slowly add flour mixture until batter comes together.
3. In a clean bowl beat egg whites with clean beaters to soft peak (tips curl); fold into batter. Divide batter among three bowls. Stir matcha and, if desired, green food coloring into one. Stir hibiscus and, if desired, purple food coloring into another. Leave the third plain.
4. Spread each batter evenly into prepared pans. Bake 15 minutes or until risen and firm when pressed with finger. Cool in pans on wire racks. Invert onto a cutting board.
5. In a small bowl whisk together tahini and honey. Place the purple cookie layer in one of the baking pans. Spread evenly with half the tahini mixture. Top with plain cookie layer. Spread with remaining tahini mixture. Top with green cookie layer.
6. In a small microwavable bowl heat chocolate chips and coconut oil on high (100% power) 30 seconds to 1 minute or until melted. Stir until smooth. Evenly spread half the chocolate mixture on cookies. Chill 30 minutes or until firm.
7. Invert uncut cookies onto a cutting board. Spread remaining chocolate evenly over top. Return to refrigerator; chill 30 minutes.
8. Trim edges. Cut into 1½-inch squares. Makes 48 cookies.
PER COOKIE *158 cal, 12 g fat, 41 mg chol, 40 mg sodium, 11 g carb, 1 g fiber, 8 g sugars, 4 g pro.*

COCONUT-HALVA MACAROONS

Halva, a sweet, dense confection originating in the Middle East, has two main types: flour-based and more common nut-based. Find it at specialty food stores and online.

HANDS-ON TIME 20 min.
TOTAL TIME 1 hr. 20 min.

1 14-oz. bag sweetened shredded coconut
1 14-oz. can sweetened condensed milk or 1 cup canned unsweetened coconut milk
2 Tbsp. matzo meal or coconut flour
¾ tsp. salt
¼ tsp. ground cinnamon
¼ tsp. ground cardamom
2 eggs, separated
½ cup crumbled halva (optional)

1. Preheat oven to 325°F. Line two baking sheets with parchment paper. In a large bowl combine coconut, condensed milk, matzo meal, ½ tsp. salt, cinnamon, cardamom, and egg yolks.
2. In a medium bowl beat egg whites and remaining ¼ tsp. salt with a mixer until stiff peaks form (tips stand straight). Fold into coconut mixture; if desired, fold in halva.
3. Scoop 2 Tbsp. mounds onto baking sheets 2 inches apart. Bake 20 minutes or until golden. Remove from oven; let cool completely on wire racks. Makes 24 cookies.
PER COOKIE *144 cal, 8 g fat, 21 mg chol, 105 mg sodium, 17 g carb, 1 g fiber, 16 g sugars, 2 g pro.*
Tip For picture-perfect macaroons, bake 10 minutes. Dip a 3-inch round cookie cutter in water, then place it over a cookie and roll it around the edges to smooth and reshape cookies into tight mounds. Return to oven and bake remaining 10 minutes; repeat with wet cookie cutter after baking.

JAKE COHEN

For Jake, the editorial and test kitchen director of the social-driven cooking site *thefeedfeed.com*, Passover is an occasion to blend his Eastern-European-Jewish heritage with those of his husband's Persian and Iraqi-Jewish roots through food. Jake adds halva, a Middle Eastern candy made from sesame, to chewy macaroons and he layers tahini in cakey cookies. Because using leaveners is forbidden during Passover, bakers get creative. "It's all about meringue," says Jake, who uses whipped egg whites to lift dessert recipes.

JAKE USES MATCHA POWDER AND GROUND HIBISCUS TO SUBTLY COLOR RAINBOW COOKIE LAYERS.

CUCUMBER TEA SANDWICHES
Recipe on page 111

may

Deliciously beautiful fare to serve at Derby parties, Mom's Day celebrations, and backyard gatherings. Plus, new twists on family favorites and cool-as-a-cucumber cuisine.

105

116

124

FLOWERS FOR MOM

This Mother's Day present Mom with a luscious lemon verbena ice cream pie sprinkled with edible flowers.

LEMON VERBENA ICE CREAM PIE

Lemon verbena is an easy-to-grow container plant with leaves that impart a strong citrus flavor. Find it in nurseries in the spring. In addition to flavoring this ice cream, the herb brightens baked goods and salads. Or pop a sprig into ice tea and other drinks.

HANDS-ON TIME 50 min.
TOTAL TIME 6 hr., includes chilling

LEMON VERBENA ICE CREAM
1 cup milk
½ cup fresh lemon verbena leaves or 4 tsp. lemon zest
½ tsp. kosher salt
¾ cup sugar
3 egg yolks
1½ cups heavy cream
2 tsp. vanilla

GINGER SHORTBREAD CRUST
½ cup butter, softened
1 cup all-purpose flour
¼ cup sugar

2 Tbsp. finely chopped candied ginger
1 tsp. ground ginger
½ tsp. kosher salt
Herbs and edible flowers, such as lemon verbena, phlox, and/or roses

1. For Lemon Verbena Ice Cream: In a medium saucepan heat milk and verbena just to a simmer over high heat. Remove from heat; let steep 30 minutes. Stir in salt.

2. In a medium bowl whisk together sugar and egg yolks until thick and pale. Return milk to a simmer. Gradually whisk ½ cup milk mixture into egg mixture. Continue whisking until smooth. Slowly add egg mixture to saucepan, stirring constantly. Cook and stir over medium-low until thick enough to coat the back of a spoon and just starting to bubble. Stir in cream. Press through a fine-mesh sieve into a bowl; discard solids. Stir in vanilla.

3. Set mixture in an ice bath to chill, stirring occasionally. Transfer to a 2-qt. ice cream freezer. Freeze according to manufacturer's directions.

4. For Ginger Shortbread Crust: Grease a 9-inch pie plate. Preheat oven to 350°F. In a large bowl beat butter with a mixer on medium 30 seconds. Add flour, sugar, candied ginger, ground ginger, and salt. Beat until a soft dough forms.

5. Evenly press dough into prepared pie plate. Line with a double thickness of greased foil. Fill to top with pie weights. Bake 25 minutes. Remove weights and foil. Bake 10 to 12 minutes more or until dark golden brown. Cool completely. Freeze at least 1 hour.

6. Spread ice cream into crust. Freeze at least 4 hours or until ice cream is firm. Let stand at room temperature 10 to 15 minutes before serving. Top with herbs and edible flowers. Makes 10 servings.

PER SERVING *369 cal, 24 g fat, 122 mg chol, 200 mg sodium, 34 g carb, 22 g sugars, 4 g pro.*

LEMON AND GINGER ARE AN IRRESISTIBLY BRIGHT COMBO, ESPECIALLY IN THIS CRISP DOUBLE-GINGER SHORTBREAD CRUST. THE ICE CREAM IS MADE AROMATIC BY STEEPING LEMON VERBENA IN MILK (LEMON ZEST IS A DELICIOUS SUBSTITUTE).

entertaining
WINNER'S CIRCLE

The race itself lasts only about two minutes, but this make-ahead spread will keep your Kentucky Derby-watching party going for several more laps of fun.

HOT BROWN STROMBOLI

Made famous by The Brown Hotel in Louisville, a hot brown is an open-face turkey sandwich with cheese sauce and bacon. This version rolls the ingredients into a sliceable stromboli.

HANDS-ON TIME 25 min.
TOTAL TIME 1 hr. 30 min.

2 tsp. olive oil
1 Tbsp. cornmeal
1 16-oz. pkg. refrigerated or frozen pizza dough, thawed
3 Tbsp. Dijon mustard
8 oz. sliced deli cooked turkey
1½ cups shredded Gruyère cheese (6 oz.)
4 slices bacon, crisp-cooked and crumbled
1 cup chopped roma tomatoes
1 egg yolk
1 Tbsp. sesame seeds

1. Preheat oven to 375°F. Line a 15×10-inch baking pan with foil. Brush with oil. Sprinkle with cornmeal.
2. On a lightly floured surface, roll dough to a 13×10-inch rectangle. Transfer to prepared pan. Spread dough with mustard then arrange half the turkey on dough, leaving ½-inch borders. Sprinkle with half the cheese. Top with bacon, tomatoes, and remaining turkey and cheese.
3. Starting from a long side, roll up dough around filling. Pinch seam and ends to seal. Lightly beat egg yolk with 1 tsp. water. Brush dough with egg yolk mixture; sprinkle with sesame seeds. Using a sharp knife, cut shallow slits on top to vent.
4. Bake 40 minutes or until golden brown. Let cool 20 minutes. Makes 8 servings.
PER SERVING *310 cal, 13 g fat, 63 mg chol, 787 mg sodium, 28 g carb, 1 g sugars, 18 g pro.*

PIMIENTO CHEESE DIP

HANDS-ON TIME 15 min.
TOTAL TIME 1 hr. 15 min.

2 cups smoked cheddar cheese
¾ cup mayonnaise
8 oz. softened cream cheese
1 tsp. freshly cracked black pepper
¼ tsp. kosher salt
 Pinch of cayenne pepper
4 oz. diced pimiento
 Crackers and crudites

In a food processor combine cheddar cheese, mayo, cream cheese, black pepper, salt, and cayenne. Stir in pimiento. Serve with crackers and crudites. Makes 10 servings.
PER SERVING *243 cal, 24 g fat, 42 mg chol, 330 mg sodium, 2 g carb, 1 g sugars, 7 g pro.*

BOURBON-BROWN SUGAR NUTS

HANDS-ON TIME 20 min.
TOTAL TIME 1 hr.

½ cup packed brown sugar
3 Tbsp. bourbon
1 cup toasted whole almonds
½ tsp. salt
½ tsp. black pepper
½ tsp. ground cinnamon
⅛ to ¼ tsp. cayenne pepper

1. Line a shallow baking pan with foil; grease foil.
2. In a medium saucepan combine brown sugar and bourbon. Bring to boiling over medium-high heat, stirring to dissolve sugar. Stir in almonds. Reduce heat to medium; cook 4 minutes or until syrup thickens slightly, stirring often. Reduce heat to medium-low. Stir in salt, black pepper, cinnamon, and cayenne. (Mixture will be foamy.) Cook 7 minutes more or until syrup thickens and coats nuts, stirring frequently.
3. Spread nuts in a single layer in prepared pan. Cool completely. Break apart. Store in an airtight container up to 1 week. Makes 6 servings.
PER SERVING *225 cal, 12 g fat, 99 mg sodium, 23 g carb, 3 g fiber, 19 g sugars, 5 g pro.*

BLACKBERRY-MINT JULEP SPARKLER

HANDS-ON TIME 10 min.
TOTAL TIME 20 min.

½ cup sugar
1 cup chopped mint
3 fresh mint leaves
2 fresh blackberries
2 oz. bourbon
 Crushed ice
 Club soda or sparkling water

1. For mint syrup: In a saucepan combine sugar, 2 cups water, and chopped mint over medium-high heat. Bring to boiling, stirring to dissolve sugar. Reduce heat; simmer 5 minutes. Pour through a fine-mesh sieve, pressing on mint to release water; discard mint. Cool 10 minutes.
2. In a tall glass muddle mint leaves and blackberries. Add bourbon and 2 Tbsp. mint syrup; stir. Add crushed ice and top with club soda or sparkling water. Makes 1 serving.
PER SERVING *125 cal, 14 mg sodium, 7 g carb, 7 g sugars.*

DERBY SKILLET COOKIE

Topping the gooey cookie with a scoop of ice cream is strongly encouraged.

HANDS-ON TIME 15 min.
TOTAL TIME 3 hr., includes cooling

2½ cups all-purpose flour
1 tsp. baking soda
½ tsp. salt
1 cup butter, softened
1 cup packed brown sugar
½ cup granulated sugar
2 eggs
1 Tbsp. vanilla
1 10-oz. pkg. bittersweet chocolate chips
½ cup walnuts or pecans, toasted and coarsely chopped (tip, page 37)

1. Place rack in middle of oven. Preheat oven to 350°F. In a bowl whisk together flour, baking soda, and salt.
2. In a large bowl beat butter and sugars with mixer on medium-high 2 to 3 minutes or until pale and fluffy. Add eggs one at a time, beating until combined after each. Beat in vanilla.
3. One-third at a time, beat flour mixture into butter mixture just until combined. Fold in chocolate chips and walnuts. Spread into an ungreased 9- to 10-inch cast-iron skillet. Bake 40 to 45 minutes for a 9-inch skillet (30 minutes for 10-inch) or until evenly browned. Cool in skillet on a wire rack at least 2 hours. Makes 10 to 12 servings.
PER SERVING *607 cal, 35 g fat, 86 mg chol, 410 mg sodium, 72 g carb, 43 g sugars, 7 g pro.*

great starts
EXTRA CHEESE, *please*

The genius behind this irresistible breakfast sandwich is frying the eggs on top of a thin, lacy cheese crisp, known as a frico.

FRICO FRIED EGG AND CHEESE BREAKFAST SANDWICHES

The best cheeses for fricos are hard and have low moisture content, such as Asiago, Grana Padano, and Parmesan.

TOTAL TIME 20 min.

1   cup shredded Parmesan cheese (4 oz.)
4   eggs
4   English muffins, split and toasted
4   slices provolone cheese
1   cup baby arugula
¼   cup dried tomato pesto or tomato jam

1. Heat a 12-inch griddle or nonstick skillet over low heat. Sprinkle ¼ cup cheese into four 4- to 5-inch circles on hot griddle. Cook 1 minute or just until cheese begins to melt.
2. Break eggs onto fricos; sprinkle with pepper. Cook 4 to 5 minutes or until egg whites are completely set and yolks are desired doneness.
3. Layer English muffin bottoms with provolone slices, arugula, frico and egg, pesto, and muffin tops. Serve immediately. Makes 4 sandwiches.
PER SANDWICH *389 cal, 19 g fat, 219 mg chol, 959 mg sodium, 32 g carb, 1 g fiber, 2 g sugars, 23 g pro.*

TYPICALLY SERVED WITH SALADS, FRICOS ORIGINATED IN NORTHERN ITALY AS A WAY TO USE RINDS AND/OR CHEESE-MAKING SCRAPS.

COOL CUKES

Discover novelty varieties to grow plus fresh ideas to keep up with a bumper crop of this versatile, seasonal fruit.

CUCUMBER-GINGER COCKTAIL
Recipe on page 111

CUCUMBER-CORN SALAD

PICKLED CUCAMELONS

CUCUMBER TEA SANDWICHES

WHITE GAZPACHO

CUCUMBER-GINGER COCKTAIL

Photo on page 109.

Thin slices of cucumber make this fizzy gin- and ginger-spiked cooler extra refreshing. Use a peeler to shave lengthwise ribbons from a cucumber to lay inside the glass before filling. Add Pimm's No. 1 for a spin on a Pimm's Cup cocktail or leave out the spirits for a spa-like thirst-quencher.

TOTAL TIME 10 min.

1   small cucumber
6   thin slices peeled fresh ginger
1   tsp. sugar
2   oz. gin
4   oz. Pimm's No. 1 (optional)
    Club soda, chilled
2   lemon slices

Halve cucumber lengthwise; cut one half lengthwise into two spears. Slice remaining half; muddle in a cocktail shaker along with four ginger slices and the sugar. Stir in gin and Pimm's, if using. Strain into two ice-filled highball glasses; top with club soda. Garnish with remaining ginger slices, cucumber spears, and lemon slices. Makes 2 servings.

PER SERVING *87 cal, 21 mg sodium, 6 g carb, 1 g fiber, 3 g sugars.*

CUCUMBER-CORN SALAD

Yellow and green cucumbers tossed with sweet corn and herbs will have you toting this fresh salad to backyard barbecues all summer. Because mint, basil, and chives are easy to grow, it's possible for even novice gardeners to harvest most of the ingredients from their backyard. Serve with grilled chicken or fish for a light summertime dinner.

HANDS-ON TIME 20 min.
TOTAL TIME 1 hr. 20 min., includes chilling

¼   cup lemon juice
¼   cup olive oil
½   tsp. salt
½   tsp. black pepper
½   cup each chopped fresh basil, mint, and chives
4   cups chopped fresh cucumbers
1½ cups fresh corn kernels

In a large bowl whisk together lemon juice, olive oil, salt, and black pepper. Stir in herbs, cucumbers, and corn. Cover; chill at least 1 hour. Season with salt and pepper. Makes 10 servings.

PER SERVING *81 cal, 6 g fat, 119 mg sodium, 8 g carb, 1 g fiber, 2 g sugars, 1 g pro.*

CUCUMBER TEA SANDWICHES

The cucumber sandwich is a tea party staple because it's light yet fancy. In this version, radishes spice up thinly sliced cucumbers on a bed of creamy herbed cheese.

TOTAL TIME 10 min.

12 very thin slices firm white bread, toasted
1   5.3-oz. container semisoft cheese with garlic and fine herbs
2   cups thinly sliced cucumbers
6   radishes, thinly sliced
¾   cup fresh basil, dill, and/or oregano
    Freshly ground black pepper
    Sea salt

Spread bread slices with cheese. Top with cucumbers, radishes, and herbs. Sprinkle with black pepper and salt. Makes 12 servings.

PER SERVING *112 cal, 6 g fat, 14 mg chol, 208 mg sodium, 13 g carb, 2 g sugars, 3 g pro.*

WHITE GAZPACHO

Based on the centuries-old Spanish recipe ajo blanco, this creamy soup combines a handful of improbable ingredients: almonds, bread, cukes, yogurt, sherry vinegar, and grapes. Any variety of cucumber will work as long as you remove tough seeds and peel thick skins to keep texture smooth and color pale green.

HANDS-ON TIME 15 min.
TOTAL TIME 2 hr. 15 min., includes chilling

1¼ lb. cucumbers, peeled and chopped
1   cup seedless green grapes
1   slice country Italian bread, crusts removed and cubed (½ cup)
½   cup slivered almonds
¼   cup finely chopped shallot
½   tsp. salt
1   cup plain whole milk Greek yogurt
1   Tbsp. sherry vinegar
    Mint leaves and cucumber slices, for topping

1. In a medium bowl combine cucumbers, grapes, bread, almonds, shallot, and salt. Cover; chill 2 hours.
2. Using an immersion blender, blend until nearly smooth. Press through a fine-mesh sieve into a bowl; discard solids. Whisk in yogurt and vinegar. Serve immediately, or chill, covered, up to 24 hours. Top with mint and cucumber just before serving. Makes 5 to 6 servings.

PER SERVING *184 cal, 11 g fat, 9 mg chol, 150 mg sodium, 16 g carb, 2 g fiber, 10 g sugars, 7 g pro.*

PICKLED CUCAMELONS

Refrigerator pickles are a tasty way to preserve your cucumbers as they ripen without using special canning equipment. Vinegar, dill seeds, and celery seeds play nicely with a variety of cucumbers, including cucamelons, Boston pickling, or Parisian gherkin. Each batch will last up to two weeks in the fridge.

HANDS-ON TIME 20 min.
TOTAL TIME 24 hr. 40 min., includes chilling

8   oz. cucamelons, halved, or any other pickling cucumbers, cut into ½-inch slices (1½ cups)
1   tsp. dill seeds
½   tsp. celery seeds
¾   cup cider vinegar
1   Tbsp. sugar
1   tsp. salt

1. In a clean pint canning jar combine cucamelons, dill seeds, and celery seeds.
2. In a small saucepan combine vinegar, ⅓ cup water, the sugar, and salt. Bring to boiling, stirring to dissolve sugar. Pour over cucamelon mixture, leaving ¼-inch headspace. Seal. Cool 20 minutes. Chill at least 24 hours and up to 2 weeks. Makes 6 servings.

PER SERVING *15 cal, 55 mg sodium, 4 g carb, 3 g sugars.*

thoroughly
MODERN MEXICAN

When blogger Kate Ramos hosts a gathering, she blends her family's Midwestern and Mexican roots for a playful, multicultural menu.

RHUBARB AGUA FRESCA

Kate gets the party going with a big batch of agua fresca but flavoring the Mexican drink with rhubarb, which recalls her native Des Moines, Iowa.

HANDS-ON TIME 10 min.
TOTAL TIME 3 hr. 55 min.

1   lb. fresh rhubarb, chopped, or one 16-oz. pkg. frozen cut rhubarb
1½   cups sugar
½   cup fresh lemon juice

1. In a 4-qt. pot combine rhubarb, sugar, and 6 cups water. Bring to boiling, stirring to dissolve sugar; reduce heat. Simmer, uncovered, 30 minutes or until rhubarb has broken down. Cool 1 hour. Chill, covered, 2 to 4 hours.
2. Strain through a fine-mesh sieve into a pitcher; discard solids. Stir in lemon juice. Serve immediately or chill, covered, until ready to serve. Serve over ice. Makes 6 servings.
PER SERVING *207 cal, 9 mg sodium, 54 g carb, 1 g fiber, 51 g sugars.*

KATE RAMOS TRADES MARGARITAS, GUACAMOLE, AND CHIPS FOR A LESS EXPECTED PARTY TRIO.

CHIPOTLE CARROT-ONION DIP

Kate's take on sour cream-onion dip features chipotles in adobo for a smoky kick.

HANDS-ON TIME 25 min.
TOTAL TIME 8 hr. 40 min., includes chilling

2   Tbsp. olive oil
1½   cups chopped sweet onions
1½   cups chopped carrots
3   cloves garlic, minced
2   canned chipotle peppers in adobo sauce, minced
1   16-oz. container sour cream
¾   tsp. salt
¼   tsp. black pepper
     Amaranth Crackers (right)
     Assorted vegetables, such as sliced jicama, baby carrots, cucumber slices, cauliflower florets, and/or mini bell peppers

1. In a large skillet heat oil over medium-high heat. Add onions and chopped carrots. Cook 15 minutes or until onions are dark golden and starting to char and carrots are tender, stirring occasionally.
2. Add garlic and chipotles; cook 1 minute more. Cool completely.
3. In a medium bowl combine onion mixture, sour cream, salt, and black pepper. Chill, covered, 8 hours. Serve with Amaranth Crackers and assorted vegetables. Makes 20 servings.
PER SERVING *67 cal, 6 g fat, 13 mg chol, 63 mg sodium, 3 g carb, 2 g sugars, 1 g pro.*

AMARANTH CRACKERS

Homemade crackers made with puffed amaranth (a nutty grain popular in Mexico) snap with cumin and pepitas as well as sunflower kernels and chia seeds.

TOTAL TIME 25 min.

¾   cup all-purpose flour
½   cup puffed amaranth
1   Tbsp. pepitas
1   Tbsp. sunflower kernels
1   tsp. kosher salt
¼   cup vegetable oil
1   Tbsp. black sesame seeds
1   Tbsp. white sesame seeds
1   Tbsp. chia seeds
1   tsp. cumin seeds
1   tsp. flaky sea salt

1. Preheat oven to 375°F. In a medium bowl combine flour, amaranth, pepitas, sunflower kernels, and salt. Add oil and ¼ cup water. Using your hands, mix until evenly moistened; form into a ball.
2. Place dough between two sheets of parchment paper. Roll to ⅛-inch thickness. Peel off top sheet of parchment paper; use bottom sheet to transfer dough to a baking sheet. Sprinkle evenly with sesame seeds, chia seeds, cumin seeds, and sea salt. Press seeds into dough.
3. Bake 15 minutes or until golden and crisp. Let cool. Break into pieces. Store at room temperature up to 3 days. Makes 6 to 8 servings.
PER SERVING *231 cal, 13 g fat, 482 mg sodium, 24 g carb, 2 g fiber, 5 g pro.*

Fried chicken probably isn't the first thing that comes to mind when you think of a Mexican menu. But for Kate Ramos, creating untraditional dishes with Mexican flavors celebrates the culture's vibrant and varied foods. Kate, who lives with her family in Southern California, became enamored with Mexican cooking while working in restaurants in Northern California. When she met her husband, Armando, a first-generation American, her connection to the cuisine became deeper and more personal.

On her blog, *¡Hola! Jalapeño,* Kate shares recipes that are both a reflection of her multicultural family and her Midwestern background. "For my kids (Louisa, 10, and Hiro, 7), I think of it as a running recipe box of all the things that I've made. I want them to honor their Mexican-American heritage and, for me, that starts in the kitchen."

Kate has a knack for presenting authentic ingredients in fresh, new ways. "Often when we think of Mexican food, we default to the same dishes over and over," Kate says. "But the ingredients are so vast and versatile. I like to create dishes that are surprising and don't take themselves too seriously."

Like her fried chicken. It turns out that a jar of pickled jalapeños makes a delicious brine that yields flavorful, moist chicken. And her stuffed poblanos are equally unexpected. She fills the charred peppers with spoon bread—a soufflé-like Southern corn bread—with a little Maytag blue cheese from Iowa stirred in to merge the flavors of her present and past.

Gathering around the table to share meals and stories preserves her families' traditions. "We've always lived away from our families, so cooking dishes that blend our cultures has become a way to connect to our roots."

PICKLED-JALAPEÑO FRIED CHICKEN
Recipe on page 117

SPOON BREAD-STUFFED POBLANOS
Recipe on page 117

**GEM LETTUCE
SALAD WITH
CHAMOY DRESSING**
Recipe on page 117

**SPICY PICKLED
EGGS AND BEETS**
Recipe on page 118

BURNT-ORANGE AÑEJO SOUR

This mash-up between a margarita and a whiskey sour features añejo, a dark aged tequila that has woodsy, caramel flavors.

TOTAL TIME 10 min.

- 1 orange slice
- ¼ tsp. sugar
- 4 mint leaves
- 1½ oz. añejo tequila
- 1 oz. fresh lime juice
- 1 oz. Cointreau or orange liqueur
- 1 oz. sweet vermouth
- 1 oz. pasteurized liquid egg whites
  Blood orange soda

1. Place orange slice on a sheet of foil; sprinkle with sugar. Use a kitchen torch to heat sugar until it is dark golden and charred in some spots. Cool.
2. In a cocktail shaker muddle mint. Add tequila, lime juice, Cointreau, vermouth, and egg whites. Cover; shake vigorously until pressure builds and mixture sounds less sloshy and looks frothy. Add ice; cover and shake vigorously until cold.
3. Strain into a glass and top with blood orange soda. Float the burnt orange slice on top. Makes 1 serving.
PER SERVING *267 cal, 57 mg sodium, 7 g carb, 1 g fiber, 4 g sugars, 4 g pro.*

KATE TOPS THE DRINK WITH AN ORANGE SLICE THAT IS CARAMELIZED WITH A KITCHEN TORCH. (A BROILER WORKS AS WELL.)

PICKLED-JALAPEÑO FRIED CHICKEN

Photo on page 115.

"The pickled jalapeño brine is insurance for moist chicken," Kate says. "I brine overnight to guarantee the result is juicy and flavor-packed." If you can't find canned pickled jalapeños with carrots and onions, such as La Costeña, plain pickled jalapeños work too.

HANDS-ON TIME 40 min.

TOTAL TIME 3 hr. 55 min., includes chilling

1   28.2-oz. can pickled jalapeños with carrots and onions
3½ to 4 lb. meaty bone-in chicken pieces (breast halves, thighs, and drumsticks)
2½ cups all-purpose flour
⅔ cup cornstarch
2   Tbsp. kosher salt
2   Tbsp. ground cumin
2   Tbsp. smoked paprika
2   tsp. black pepper
1   egg
8   cups vegetable oil

1. For marinade: Place pickled jalapeños, carrots, onions, and juices into a food processor. Process until nearly smooth. Using a large chef's knife, cut chicken breast pieces in half crosswise. In a large bowl combine all chicken and marinade, turning chicken to coat evenly. Chill, covered, at least 2 hours or up to 8 hours.
2. In a large bowl whisk together flour, cornstarch, salt, cumin, smoked paprika, and black pepper. Remove chicken from marinade one piece at a time, letting excess drip back into bowl. Dip chicken into flour mixture, turning to coat. Place on a wire rack set in a 15×10-inch pan.
3. For batter: Whisk egg into marinade until combined. Stir in remaining flour mixture until combined. (Batter will be very thick.) Spoon batter over chicken pieces, one at a time, to coat. Chill batter-coated chicken at least 30 minutes or up to 2 hours. Discard any remaining batter.
4. Preheat oven to 300°F. In a 5- to 6-qt. heavy-bottom pan heat oil to 325°F. Cover a baking sheet with paper towels; set a wire rack on paper towels. Add chicken, three to four pieces at a time, to hot oil. Fry 15 to 18 minutes or until deep golden brown and cooked through (170°F for breast pieces, 175°F for thighs and drumsticks). Transfer to wire rack; let drain 5 minutes. Transfer to a baking sheet; place in warm oven while frying remaining chicken. Makes 6 servings.
PER SERVING *685 cal, 40 g fat, 151 mg chol, 1,459 mg sodium, 29 g carb, 1 g fiber, 43 g pro.*

SPOON BREAD-STUFFED POBLANOS

Photo on page 114.

Charring poblanos (which you can do ahead of time) tenderizes the peppers and gives this comforting side dish a deep smoky flavor. Just before serving, top with skillet-toasted corn kernels.

HANDS-ON TIME 30 min.

TOTAL TIME 1 hr. 20 min.

6   poblano chile peppers
    Nonstick cooking spray
¾ cup yellow cornmeal
¾ cup fresh corn kernels or frozen fire-roasted whole kernel corn, thawed
¼ cup all-purpose flour
¼ cup sugar
1   tsp. baking powder
½ tsp. salt
¼ tsp. black pepper
½ cup buttermilk
½ cup heavy cream
1   egg
¾ cup crumbled blue cheese (3 oz.)

1. Preheat broiler. Arrange peppers on a baking pan lined with foil. Broil 4 to 6 inches from heat 15 minutes or until skin is blackened on all sides, turning occasionally. Transfer to a heatproof bowl. Cover with plastic wrap. Cool.
2. Once cool enough to handle, peel off skin. Cut a small slit on one side, keeping pepper intact; gently scoop out seeds. Gently swish in a bowl of water to remove all seeds. Pat dry.
3. Preheat oven to 375°F. Coat a 3-qt. baking dish with cooking spray. In a bowl combine cornmeal, corn, flour, sugar, baking powder, salt, and black pepper.
4. In a separate bowl whisk together buttermilk, cream, and egg. Pour into dry mixture; stir to combine. Fold in half the blue cheese.
5. Arrange poblanos in a single layer in prepared dish. Gently fill each pepper with spoon bread batter. Spoon remaining batter around peppers. Sprinkle top with remaining blue cheese. Bake 25 minutes or until spoon bread is puffed and golden yet still tender. Let stand 10 minutes. Makes 6 servings.
PER SERVING *315 cal, 14 g fat, 65 mg chol, 405 mg sodium, 40 g carb, 2 g fiber, 12 g sugars, 10 g pro.*

GEM LETTUCE SALAD WITH CHAMOY DRESSING

Photo on page 115.

Chamoy is a popular salty-sweet Mexican condiment of fruit and chiles. Often served as a dip for fresh fruit, it's especially delicious with mangoes and peaches.

TOTAL TIME 25 min.

1   lb. baby gem lettuce, washed and dried thoroughly, or two 8-oz. romaine lettuce hearts, cored and leaves separated
1   ripe avocado, sliced
1   mango, peeled and sliced
1   large watermelon radish or large red radishes, sliced (about ¾ cup)
2   Tbsp. apricot or peach preserves
¾ tsp. chile de árbol powder or ¼ tsp. crushed red pepper
¼ cup fresh lime juice
2   Tbsp. olive oil
½ tsp. salt
½ Tbsp. finely chopped green onion
¼ cup cilantro leaves

1. Arrange lettuce, avocado, mango, and radish on a large serving platter.
2. For dressing: In a small bowl whisk together preserves, árbol chile powder, lime juice, olive oil, and salt. Add green onion. Drizzle dressing over salad. Top with cilantro leaves. Makes 8 servings.
PER SERVING *100 cal, 7 g fat, 90 mg sodium, 12 g carb, 3 g fiber 7 g sugars, 1 g pro.*

"I LOVE TO TAKE FOODS I GREW UP EATING AND INCORPORATE MEXICAN INGREDIENTS TO GIVE THEM A MODERN TWIST."

SPICY PICKLED EGGS AND BEETS

Photo on page 115.

Kate reinvents her grandmother's recipe by adding chiles to the spice mix for complex flavor.

HANDS-ON TIME 40 min.
TOTAL TIME 9 hr. 40 min., includes chilling

2	lb. small red beets, trimmed, peeled, and quartered
12	cloves garlic
1	cup sugar
1	cup distilled white vinegar
1	Tbsp. kosher salt
1	Tbsp. black peppercorns
1	Tbsp. crab boil spice mix, such as Zatarain's
6	bay leaves
3	dried árbol chiles
6	hard-boiled eggs

1. In a large saucepan combine beets and garlic. Cover with lightly salted water. Bring to boiling over high heat; reduce heat. Simmer, uncovered, 10 to 12 minutes or until beets are easily pierced with a knife; drain.
2. In the same saucepan combine 1 cup water, the sugar, vinegar, salt, peppercorns, spice mix, bay leaves, and árbol chiles. Bring to boiling over high heat, whisking to dissolve sugar. Remove from heat.
3. Divide beets, garlic, eggs, bay leaves, and chiles among three clean pint canning jars. Pour hot brine over beets and eggs to cover, leaving ¼-inch headspace. Seal. Chill 8 hours or up to 1 week. Makes 6 servings.
PER SERVING *284 cal, 5 g fat, 186 mg chol, 267 mg sodium, 50 g carb, 4 g fiber, 44 g sugars, 9 g pro.*

TRES LECHES STRAWBERRY SHORTCAKE

Iconic Mexican and American desserts meet in this heavenly combo. Tres leches (three milks) typically includes evaporated milk, sweetened condensed milk, and cream. Kate trades evaporated milk for buttermilk—and the tangy wild card complements the cake's sweetness.

HANDS-ON TIME 25 min.
TOTAL TIME 4 hr. 20 min., includes chilling

1½	cups all-purpose flour
¾	tsp. baking powder
¼	tsp. kosher salt
½	cup butter, softened
½	cup plus 1 Tbsp. granulated sugar
2	large eggs, room temperature
½	cup buttermilk
½	tsp. almond extract
1	14-oz. can sweetened condensed milk
⅔	cup buttermilk
1½	cups heavy cream
2	lb. fresh strawberries, hulled and sliced
1	Tbsp. fresh lemon juice
1	Tbsp. powdered sugar

1. Preheat oven to 350°F. Grease a 10-inch round cake pan. Line with parchment paper. Grease parchment.
2. In a medium bowl whisk together flour, baking powder, and salt.

3. In the bowl of a mixer fitted with paddle attachment combine butter and ½ cup sugar; beat on high until fluffy. Add eggs; beat until smooth. Scrape down sides of bowl. Add ½ cup buttermilk and the almond extract; beat until smooth. Add flour mixture; beat just until combined.
4. Spoon into prepared baking pan; spread evenly. Bake 30 minutes or until cake is golden and a toothpick inserted in center comes out clean.
5. In a medium bowl whisk together sweetened condensed milk, ⅔ cup buttermilk, and ½ cup cream. Using a skewer, poke cake all over. Pour milk mixture over warm cake. Chill, covered, at least 3 hours or overnight. Invert cake onto a wire rack. Remove parchment. Transfer to a serving plate and bring to room temperature at least 30 minutes before serving.
6. Meanwhile, in a large bowl combine strawberries, lemon juice, and remaining 1 Tbsp. granulated sugar. Let stand at room temperature at least 30 minutes.
7. In a medium bowl beat remaining 1 cup cream and the powdered sugar with a mixer on medium-high until stiff peaks form (tips stand straight). Spread over cake. Top with berries. Makes 10 servings.
PER SERVING *501 cal, 27 g fat, 117 mg chol, 196 mg sodium, 57 g carb, 2 g fiber, 40 g sugars, 9 g pro.*

TRES LECHES
STRAWBERRY
SHORTCAKE

BARBECUE

MUSTARD-
TARRAGON

CHIPOTLE

CAJUN-GARLIC

FRESH HERB

DINNER IN AMERICA

A deep dive—via reader surveys and data on recipe searches—reveals steady diets of chicken, pasta, and tacos. To stave off monotony while enlivening familiar foods, these recipes have been refreshed with flavor spins and creative techniques. Here's to deliciously new weeknight dishes!

COLD OVEN CHICKEN

Our cold-oven chicken delivers juicy, tender results every time. Season with salt and pepper before baking or try these spice blends for more variety.

HANDS-ON TIME 5 min.
TOTAL TIME 35 min.

4   6-to 8-oz. skinless, boneless chicken breast halves
2   Tbsp. vegetable oil
     Salt and black pepper
     Spice blend (right) (optional)

1. Line a 15×10-inch baking pan with foil. Drizzle chicken with oil; season with salt and black pepper or one of the spice blends.
2. Place baking pan in a cold oven. Set oven temperature to 450°F. Bake 25 to 30 minutes or until chicken is done (165°F).*

*Tip Because ovens and the size of chicken breasts vary, use an instant-read thermometer to check for doneness. Chicken breasts at 165°F can have the slightest pink hue, but this temperature is proven to be safe and is hot enough to destroy harmful bacteria. For best results, use chicken breast halves of even thickness. If portions are thicker, you may need to add 5 to 7 minutes cooking time. Makes 4 servings.
PER SERVING *262 cal, 11 g fat, 124 mg chol, 207 mg sodium, 38 g pro.*

Barbecue Spice Blend ¼ cup barbecue seasoning, 2 Tbsp. garlic powder, 2 tsp. onion powder, 1 tsp. ground celery seeds, and ½ tsp. cayenne.

Mustard–Tarragon Spice Blend 2 Tbsp. Dijon mustard; 2 tsp. coarse salt; and 1 Tbsp. each cracked black pepper, chopped fresh tarragon, and olive oil.

Chipotle Spice Blend 2 Tbsp. smoked paprika; 2 tsp. each ground cumin and chipotle chili powder; 1 tsp. each salt, coriander, and black pepper; and ½ tsp. cayenne.

Cajun–Garlic Spice Blend 1 to 2 Tbsp. black pepper or white pepper; 1 tsp. cayenne; 2 tsp. crushed dried thyme; 2 tsp. each garlic powder and onion powder; and 1 tsp. salt.

Fresh Herb Spice Blend ⅓ cup chopped fresh basil, 3 Tbsp. chopped fresh thyme, 1 Tbsp. each chopped fresh rosemary and chopped fresh mint, 3 cloves minced garlic, 3 Tbsp. olive oil, and ½ tsp. each salt and black pepper.

CHICKEN IS THE NO. 1 WEEKNIGHT PROTEIN— ITS VERSATILITY IS UNMATCHED! THIS FAILPROOF COOKING METHOD RESULTS IN JUICY, TENDER RESULTS.

CRISPY RICOTTA
MEATBALLS
WITH SHEET-PAN
TOMATO SAUCE

A TYPICAL HOMEMADE SAUCE SIMMERS FOR HOURS ON THE STOVE TOP TO MELD FLAVORS. ROASTING A MIXTURE OF FRESH AND CANNED TOMATOES, CHOPPED GARLIC, AND FRESH HERBS ON A SHEET PAN GETS YOU THERE IN ONLY 20 MINUTES.

CRISPY RICOTTA MEATBALLS WITH SHEET-PAN TOMATO SAUCE

The secret for crispy, tender-on-the-inside meatballs, plus a sheet pan tomato sauce, will revamp Spaghetti Night.

HANDS-ON TIME 45 min.
TOTAL TIME 1 hr. 15 min.

1   cup ricotta cheese
1   egg
¼   cup chopped fresh parsley
3   Tbsp. chopped fresh basil
1   Tbsp. chopped fresh sage, oregano, or thyme
¾   tsp. salt
½   tsp. black pepper
1   lb. ground beef
1   pt. cherry tomatoes
1   28-oz. can crushed tomatoes
3   cloves garlic, chopped
1   Tbsp. chopped flat-leaf parsley
¾   cup panko
1   Tbsp. canola oil or vegetable oil
1   Tbsp. olive oil
12 oz. linguine or spaghetti
    Grated Parmesan cheese (optional)

1. For meatballs: In a large bowl combine ricotta, egg, parsley, 2 Tbsp. basil, the sage, ½ tsp. salt, and ¼ tsp. black pepper. Add ground beef; gently mix until just combined. Form into twenty-four 1-inch meatballs.

2. Preheat oven to 425°F. For sauce: In a 15×10-inch pan combine cherry and crushed tomatoes, garlic, remaining basil, and 1 Tbsp. parsley. Roast 20 minutes, stirring once halfway through. Season with ¼ tsp. each salt and black pepper. For a smooth sauce, use an immersion blender or a blender to puree.

3. Meanwhile, place panko in a shallow dish. Working in batches, add meatballs; roll gently to coat.

4. In a large skillet heat oils over medium-high heat. Working in batches, cook meatballs 4 minutes each side or until golden brown and cooked through (160°F). Transfer to a paper towel-lined plate. Cover; keep warm.

5. Bring a large pot of salted water to boiling. Cook pasta according to package directions; drain. Toss pasta with sauce, top with meatballs, and, if desired, sprinkle with Parmesan cheese. Makes 5 servings.

Make Ahead Prepare meatballs through Step 1. Cover and chill up to 1 day. To freeze, place on a parchment-lined baking pan. Freeze 4 to 6 hours or until firm. Transfer to a freezer bag; freeze up to 6 months. Before cooking, thaw in the refrigerator overnight.

PER SERVING *677 cal, 29 g fat, 115 mg chol, 798 mg sodium, 73 g carb, 6 g fiber, 11 g sugars, 35 g pro.*

FOR MEATBALLS THAT WOULD MAKE AN ITALIAN GRANDMOTHER PROUD

Use 80-percent-lean beef (superlean meat equals dry meatballs) and add a few spoonfuls of whole milk ricotta. Use your fingertips and a light touch when forming meatballs. (Squeezing and overhandling can make them tough.) Finally, roll each meatball in panko then pan-fry for a crisp crust that traps moisture inside.

PAD THAI STIR-FRY

Add shredded chicken or cooked shrimp to boost the protein.

TOTAL TIME 25 min.

8   oz. pad Thai or flat rice noodles
¼   cup fish sauce
2   Tbsp. sugar
2   Tbsp. lime juice
1   Tbsp. Asian chili-garlic sauce
2   Tbsp. tamarind paste (optional)
2   Tbsp. canola oil or vegetable oil
2   eggs
¼   tsp. black pepper
3   green onions, trimmed and cut into
    1½- to 2-inch pieces
1   cup fresh bean sprouts
⅔   cup salted peanuts, chopped
2   Tbsp. chopped fresh cilantro
    Lime wedges

1. Bring a small pot of water to boiling. Place noodles in a heatproof bowl; pour boiling water over. Let soak according to package directions or until softened but still firm. Drain.
2. Meanwhile, for sauce: In a small bowl whisk together fish sauce, sugar, lime juice, Asian chili-garlic sauce and, if desired, tamarind paste.
3. In large heavy skillet heat 1 Tbsp. oil over medium heat. In a small bowl whisk together eggs and black pepper. Add eggs to hot skillet; tilt to spread to even layer. (They may not cover the bottom.) Cook, without stirring, 30 seconds. Using a wide spatula, carefully turn eggs over; cook 30 to 60 seconds more or just until set. Transfer to a plate. Roll egg and cut into ¼-inch-wide strips.
4. Return skillet to medium-high heat; add remaining 1 Tbsp. oil and the green onions. Cook 30 seconds. Add bean sprouts, ½ cup peanuts, and cilantro. Cook and stir 20 seconds. Add noodles and sauce. Cook 1 to 2 minutes more, tossing to coat.
5. Serve hot topped with egg strips, remaining peanuts, lime wedges, and cilantro leaves. Makes 4 servings.
PER SERVING *440 cal, 18 g fat, 93 mg chol, 1,610 mg sodium, 58 g carb, 3 g fiber, 10 g sugars, 14 g pro.*

SOBA NOODLES WITH SESAME-GINGER SAUCE

TOTAL TIME 25 min.

⅓   cup reduced-sodium soy sauce
2   Tbsp. red wine vinegar
2   Tbsp. mirin (Japanese rice wine)
    (optional)
1½ Tbsp. grated fresh ginger
1   Tbsp. plus 1 tsp. sesame oil
½   to 1 tsp. chili paste (sambel oelek)
6   oz. soba noodles
1½ Tbsp. canola oil or vegetable oil
2   Tbsp. finely chopped fresh ginger
2   tsp. chopped garlic
½   to 1 tsp. chili oil
5   cups vegetables, such as quartered
    baby bok choy, broccoli florets,
    and/or halved, or quartered
    stemmed shiitake mushrooms
1   cup frozen shelled edamame
1   Tbsp. sesame seeds, toasted
    (tip, page 37)

1. For sauce: In a small bowl combine soy sauce, vinegar, mirin (if using), grated ginger, 1 Tbsp. sesame oil, and the chili paste.
2. Bring a large pot of salted water to boiling. Add noodles; cook according to package directions. Drain; rinse under cold water and drain again.
3. Heat a wok or large heavy skillet over medium-high heat 1 minute. Add canola oil; heat 10 seconds. Add chopped ginger and garlic; cook and stir 10 seconds. Stir in remaining 1 tsp. sesame oil, the chili oil, vegetables, and edamame. Cook, without stirring, 2 minutes. Cook, stirring constantly, 3 to 4 minutes or until crisp-tender.
5. Add noodles. Cook 1 minute, stirring constantly. Add sauce; stir to coat. Cook 1 minute more or until noodles are heated through. Top with sesame seeds. Makes 4 servings.
PER SERVING *369 cal, 13 g fat, 1,020 mg sodium, 53 g carb, 7 g fiber, 6 g sugars, 15 g pro.*

VIETNAMESE-STYLE NOODLE SALAD

TOTAL TIME 30 min.

⅓   cup Asian fish sauce
3   Tbsp. rice vinegar
3   Tbsp. lime juice
2   Tbsp. packed brown sugar
1   large clove garlic, minced
2   Tbsp. finely chopped fresh ginger
½   jalapeño, stemmed and seeded
    if desired, finely chopped (tip,
    page 127)
3   Tbsp. finely chopped green onion
1   Tbsp. chopped fresh basil or mint
8   oz. dried rice vermicelli noodles,
    broken in half
1   Tbsp. canola oil or vegetable oil
1   Tbsp. chopped fresh ginger
4   cups vegetables, such as sliced bell
    peppers, snow pea pods, and/or
    julienned carrots
1   cup shredded romaine lettuce
¼   cup fresh basil and/or mint leaves
    Salted peanuts and lime wedges

1. For dressing: In a screw-top jar combine fish sauce, rice vinegar, lime juice, brown sugar, garlic, finely chopped ginger, jalapeño, green onion, and chopped basil.
2. Bring a pot of water to boiling. Remove from heat. Add noodles. Let stand 5 minutes or according to package directions until softened. Drain; rinse under cold water and drain again.
3. Heat a wok or large heavy skillet over medium-high heat 1 minute. Add oil; heat 10 seconds. Add chopped ginger; cook and stir 10 seconds. Add vegetables; cook and stir 2 minutes or until crisp-tender.
4. Divide noodles, vegetables, and romaine among six bowls. Drizzle with dressing. Top with herb leaves. Serve with peanuts and lime wedges. Makes 6 servings.
PER SERVING *211 cal, 3 g fat, 1,292 mg sodium, 43 g carb, 2 g fiber, 8 g sugars, 4 g pro.*

A STIR-FRY TURNED TRENDY NOODLE BOWL ALLOWS FOR TOTAL CUSTOMIZATION.

PAD THAI
STIR-FRY

VIETNAMESE-
STYLE NOODLE
SALAD

SOBA NOODLES
WITH SESAME-
GINGER SAUCE

SALSA VERDE
BLENDER SAUCE

TACO SEASONING

SAUCY CHILI
CHICKEN

CHIPOTLE MOJO
BLENDER SAUCE

AT LEAST A QUARTER OF YOU HAVE DESIGNATED NIGHTS FOR SPECIFIC RECIPES. (TACOS ON TUESDAY, ANYONE?) SWITCH UP THE ROUTINE WITH THESE.

TACO SEASONING

You'll think of restaurant flavor when you taste this taco mix.

TOTAL TIME 5 min.

- 1½ Tbsp. Dried Chile Powder or purchased chili powder
- 1 Tbsp. sugar
- 1 Tbsp. ground cumin
- 1½ tsp. garlic powder
- 1½ Tbsp. salt
- ½ tsp. black pepper
- ½ tsp. crushed dried oregano
- ¼ to ½ tsp. crushed red pepper

In a small airtight container stir together all of the ingredients. Store in a cool, dark place up to 1 year. Makes 16 servings (6 Tbsp.).

Dried Chile Powder Remove stems from 1 lb. fresh chile peppers, such as poblano, habanero, Anaheim, jalapeño, banana, Fresno, serrano, and/or Thai chiles (do not seed peppers)*. Cut large peppers into 1-inch-wide strips; quarter or halve small peppers. Place peppers, cut sides down, on mesh-lined dehydrator trays, leaving space between peppers. Dehydrate at 135°F 24 to 28 hours or until evenly dried and brittle. Cool completely. In a well-ventilated area crumble cooled peppers and place in a spice mill or food processor. Cover and grind or process until a powder forms. When grinding peppers, turn away to avoid inhaling fumes or particles from peppers. Store in an airtight container in a cool, dark place up to 6 months. Makes about ¼ cup.

*Tip Chile peppers contain oils that can irritate skin and eyes. Wear plastic or rubber gloves when working with them.

PER 1-TSP. SERVING *8 cal, 213 mg sodium, 2 g carb, 1 g sugars.*

SAUCY CHILI CHICKEN

TOTAL TIME 10 min.

- 1 8-oz. can tomato sauce
- 1 Tbsp. Chili Bouillon Base or jarred chili bouillon base
- 2 cups shredded cooked chicken
- 4 flour tortillas
- 2 radishes, cut into matchsticks

In a saucepan combine tomato sauce and Chili Bouillon Base. Bring to boiling; stir in chicken. Heat through. Serve in tortillas topped with radishes. Makes 4 servings.

Chili Bouillon Base In a small bowl combine 2 tsp. chili powder, 1 tsp. paprika, and ½ tsp. each onion powder, garlic powder, and salt. Stir in 1 Tbsp. water.

PER SERVING *252 cal, 8 g fat, 62 mg chol, 702 mg sodium, 19 g carb, 2 g fiber, 3 g sugars, 24 g pro.*

SALSA VERDE BLENDER SAUCE

Serve this green salsa on enchiladas and tacos, or as a dip with tortilla chips.

TOTAL TIME 30 min.

- 1 lb. husked tomatillos
- ½ cup chopped onion
- 1 jalapeño, halved and seeded (tip, left)
- 2 smashed garlic cloves
- ⅓ cup fresh cilantro leaves
- 3 Tbsp. toasted pepitas (tip, page 37)
- 1 tsp. honey
- ¼ tsp. kosher salt

1. In a saucepan cook tomatillos, onion, jalapeño, and garlic in a boiling water 8 minutes or until tomatillos turn light green. Drain.

2. In a blender combine the tomatillo mixture, cilantro, pepitas, honey, and salt. Cover and blend until smooth. Makes 4 servings (2½ cups).

PER SCANT ⅔-CUP SERVING *264 cal, 13 g fat, 83 mg chol, 370 mg sodium, 8 g carb, 2 g fiber, 4 g sugars, 29 g pro.*

CHIPOTLE MOJO BLENDER SAUCE

Spoon this mildly spicy smoky sauce on tacos as well as chicken, pork, or salmon.

TOTAL TIME 40 min.

- 6 smashed garlic cloves
- ¼ cup olive oil
- 1 tsp. orange zest
- ¼ cup orange juice
- 1 14.5-oz. can fire-roasted tomatoes, drained
- 1 chipotle chile pepper in adobo sauce
- ¼ tsp. salt

1. In a saucepan cook garlic in hot oil 10 minutes or until garlic is softened. Remove from heat; stir in orange zest and juice.

2. In a blender combine garlic mixture, fire-roasted tomatoes, chipotle chile pepper in adobo, and salt. Cover and blend until smooth. Makes 4 servings (2 cups).

PER ¼-CUP SERVING *350 cal, 21 g fat, 91 mg chol, 725 mg sodium, 9 g carb, 1 g fiber, 5 g sugars, 31 g pro.*

CHARRED CORN WITH POBLANOS AND FETA
Recipe on page 147

BROASTED RED PEPPER PANZANELLA
Recipe on page 147

june

Welcome summer with an unfussy backyard barbecue that promises make-ahead bites, big batch drinks, and steaks and ribs to keep the kitchen cool.

134

136

148

entertaining

GRAB A SPOON

When hosting a low-key summertime dinner for friends, keep dessert simple—or at least made well ahead. This impressive elegant yet simple-to-pull-off dessert is an entertaining dream.

CHERRY-THYME CRISPS

Present this dessert deconstructed. Set out cherry filling, crumb topping, and meringue for guests to build their own.

HANDS-ON TIME 10 min.
TOTAL TIME 45 min.

6   cups pitted fresh tart red cherries or two 16-oz. pkg. frozen pitted tart red cherries
2   cups crumbled shortbread cookies
⅓   cup butter, melted
¼   tsp. ground cinnamon
2   tsp. chopped fresh thyme
⅔   cup sugar
3   Tbsp. cornstarch
4   fresh pasteurized egg whites
1   tsp. vanilla
½   tsp. cream of tartar
½   cup sugar

1. Preheat oven to 400°F. If using frozen cherries, thaw then drain, reserving ¼ cup juice. For crumb topping: In a medium bowl stir together cookie crumbs, butter, and cinnamon. Spread evenly on a baking sheet lined with parchment paper. Bake 8 minutes or until browned and crisp. Toss with thyme. Set aside to cool.*
2. For filling: In a large saucepan stir together cherries, reserved juice if using frozen, ⅔ cup sugar, and the cornstarch.

3. Cook and stir cherry mixture over medium heat until thickened and bubbly. Cook and stir 2 minutes more.* Divide filling among 8 to 10 dessert dishes. (Use immediately or let stand up to 2 hours.)
4. For marshmallow meringue: Preheat broiler. Line a baking sheet with foil; set aside. In a large bowl beat egg whites, vanilla, and cream of tartar with a mixer on medium about 1 minute or until soft peaks form (tips curl). Gradually add the ½ cup sugar, 1 Tbsp. at a time, beating on high. Beat continuously until meringue forms stiff, glossy peaks and sugar dissolves. Spoon into mounds or spread in a rectangle on the prepared baking sheet (photo, right). Broil 4 to 5 inches from heat source 30 to 60 seconds or until browned, or use a culinary torch to brown tops.*
5. Top cherry filling with crumb topping then spoon toasted meringue over each. Makes 8 to 10 crisps.
*Make Ahead Prepare and store crumb topping in an airtight container at room temperature up to 24 hours. Prepare cherry filling, cool 30 minutes, then cover and chill 8 hours; reheat before serving. Chill meringue up to 4 hours before toasting or up to 2 hours after toasting.
PER CRISP *337 cal, 13 g fat, 26 chol, 165 mg sodium, 56 g carb, 2 g fiber, 40 sugars, 4 g pro.*

PICK A SHAPE

To make mini crisps, drop meringue by spoonfuls. If serving family-style, spread, swirl, and let guests scoop their own.

SCOOP A SPOONFUL Spoon meringue into 8 to 10 dollops on a baking sheet lined with foil. Brown as in Step 4, left. If tops brown too quickly, move rack away from heat.

SWOOP AND SWIRL Spread the meringue into a ½-inch-thick rectangle. Use the back of a spoon to swirl. Peaks crisp well for more crunch. Brown as in Step 4, left.

CUCUMBER-LIMEADE

HIBISCUS-LEMON WATER

PINEAPPLE-SAGE SANGRIA

PEACH-BASIL ROSÉ SANGRIA

gatherings
SUMMER SOIRÉE

Big-batch drinks, make-ahead snacks, and tropical decor set the scene for a summer party that's about as stressful as sipping sangria on the patio.

CUCUMBER LIMEADE

HANDS-ON TIME 20 min.
TOTAL TIME 4 hr. 20 min., includes chilling

1   sliced cucumber
6¼ cups water
1   cup lime juice
½   cup honey
     Lime slices
     Cucumber slices

In a blender combine cucumber and ¼ cup water. Cover and pulse until liquefied. Strain through a fine-mesh sieve into a pitcher, pressing to extract juice. Discard solids. Add 6 cups water, lime juice, and honey. Refrigerate 4 hours or until thoroughly chilled. Serve with lime and cucumber slices. Makes 9 servings.
PER SERVING *69 cal, 7 mg sodium, 19 g carb, 1 g fiber, 15 g sugar, 1 g pro.*

HIBISCUS-LEMON WATER

HANDS-ON TIME 10 min.
TOTAL TIME 20 min.

8   cups water
2   Tbsp. honey
2   hibiscus tea bags
2   Tbsp. lemon juice
     Ice cubes
1   lemon, sliced

In a large pitcher combine water and honey; stir to dissolve honey. Add tea bags; steep 15 minutes or until water has turned vibrant pink. Remove and discard tea bags. Add lemon juice. Refrigerate 4 hours or until thoroughly chilled. Add ice and lemon slices just before serving. Makes 8 servings.

Tip If using loose hibiscus flowers, place on a square of cheesecloth, gather into a bundle and tie closed with 100%-cotton kitchen string.
PER SERVING *16 cal, 7 mg sodium, 4 g carb, 4 g sugars.*

PEACH-BASIL ROSÉ SANGRIA

HANDS-ON TIME 10 min.
TOTAL TIME 2 hr. 10 min., includes chilling

2   cups apricot nectar
½   cup apricot brandy
¼   cup fresh lemon juice
2   cups sliced peaches
½   cup raspberries
1   750-milliliter bottle sparkling rosé wine, chilled
     Fresh basil leaves

In a large pitcher combine apricot nectar, apricot brandy, and lemon juice; stir in peaches and raspberries. Refrigerate 2 hours or until thoroughly chilled. To serve, gently pour in sparkling rosé. Add basil leaves. Makes 8 servings.
PER SERVING *189 cal, 8 mg sodium, 23 g carb, 2 g fiber, 21 g sugars, 1 g pro.*

PINEAPPLE-SAGE SANGRIA

HANDS-ON TIME 15 min.
TOTAL TIME 1 hr. 15 min., includes chilling

4   sprigs fresh sage
1   cup ice cubes
1   750-milliliter bottle fruity white wine, such as Sauvignon Blanc or Pinot Blanc, chilled
2   cups pineapple juice
¼   cup orange liqueur
1   orange, halved and sliced
2   cups fresh pineapple cubes
1   cup blueberries

In a large pitcher combine sage and ice cubes. Muddle and stir until sage is bruised and fragrant. Add wine, pineapple juice, and orange liqueur; stir. Add orange, pineapple, and blueberries. Refrigerate at least 1 hour or up to 8 hours. Add additional sage. Makes 8 servings.
PER SERVING *167 cal, 2 mg sodium, 22 g carb, 1 g fiber, 13 g sugars, 1 g pro.*

LOW- AND NO-ALCOHOL SIPPERS FLOW FROM AFTERNOON INTO EVENING.

THREE-MELON
KABOBS

THREE-MELON KABOBS

Serve melon kabobs on a Himalayan salt plate to impart a subtle salty note. Finish them with a quick fresh herb dressing or a sprinkle of citrus zest, salt, and chile pepper.

TOTAL TIME 30 min.

- 4 cups cubed seedless watermelon
- 4 cups cubed cantaloupe
- 4 cups cubed honeydew melon
- 3 Tbsp. lime juice
  Mint-Lime Dressing or Chile-Lime Salt

1. Thread melon cubes onto sixteen 10-inch bamboo skewers. Sprinkle with lime juice. Serve immediately or refrigerate, covered, up to 8 hours.
2. Drizzle skewers with Mint-Lime Dressing or sprinkle with Chile-Lime Salt just before serving. Makes 16 servings.
Mint-Lime Dressing In a small food processor or using an immersion blender, blend 1 cup coarsely chopped fresh mint or basil, 2 Tbsp. olive oil, 1 Tbsp. lime juice, a pinch salt, and 2 Tbsp. cold water until nearly smooth.
Chile-Lime Salt Combine 1 Tbsp. flaky sea salt, zest of one lime, and one finely minced Thai chile pepper.
PER SERVING *58 cal, 2 g fat, 25 mg sodium, 11 g carb, 1 g fiber, 9 g sugars, 1 g pro.*

PIMM'S POPS

Alcohol, which has a much lower freezing point than water, doesn't freeze solid. Juice and mixers dilute alcohol enough that the pops freeze solid, but will melt faster than nonalcoholic ones.

HANDS-ON TIME 15 min.
TOTAL TIME 12 hr. 15 min., includes freezing

- 4 small strawberries, hulled and chopped
- ½ navel orange, peeled and chopped
- 8 thin slices English cucumber, quartered
- 8 fresh mint leaves, thinly sliced
- 1 cup ginger ale
- ½ cup Pimm's No. 1

Divide strawberries, orange, cucumber, and mint among eight 3-oz. ice-pop molds. In a 2-cup liquid measure combine ginger ale and Pimm's No. 1. Pour into molds; insert sticks. Freeze pops at least 8 hours. Makes 8 servings.
PER SERVING *50 cal, 3 mg sodium, 4 g carb, 4 g sugars.*

APEROL SPRITZ POPS

Aperol spritz, a fizzy cocktail from Italy, gets a pretty blush from Aperol—a bitter low-alcohol aperitif—and fizz from a splash of Prosecco and/or club soda.

HANDS-ON TIME 10 min.
TOTAL TIME 12 hr. 10 min., includes freezing

- 2½ oranges
- ¾ cup Prosecco
- ¼ cup Aperol
- 3 Tbsp. club soda

Squeeze ⅓ cup juice from the two whole oranges. Cut the orange half into bite-size pieces and divide among six 3-oz. ice-pop molds. In a 2-cup liquid measure combine orange juice and remaining ingredients. Pour into molds; insert sticks. Freeze pops at least 8 hours. Makes 6 servings.
PER SERVING *44 cal, 4 mg sodium, 4 g carb, 3 g sugars.*

APEROL SPRITZ
POPS

PIMM'S POPS

FAST & FRESH

Easy, delicious recipes for a better dinner tonight.

OPEN-FACE CRISPY-FISH SANDWICHES

Any firm whitefish, such as haddock, cod, or catfish, will work well here. If frying the fish in batches, keep cooked fish warm on a sheet pan in a 200°F oven.

TOTAL TIME 25 min.

⅓ cup all-purpose flour
2 eggs
  Salt
⅔ cup cornmeal
4 firm whitefish fillets (about 1½ lb.)
  Black pepper
1½ cups vegetable oil
¼ cup mayonnaise
1 Tbsp. capers
¼ tsp. cayenne pepper
4 1-inch slices Italian bread, toasted
½ red onion, thinly sliced

1. Place flour in a shallow dish. In another shallow dish whisk together eggs and a pinch of salt. In a third shallow dish combine cornmeal and ½ tsp. salt. Lightly season fish with salt and black pepper. Dip fish into flour, then egg mixture, then cornmeal mixture to coat.
2. In a 12-inch skillet heat oil over medium-high heat until it sizzles when a few cornmeal crumbs are added (about 350°F). Add fish to skillet. Cook 3 minutes on each side or until fish is golden and flakes when tested with a fork. Transfer to paper towels to drain.
3. In a small bowl combine mayonnaise, capers, and cayenne pepper. Spread on bread. Top with fish, onion, and additional capers. Makes 4 servings.
PER SERVINGS *546 cal, 26 g fat, 191 mg chol, 859 mg sodium, 41 g carb, 3 g fiber, 2 g sugars, 37 g pro.*

SESAME CHICKEN AND GREENS STIR-FRY

Japanese tamari, a by-product of making miso, is darker, slightly richer, and less salty than most soy sauces.

TOTAL TIME 25 min.

1   Tbsp. vegetable oil
2   Tbsp. toasted sesame oil
2   halves skinless, boneless chicken breast, thinly sliced (1¼ lb.)
2   Tbsp. fresh ginger, finely chopped
2   cloves garlic, finely chopped
¾   lb. snow peas, trimmed
3   Tbsp. reduced-sodium tamari or soy sauce
1   orange, juiced
4   cups mustard greens, chopped
¼   cup sesame seeds, toasted (tip, page 37)
    Crushed red pepper (optional)

1. In an extra-large skillet heat vegetable oil and 1 Tbsp. sesame oil over medium-high heat; add chicken in a single layer. Cook, without stirring, 2 minutes or until browned. Cook and stir 2 minutes more or until chicken is cooked through. Transfer to a plate.
2. Add remaining sesame oil to skillet; heat over medium-high heat. Add ginger and garlic; cook and stir 30 seconds. Add peas; cook and stir 1 to 2 minutes or until crisp-tender. Add tamari and orange juice; simmer 1 minute. Stir in greens, chicken, and sesame seeds. If desired, sprinkle with crushed red pepper. Makes 4 servings.
PER SERVING *382 cal, 19 g fat, 103 mg chol, 405 mg sodium, 15 g carb, 5 g fiber, 6 g sugars, 39 g pro.*

STEAK OUT

Grab your tongs and fire up the grill. You're about to be the envy of the neighborhood and master of the steak house steak.

REVERSE-SEARED RIBEYE STEAKS

Every season a gadget or technique gets backyard cooks buzzing. This year it's the reverse sear, and for good reason. Start by grilling a thick-cut steak low and slow, which ensures the meat cooks evenly from center to surface. Then finish by searing over fiery heat. Because the steak is warm and the surface is dry, it gets that seared, browned crust rapidly. (Searing a moist steak straight from the fridge takes more time, potentially making the first bite tough.)

HANDS-ON TIME 15 min.

TOTAL TIME 5 hr, includes chilling

4   1¼- to 1½-inch bone-in or
     boneless beef ribeye steaks
2   tsp. kosher salt
1½   Tbsp. extra virgin olive oil
1½   tsp. coarsely ground black pepper

1. Trim outer fat of steak to ¼ inch or less. Sprinkle steaks evenly with salt; set on a wire rack in a shallow pan. Refrigerate, uncovered, 4 to 48 hours.

2. Prepare grill for indirect heat. Meanwhile, pat steaks dry, rub with oil, then season evenly with pepper. Let stand at room temperature while grill heats. Grill steaks, covered, over indirect low heat (300°F) 15 to 20 minutes or until an instant-read thermometer inserted in centers registers 100°F. Transfer steaks to a platter; let stand 20 minutes while preparing grill for high heat.

3. Finish steaks by searing on grill over direct high heat. For gas: Ignite center burner and increase heat to high (450°F to 500°F). For charcoal: Open vents, reignite coals by adding additional briquettes, spread coals evenly over grate, and let burn to high (450°F to 500°F) with rack in place. If using hardwood charcoal, light new charcoal using a chimney, then add to the grill. Grill steaks, covered, 4 to 5 minutes or until well-browned and crusty and an instant-read thermometer registers 130°F for medium-rare, turning often. Let steaks stand 5 minutes before slicing. Makes 8 servings.

PER SERVING *531 cal, 44 g fat, 137 mg chol, 391 mg sodium, 35 g pro.*

TOP THIS

Even purists appreciate a spoonful of flavor. Each of these is enough to top four steaks.

BLUE CHEESE WITH TARRAGON Stir together 1 cup crumbled blue cheese, 4 tsp. chopped fresh tarragon, and 1 tsp. lemon zest. Cover; let stand 30 minutes before serving. Makes 1 cup.

CHARRED CHERRY TOMATOES Drizzle 1 Tbsp. olive oil over 2 lb. cherry tomatoes; sprinkle with ½ tsp. each kosher salt and black pepper. Grill in a hot cast-iron skillet 5 to 10 minutes or until charred and softened. Splash with 1 Tbsp. red wine vinegar. Makes 2 cups.

BASIL CHIMICHURRI In a food processor combine ½ cup olive oil, 3 Tbsp. red wine vinegar, 2 cloves garlic, 1½ tsp. kosher salt, and ½ tsp. crushed red pepper. Add 1¾ cups packed fresh basil, ¼ cup each packed fresh cilantro, Italian parsley, and chopped shallot; process until finely chopped. Makes 1 cup. Chill up to 5 days.

KOREAN-STYLE STEAK SAUCE In a saucepan whisk together ¼ cup olive oil, ¼ cup minced green onions, 3 Tbsp. soy sauce, 2 Tbsp. toasted sesame seeds, 2 Tbsp. toasted sesame oil, 1½ Tbsp. brown sugar, 1 Tbsp. grated fresh ginger, 2 tsp. minced garlic, and ¼ tsp. cayenne pepper; heat through. Makes 1 cup. Chill up to 1 week.

THE REVERSE SEAR WARRANTS A SERIOUSLY THICK CUT OF BEEF. NEW YORK STRIP AND RIBEYE ARE MOST COMMONLY GRILLED THIS WAY. RIBEYE (LEFT) HAS A WINNING COMBO OF FLAVOR AND TEXTURE.

CROWD PLEASER

Food blogger Gaby Dalkin shares her formula for a never fussy, always delicious backyard barbecue.

If Gaby Dalkin could bottle anything and share it with the world—other than her delicious vinaigrettes—it would be the California lifestyle. She hasn't figured out how to put that in a jar, but she has been serving it up for the past decade on her popular site, *What's Gaby Cooking,* and continues in her latest cookbook.

"To me, California is a state of mind more than it is a place," says Gaby, who lives in Los Angeles with her husband, Thomas Dawson. "Everything here is refreshingly laid-back, which is exactly how I feel about making meals and entertaining. Nothing should ever be too fussy or require too much work." Helping people relax and enjoy the process of cooking and entertaining is a primary goal of Gaby's blog.

During summer, when Gaby regularly hosts backyard get-togethers, her aim is to serve flavorful food that people will flip over, without Gaby spending hours in the kitchen. Fresh summer produce is key: "The vegetables are perfect and bright and need little interference, so I fill the table with all their beautiful color and goodness." Her relatively simple menu can mostly be made ahead and served at room temperature.

This spread centers around baby back ribs Gaby bakes in advance then throws on the grill at party time. A day or two before, she preps the vegetables, whips up a couple easy dips for a crudité platter, and makes s'mookies (chocolate chip cookie and s'mores hybrid) that Gaby's friends regularly beg for).

"FORGET FORMAL DINNER PARTIES. I LIKE A PICNIC TABLE UNDER A TREE WITH FRIENDS CRAMMED AROUND GOOD FOOD, EATING FAMILY-STYLE."

IF YOU'RE AT ALL INTIMIDATED BY ENTERTAINING, THE BEAUTY OF PREPPING AHEAD IS THAT YOU CAN DO IT AT YOUR OWN PACE WHILE NO ONE IS WATCHING.

GREEN GODDESS WHITE BEAN DIP

"California is the land of green goddess dressing," says Gaby Dalkin. "It's practically a food group. I translated it to a hearty dip that brings raw vegetables to life. You can throw in whatever savory green herbs you have on hand; you can't mess it up."

TOTAL TIME 15 min.

1   15-oz. can cannellini beans, rinsed and drained
3   Tbsp. lemon juice
2   large cloves garlic
1   tsp. kosher salt
½   cup chopped, loosely packed flat-leaf parsley
½   cup chopped, loosely packed fresh basil
¼   cup chopped fresh chives

In a blender combine beans, lemon juice, garlic, and salt; blend until smooth. With blender running, drizzle in 1 Tbsp. water at a time until mixture is silky smooth (1 to 3 Tbsp. total). Add herbs; blend until smooth. Season to taste. Serve with pita wedges and assorted crudités. Makes 10 to 12 servings.

PER SERVING *34 cal, 195 mg sodium, 7 g carb, 2 g fiber, 2 g pro.*

ROMESCO DIP

Gaby considers this chunky dip made with roasted red peppers and almonds to be the thicker, smokier, spicier Spanish cousin of tomato sauce.

TOTAL TIME 15 min.

½   cup jarred roasted red bell peppers, drained
1   to 2 cloves garlic
¾   cup unsalted almonds, cashews, or walnuts
1   Tbsp. tomato paste
6   to 8 large fresh basil leaves
2   Tbsp. red wine vinegar
½   tsp. smoked paprika
½   tsp. crushed red pepper
½   tsp. kosher salt
½   tsp. black pepper
¼   cup olive oil

In a blender or food processor combine peppers, garlic, nuts, tomato paste, basil, vinegar, paprika, crushed red pepper, salt, and black pepper. Blend or process 1 minute until nearly smooth. (If necessary, add 1 to 2 Tbsp. water to help blend.) With blender or food processor running, add olive oil in a thin, steady stream. Process 1 to 2 minutes more or until completely smooth. Serve with pita wedges and assorted crudités. Makes 12 servings.

PER SERVING *96 cal, 9 g fat, 88 mg sodium, 3 g carb, 1 g fiber, 1 g sugars, 2 g pro.*

HOST LIKE GABY

START WITH A BOARD "I'm a fan of having everything ready when people arrive, especially appetizers. Grab a big board and blanket it with bright veggies and a few fun dips you've already whirled up in the blender. Bam, you're done."

SET UP A SELF-SERVE BAR "There's no line at the bar at my parties," Gaby says. "My friends make their own drinks because I'm the queen of the DIY cocktail bar. All I have to do is make a yummy base ahead of time and guests can help themselves."

KEEP IT CASUAL Gaby keeps the table as simple as possible. She adds color with flowers—like peonies from the garden—and the food serves as the main decoration. "A relaxed table means relaxed guests," she says.

THE MORNING OF THE PARTY, GABY BAKES THE RIBS IN A BEER BATH SO THEY TURN OUT SUPER-MOIST THEN MAKES A BATCH OF PICKLES TO SERVE WITH THEM. WHEN GUESTS ARRIVE, ALL SHE HAS TO DO IS GRILL THE RIBS ABOUT 15 MINUTES TO "GET THOSE BEAUTIFUL CHAR MARKS."

BABY BACK RIBS AND QUICK PICKLES

"There's not much worse than a dry rib, so you have to lock in the moisture," Gaby says. *"I wrap the ribs tightly in foil when I cook them. The beer in the pan circulates all around them and keeps them wet, so the meat will practically fall off the bone when you take the first bite."*

HANDS-ON TIME 15 min.
TOTAL TIME 6 hr. 30 min., includes chilling

RIBS

2	Tbsp. granulated sugar
1	Tbsp. chili powder
1	Tbsp. kosher salt
½	tsp. granulated garlic
2	3-lb. racks pork loin back ribs
1	cup beer
1	Tbsp. olive oil
¾	cup chopped yellow onion
2	cloves garlic, minced
1	cup chopped mango
½	cup tomato sauce
2	Tbsp. packed brown sugar
2	Tbsp. Worcestershire sauce
2	Tbsp. balsamic vinegar
1	canned chipotle pepper in adobo sauce plus 1 Tbsp. adobo sauce
4	green onions, chopped
2	Tbsp. chopped fresh cilantro
1	jalapeño, stemmed and thinly sliced (tip, page 127)

QUICK PICKLES

1	lb. Persian cucumbers, sliced ½ inch thick
6	green onions, chopped
5	Tbsp. rice vinegar
1	jalapeño, stemmed, thinly sliced, and seeded if desired (tip, page 127)
2	to 4 cloves garlic, thinly sliced
1	Tbsp. grated fresh ginger
1	Tbsp. honey

1. For Ribs: In a small bowl combine sugar, chili powder, salt, and granulated garlic. Place ribs in a roasting pan. Rub spice mixture onto both sides. Cover with foil. Refrigerate 4 to 24 hours.
2. Preheat oven to 350°F. Pour beer around ribs, then recover pan with foil. Bake 2 hours or until meat is very tender.*
3. Meanwhile, for barbecue sauce: In a medium saucepan heat olive oil over medium-high heat. Add onion and garlic. Cook and stir 2 to 3 minutes or until softened and fragrant. Add mango, tomato sauce, brown sugar, Worcestershire, vinegar, and chipotle pepper and adobo sauce. Bring to boiling; reduce heat. Simmer, uncovered, 15 to 18 minutes or until thickened, stirring occasionally. Cool slightly. Using an immersion blender, blend until smooth. Season with salt.*
4. Remove ribs from oven. Generously brush with barbecue sauce. Grill, covered, directly over medium heat 7 to 8 minutes on each side or until browned.
5. Cut ribs into individual portions. Arrange on platter. Top with green onions, cilantro, and jalapeño slices. Serve with Quick Pickles and remaining barbecue sauce. Makes 6 servings.
6. For Quick Pickles: Place cucumber slices in a colander over a bowl. Sprinkle with 1 Tbsp. kosher salt; stir to coat. Let stand 30 minutes. Rinse and drain. Blot dry with towels.
7. In a medium bowl combine cucumbers, green onions, vinegar, jalapeño, garlic, ginger, and honey. Stir to coat. Refrigerate, covered, 4 to 8 hours.

*Make Ahead Prepare ribs through Step 2. Transfer to a rimmed baking pan, reserving cooking liquid. Cool 30 minutes. Drizzle with enough cooking liquid to moisten; discard any remaining cooking liquid. Refrigerate, covered, 8 hours. Grill as directed in Step 4. Make the barbecue sauce as directed in Step 3. Refrigerate in an airtight container up to 1 week.

PER SERVING *319 cal, 14 g fat, 75 mg chol, 1,121 mg sodium, 25 g carb, 3 g fiber, 18 g sugars, 26 g pro.*

CHARRED CORN WITH POBLANOS AND FETA

BROASTED RED PEPPER PANZANELLA

BROASTED RED PEPPER PANZANELLA

The croutons should be crispy on the outside and chewy inside. Gaby suggests working the oil into the bread by hand.

HANDS-ON TIME 30 min.
TOTAL TIME 50 min.

6   large red, orange, and/or yellow bell peppers
9   Tbsp. olive oil
½   loaf country-style bread (about 12 oz.), torn into 1½- to 2-inch pieces
    Salt and black pepper
2   Tbsp. red wine vinegar
1   Tbsp. lemon juice
1   Tbsp. chopped fresh oregano
2   cloves garlic, finely chopped
½   tsp. crushed red pepper
½   cup thinly sliced red onion
6   oz. Burrata cheese, torn into 2-inch pieces
¼   cup fresh mint leaves

1. In an extra-large bowl toss bell peppers with 1 Tbsp. oil. Grill peppers, covered, directly over medium-high heat 10 to 12 minutes or until skins are blackened in spots and blistered all over, turning occasionally. Return peppers to bowl. Cover with plastic wrap. Let stand 15 minutes.
2. Meanwhile, for croutons: On a baking sheet* or grill tray toss bread with 4 Tbsp. oil; season with salt and black pepper. Place baking sheet on a grill rack directly over medium. Grill, covered, 8 to 10 minutes or until crisp on outside but still chewy in center, tossing occasionally. Cool.
3. Peel, stem, and seed peppers; cut into 2-inch-long bite-size strips. In a large serving bowl whisk together vinegar, lemon juice, oregano, garlic, crushed red pepper, and remaining 4 Tbsp. oil. Season to taste with salt and black pepper. Add peppers, croutons, and onion. Top with cheese and mint. Makes 6 servings.
***Tip** Wrap baking sheet in foil to prevent discoloration from grilling.
PER SERVING *426 cal, 28 g fat, 20 mg chol, 513 mg sodium, 37 g carb, 5 g fiber, 4 g sugars, 11 g pro.*

STRAWBERRY-BASIL SMASH

CHARRED CORN WITH POBLANOS AND FETA

Gaby uses feta cheese blocks packed in brine—they deliver true flavor and have a longer shelf life than crumbles.

TOTAL TIME 35 min.

6   ears fresh corn, shucked
½   cup plus 2 Tbsp. olive oil
2   poblano chile peppers, stemmed, halved, and seeded (tip, page 127)
1   pt. cherry tomatoes, halved
½   cup finely chopped red onion
½   cup crumbled feta cheese
1   jalapeño, stemmed, seeded, and finely chopped (tip, page 127)
2   limes, juiced
    Salt and black pepper
2   cups tightly packed fresh cilantro leaves, stems removed
¼   cup coarsely chopped shallot
2   Tbsp. red wine vinegar
1   clove garlic
½   tsp. crushed red pepper

1. Brush corn with 2 Tbsp. oil. Grill corn and poblanos skin sides down on the greased rack of a grill directly over medium-high heat 8 to 10 minutes or until charred, turning corn occasionally.
2. Remove corn from grill; let cool. Transfer peppers to a bowl; cover and let stand 15 minutes. Cut kernels from cobs; transfer to a serving bowl. Peel peppers and dice. Add to bowl with corn, along with tomatoes, onion, feta, jalapeño, and lime juice. Season with salt and black pepper.

3. For vinaigrette: In a blender combine remaining ½ cup olive oil, the cilantro, shallot, vinegar, garlic, crushed red pepper, and 1 tsp. salt. Blend 60 seconds or until very smooth. Drizzle ½ cup vinaigrette over corn mixture. Pass remaining vinaigrette. Makes 6 servings.
PER SERVING *350 cal, 27 g fat, 11 mg chol, 619 mg sodium, 26g carb, 3 g fiber, 9 g sugars, 6 g pro.*

STRAWBERRY-BASIL SMASH

TOTAL TIME 15 min.

¾   cup sugar
12 oz. strawberries, hulled (2¼ cups)
1   cup fresh lemon juice
½   cup packed fresh basil leaves
    Gin, vodka, silver tequila, or white rum
    Sparkling water, chilled

1. In a pitcher combine 4 cups water and the sugar. Stir until dissolved.
2. Add strawberries, lemon juice, and basil. Using an immersion blender, blend 2 minutes or until smooth. Strain through a fine-mesh sieve; discard solids. Skim off and discard any foam. Refrigerate, covered, up to 24 hours.
3. For each drink, pour about ¾ cup strawberry mixture into a highball glass filled with ice. Stir in 1 to 2 oz. alcohol. Top with a splash of sparkling water. If desired, garnish with sliced strawberries and additional basil leaves. Makes 6 to 8 servings.
PER SERVING *180 cal, 10 mg sodium, 30 g carb, 1 g fiber, 28 g sugars.*

"ONE OF MY PROUDEST ACHIEVEMENTS IS THIS RIFF ON S'MORES," SAYS GABY, WHO ADMITS TO AN "AGGRESSIVE ADDICTION" TO HOMEMADE COOKIES.

CHOCOLATE CHIP S'MOOKIES

"If you don't want to go to the trouble of making marshmallow creme, store-bought will do. But you haven't lived until you've tried a homemade marshmallow creme," Gaby says. She works crushed graham crackers into the chocolate-studded dough, then sandwiches marshmallow creme between the cookies to serve.

HANDS-ON TIME 30 min.
TOTAL TIME 3 hr., includes chilling

COOKIES
1   cup butter, room temperature
1   cup granulated sugar
1   cup packed brown sugar
2   large eggs
2   tsp. vanilla
2½ cups all-purpose flour
1   tsp. baking soda
1   tsp. baking powder
1   tsp. salt
1   cup semisweet chocolate chips
3   graham crackers, chopped (¾ cup)

MARSHMALLOW CREME
1½ Tbsp. unflavored gelatin
    (2 envelopes)
¾   cup sugar
½   cup light corn syrup
    Pinch salt
½   tsp. vanilla
    Nonstick cooking spray

1. For the Cookies: In a large bowl beat butter and sugars with a mixer on medium to high 2 to 3 minutes or until smooth. Add eggs and vanilla. Beat until combined, scraping sides of bowl occasionally. Add flour, baking soda, baking powder, and salt. Beat on low until combined. Stir in chocolate chips and graham crackers. Cover dough with plastic wrap. Refrigerate at least 2 hours.

2. Preheat oven to 350°F. Shape dough into 1½-inch balls. Place balls 2 inches apart on a baking sheet lined with parchment paper. Bake 9 to 10 minutes or until edges are slightly golden brown and center is still soft. Remove from oven; cool 5 minutes. Transfer to a wire rack to cool completely. Repeat with remaining dough.*

3. For the Marshmallow Creme: Place ¼ cup ice water and the gelatin in the bowl of a stand mixer fitted with the whisk attachment.

4. Meanwhile, in a small saucepan combine an additional ¼ cup ice water, the sugar, corn syrup, and salt. Bring to boiling over medium-high heat. Cook and stir 5 minutes or until sugar has dissolved. Using a pastry brush dipped in water, brush down sides of pan to wash any sugar crystals down into the syrup. Attach a candy thermometer to side of pan. Cook, without stirring, 10 minutes or until mixture reaches 240°F.

5. With mixer on low, slowly pour hot sugar mixture into gelatin in bowl. Increase speed to high. Whisk 5 minutes. Add vanilla. Whisk 1 minute more.

6. Using a rubber spatula sprayed with nonstick cooking spray, transfer creme to a piping bag fitted with a ½-inch round or star tip. For each s'mookie, pipe creme on bottom of a cookie; top with a second cookie, bottom side to creme.* Makes 36 sandwich cookies.

*Make Ahead Store unfilled cookies in an airtight container at room temperature up to 3 days. Store filled cookies in the refrigerator up to 3 days.

PER SANDWICH COOKIE *188 cal, 7 g fat, 24 mg chol, 100 mg sodium, 31 g carb, 1 g fiber, 23 g sugars, 2 g pro.*

FRUITY LAYER POPS
Recipes on page 166

july

Create a sparkling Fourth of July celebration featuring a hot dog bar, fresh salads, and refreshing desserts. Plus learn how to get smokehouse flavor from your backyard grill.

153

157

159

SMOKE OUT

Attention, aspiring pitmasters: These recipes will help you get smokehouse flavor from a standard backyard charcoal or gas grill.

SMOKED SALMON WITH WILD PEPPER

When you buy a side of salmon, the pin bones will be intact. Ask your fishmonger or grocer to remove them. Or remove them yourself with tweezers or needle-nose pliers by pulling straight toward the head.

HANDS-ON TIME 15 min.
TOTAL TIME 45 min.

1   4-lb. skin-on side of salmon
    Extra virgin olive oil
2   tsp. kosher salt
1   Tbsp. plus ¼ tsp. Voatsiperifery peppercorns or other black peppercorns, coarsely ground
5   to 6 sprigs rosemary, thyme, or dill
5   cups watercress, cleaned and trimmed
1   cup sunflower sprouts
3   Tbsp. Pickled Mustard Seeds
2   Tbsp. white wine vinegar
    Flaky sea salt
    Lemon wedges

1. Cut two sheets of heavy-duty aluminum foil 12 inches longer than salmon and place on a rimless baking sheet. Place salmon, skin side down, on the foil. Drizzle with oil; sprinkle with 1½ tsp. kosher salt and ground peppercorns. Use clean fingers to spread oil and seasonings evenly over fish. Top with herbs. Set salmon aside to marinate at room temperature while preparing grill.

2. Prepare grill for smoking (see "Smoking on Your Grill." page 154).
3. Carefully slide salmon and foil onto grill. Close grill; position vents open for smoking. Smoke 25 to 30 minutes or just until salmon is firm and flakes easily. Rotate salmon as needed to ensure even doneness. Carefully slide the foil and salmon onto baking sheet; let rest 10 minutes.
4. Meanwhile, in a bowl combine watercress and sunflower sprouts. Toss with Pickled Mustard Seeds, vinegar, and 3 Tbsp. olive oil. Sprinkle with ½ tsp. kosher salt and ¼ tsp. ground peppercorns.
5. Sprinkle salmon with flaky sea salt. Serve with watercress salad and lemon wedges. Refrigerate leftover salmon in an airtight container up to 4 days. Makes 6 to 8 servings.
Pickled Mustard Seeds Rinse ¾ cup yellow mustard seeds in a fine-mesh sieve; place in an 8-oz. glass jar or heatproof bowl. In a small heavy saucepan combine 1 cup distilled white vinegar, ⅓ cup sugar, 1 dried arbol chile, and ½ tsp. kosher salt. Bring mixture to boiling over medium, stirring to dissolve sugar. Pour the hot liquid over mustard seeds; let stand at room temperature 3 to 4 hours or until softened. Refrigerate in an airtight container up to 1 month.
PER SERVING *520 cal, 28 g fat, 157 mg chol, 618 mg sodium, 5 g carb, 2 g fiber, 1 g sugars, 60 g pro.*

CHUNKS OR CHIPS?

Length of cooking and grill type (gas versus charcoal) determine the best wood for the job. Never use pressure-treated lumber or soft woods.

CHUNKS Hardwood chunks (pieces about the size of a tennis ball) give off more smoke and burn slowly. They work best for recipes that smoke longer than 30 minutes.

CHIPS Small, light wood chips burn more quickly than chunks. Soak in water at least 30 minutes before using so they smolder instead of ignite. Use chips for recipes with short smoke times.

THE BIGGEST MISTAKE WHEN SMOKING FOODS? USING TOO MUCH WOOD. DON'T LET SMOKE OVERPOWER THE FLAVOR OF YOUR FOOD.

SMOKING ON YOUR GRILL

FOR A CHARCOAL GRILL Bank briquettes on one side of grill grate and ignite them. When coals are ashy and glowing, place a foil drip pan (about the same size as the food to be smoked) filled with ½ to 1 inch warm water opposite coals. Then place a couple of wood chunks on the coals or scatter soaked chips onto coals. When there's a steady stream of smoke, place food on cooking rack over drip pan (cool zone).

FOR A GAS GRILL Place soaked chips in a smoker box or pouch (below) on the burners under the cooking rack. Replace cooking rack and ignite burners only on the side with the smoker box. Leave remaining burners off to create a cool cooking zone. Adjust heat per recipe. Skip using a drip pan with water for short smoking times on a gas grill. For longer smoking times, place a pan of warm water on the cooking rack over direct heat. When there's a steady stream of smoke, place food on cool end of grill.

SMOKER POUCH

If you don't have a smoker box, wrap about 2 cups soaked wood chips in a double thickness of heavy-duty aluminum foil. Fold edges to seal, then cut slits for smoke to escape.

TWO SMOKED BIRDS

Two birds are better than one. Smoke two chickens; serve one for dinner and save the other to elevate chicken salad, tacos, or flautas another night.

HANDS-ON TIME 30 min.
TOTAL TIME 2 hr.

2	4- to 4½-lb. whole chickens
	Extra virgin olive oil
	Salt and black pepper
1	small onion, quartered
1	lemon, quartered
4	sprigs thyme
4	fresh bay leaves
2	sprigs rosemary

1. Drizzle chickens with oil to lightly coat. Season cavity and exterior with salt and black pepper. Place two onion quarters, two lemon quarters, two thyme sprigs, two bay leaves, and one rosemary sprig inside each cavity.
2. Position chickens on a work surface, breast side up with legs toward you.

Tuck wings under the back; tie legs together. Let stand at room temperature 30 minutes or up to 1 hour.
3. Meanwhile, prepare grill for smoking. (See "Smoking on Your Grill," left.)
4. Place chickens, breast sides up, over drip pan. Close grill vent for smoking. Smoke 35 minutes, maintaining temperature between 325°F and 350°F. (Fill and light charcoal chimney to have additional hot coals ready if needed.) Using tongs and gloved hands or a large spatula, carefully rotate the chickens on the grill from back to front. Smoke 35 to 40 minutes more or until a thermometer inserted into the thickest part of the chicken registers 165°F.
5. Transfer chickens to a cutting board. Let rest 15 minutes or up to 30 minutes. Refrigerate leftovers in an airtight container up to 5 days. Makes 8 servings.
PER SERVING *161 cal, 8 g fat, 63 mg chol, 250 mg sodium, 21 g pro.*

FAST & FRESH

Easy, delicious recipes for a better dinner tonight.

CREAMY PASTA WITH ASPARAGUS AND SMOKED FISH

This five-ingredient pasta gets intense flavor from smoked fish. Another night, toss the fish into a salad with shaved fennel, cucumber, and dill; or top avocado toast with fish, sliced radishes, and chopped green onions.

HANDS-ON TIME 15 min.
TOTAL TIME 30 min.

12 oz. pasta, such as bucatini, penne, or farfalle
1 cup heavy cream
8 oz. asparagus, trimmed and cut into 2-inch pieces
½ tsp. salt
¼ tsp. black pepper
4 to 6 oz. smoked fish, such as trout or salmon, skin removed and flaked into pieces
2 lemons, zested and juiced

1. Cook pasta according to package directions. Drain pasta, reserving ¼ cup cooking liquid.
2. Add cream to pasta pot. Bring to boiling. Add asparagus, salt, and pepper. Reduce heat to medium. Simmer, uncovered, 3 minutes or until asparagus is bright green. Add pasta and fish. Heat through. Stir in lemon zest and juice. Slowly add cooking liquid until sauce reaches desired consistency. Season with additional salt and pepper. Makes 6 servings.
PER SERVING *374 cal, 17 g fat, 57 mg chol, 248 mg sodium, 46 g carb, 3 g fiber, 4 g sugars, 13 g pro.*

TURMERIC AND CHILE HASH BROWNS

A staple in curries, turmeric has a warm, slightly peppery flavor. Also try adding the golden spice to vegetables before roasting, rice dishes, and soups and stews.

HANDS-ON TIME 15 min.
TOTAL TIME 45 min.

1½   lb. russet potatoes, peeled and cut into ½-inch pieces (4½ cups)
2   Tbsp. vegetable oil
1   tsp. mustard seeds (optional)
½   tsp. ground turmeric
1   cup chopped yellow onion
1   Tbsp. grated fresh ginger
½   tsp salt
3   fresh serrano chiles, stemmed, seeded, and chopped (tip, page 127)
4   eggs
       Plain Greek yogurt
½   bunch fresh cilantro

1. Bring a pot of salted water to boiling. Add potatoes; reduce heat. Simmer 5 minutes or just until tender but still firm when pierced with a fork. Drain.
2. In a large skillet heat oil over medium heat. Add mustard seeds (if using) and turmeric; cook 10 seconds. Add onion, ginger, and ½ tsp. salt. Cook and stir 5 minutes or until onion is beginning to soften and spices are fragrant. Add potatoes, spreading in an even layer. Reduce heat to medium-low. Cook 15 minutes or until potatoes are browned on bottom. Stir in half the chiles while turning potatoes. Cook without stirring, 10 minutes more or until potatoes are browned on bottom.
3. Meanwhile, cook eggs to your liking, such as fried, poached, or soft-boiled.
4. Divide hash browns among four plates; top each with an egg, yogurt, cilantro, and remaining chiles. Makes 4 servings.
PER SERVING *290 cal, 12 g fat, 187 mg chol, 521 mg sodium, 35 g carb, 3 g fiber, 5 g sugars, 11 g pro.*

GRILLED MOROCCAN BEEF KABOBS WITH YOGURT SAUCE

Wrap kabobs in lavash (thin unleavened Middle Eastern bread) flatbreads, or flour tortillas. Or serve them over hot cooked couscous.

HANDS-ON TIME 20 min.
TOTAL TIME 1 hr.

6   Tbsp. chopped flat-leaf parsley
4   cloves garlic, minced
2   lemons, zested and juiced
¼   cup olive oil
2   tsp. ground coriander
1   tsp. paprika
¾   tsp. salt
¾   tsp. black pepper
1   lb. boneless beef sirloin steak, cut into thin strips
1   pint grape tomatoes
1   cup plain Greek yogurt
    Lavash (optional)

1. For marinade: In a medium bowl combine 4 Tbsp. parsley, the garlic, 1½ tsp. lemon zest, ¼ cup lemon juice, the oil, coriander, paprika, and ½ tsp. each salt and pepper. Add beef; toss to coat. Chill, covered, 30 minutes.
2. Drain meat, reserving marinade. Thread meat accordion-style onto eight 10-inch skewers. Thread tomatoes onto four 10-inch skewers. Grill meat kabobs, covered, over medium heat 6 to 8 minutes or until desired doneness, turning occasionally. Add tomato kabobs the last 2 to 3 minutes, grilling until lightly charred, turning once. Place reserved marinade in a small saucepan; heat to boiling over medium.
3. For yogurt sauce: In a small bowl stir together yogurt, remaining parsley, ½ tsp. lemon zest, 2 Tbsp. lemon juice, and ¼ tsp. each salt and pepper. Serve kabobs with yogurt sauce and, if desired, over lavash. Drizzle with hot marinade. Top with additional parsley. Makes 4 servings.
PER SERVING *355 cal, 21 g fat, 81 mg chol, 297 mg sodium, 11 g carb, 2 g fiber, 6 g sugars, 32 g pro.*

CONDIMENT
GRANDSTAND
Recipes on pages 162–163

FOURTH OF JULY BLOWOUT

Make most of the recipes for this patriotic party well ahead. Then spark big-time fun with a hot dog bar, refreshing berry lemonade, and easy (handheld) desserts.

CHERRY-BERRY LEMONADE

HANDS-ON TIME 20 min.
TOTAL TIME 4 hr. 20 min., includes freezing

2   cups stemmed, pitted fresh dark sweet cherries
1   cup fresh raspberries, plus more for garnish if desired
3   cups cold water
1   cup freshly squeezed lemon juice (5 to 6 lemons)
¾   cup sugar
    Sparkling water, chilled (optional)
8   lemon slices

1. Place cherries, raspberries, and 2 Tbsp. water in a blender or food processor. Cover and puree.
2. One at a time, hold a half-pint canning jar at an angle; spoon about 3 Tbsp. berry puree into jar. Place jars at angle into 2½-inch muffin cups. Freeze 3 to 4 hours or until firm.
3. Meanwhile, in a 1½-qt. pitcher stir together the 3 cups cold water, lemon juice, and sugar until sugar is dissolved. Cover and chill. Pour over frozen puree in glasses and, if desired, top with sparkling water. Garnish glasses with lemon slices and, if desired, raspberries on wooden skewers. Makes 8 servings.
Tip Or skip the canning jars and use star-shape ice cube trays to freeze berry puree. Prepare lemonade as directed and drop frozen puree cubes into glasses.
PER SERVING 96 cal, 4 mg sodium, 25 g carb, 1 g fiber, 22 g sugars.

FROZEN FRUIT PUREE CHILLS, FLAVORS, AND NATURALLY SWEETENS HOMEMADE LEMONADE.

ROASTED POTATO
SALAD

MARINATED
VEGGIE-ORZO
SALAD

ROASTED POTATO SALAD

Oil-and-lemon juice dressing is a good safe option for salads that sit out in summer heat.

HANDS-ON TIME 10 min.
TOTAL TIME 1 hr. 40 min.

2   lb. tiny new red potatoes, halved or quartered
6   cloves garlic, halved
¼   cup plus 2 Tbsp. olive oil
1¼ tsp. salt
¾   tsp. black pepper
2½ cups chopped celery
3   Tbsp. lemon juice
1   Tbsp. Dijon mustard
    Paprika
    Celery leaves (optional)

1. Preheat oven to 425°F. In a shallow roasting pan toss together potatoes, garlic, ¼ cup of the oil, 1 tsp. salt, and ½ tsp. pepper. Roast, uncovered, 30 minutes or until very tender and browned, stirring twice. Remove; let cool. Place in a large bowl.
2. Add celery to potatoes. In a small bowl whisk together lemon juice, remaining oil, the mustard, ¼ tsp. salt, and ¼ tsp. pepper. Add to potato salad; toss to coat. Sprinkle with paprika and, if desired, celery leaves. Makes 6 servings.
PER SERVING *239 cal, 14 g fat, 579 mg sodium, 27 g carb, 3 g fiber, 3 g sugars, 3 g pro.*

MARINATED VEGGIE-ORZO SALAD

To prevent cooked orzo from soaking up dressing and becoming soggy, stir in 2 tablespoons olive oil after draining and rinsing. Make this veggie-filled salad up to 24 hours before party time.

HANDS-ON TIME 15 min.
TOTAL TIME 15 min.

1   cup dried orzo pasta
½   cup olive oil
2   lemons
¾   tsp. salt
¼   tsp. black pepper
½   cup chopped fresh herbs, such as dill, basil, mint, and/or chives
1   medium cucumber, coarsely chopped
8   oz. fresh asparagus, trimmed and cut into 1-inch pieces
1½   cups small cauliflower florets
1   cup radishes, quartered
½   cup chopped red onion
     Crumbled feta cheese

1. Cook pasta according to package directions. Drain and rinse with cold water; drain again. Place in a large bowl. Toss with 2 Tbsp. oil. Chill, covered, up to 24 hours.
2. Meanwhile, remove zest from one lemon. Juice both lemons. In a large bowl whisk together lemon zest and juice, remaining oil, salt, pepper, and about half the herbs. (Wrap and chill remaining herbs for serving.) Add cucumber; mash lightly with a potato masher to release juices. Add asparagus, cauliflower, radishes, and onion. Toss to coat. Chill, covered, up to 24 hours.
3. Add pasta to vegetables; toss to coat. Top with feta and remaining herbs. Makes 8 servings.
PER SERVING *229 cal, 15 g fat, 273 mg sodium, 20 g carb, 2 g fiber, 3 g sugars, 5 g pro.*

POTATO CHIPS DUNKED IN GARLICKY DIP HAVE MET THEIR MATCH. THIS SALAD OF ROASTED POTATOES AND GARLIC IS CRISP AND FRESH.

CONDIMENT GRANDSTAND: MAKE A FEW—OR MAKE THEM ALL!

CHIPOTLE KETCHUP

TOTAL TIME 5 min.

1 cup ketchup
2 tsp. finely chopped chipotle chile peppers in adobo sauce

In a small bowl stir together ketchup and chipotle chile peppers in adobo sauce. Makes 16 servings.
PER 1-TBSP. SERVING *41 cal, 371 mg sodium, 11 g carb, 9 g sugars.*

CUBAN MUSTARD

TOTAL TIME 15 min.

1 tsp. cumin seeds, crushed
½ cup yellow mustard
¼ cup chopped dill or sweet pickles
1 Tbsp. pickle brine
¼ cup finely chopped cooked ham

1. Heat a small skillet over medium heat. Add cumin seeds; cook 2 minutes or until toasted and aromatic. Remove; cool.
2. In a small bowl stir together mustard, pickles, pickle brine, ham, and toasted cumin seeds. Refrigerate in an airtight container up to 2 weeks. Makes 16 servings.
PER 1-TBSP. SERVING *7 cal, 1 mg chol, 139 mg sodium, 1 g carb, 1 g pro.*

OLIVE TAPENADE

TOTAL TIME 20 min.

¾ cup pitted green olives
¾ cup pitted Kalamata olives
¼ cup pitted oil-cured black olives
3 Tbsp. olive oil
1 Tbsp. drained capers
1 Tbsp. balsamic vinegar
1½ tsp. Dijon mustard
1 anchovy fillet (optional)
1 clove minced garlic
1½ tsp. snipped fresh herbs, such as flat-leaf parsley, thyme, oregano, and/or rosemary

In a food processor or blender combine olives, oil, capers, vinegar, mustard, anchovy (if using), and garlic. Pulse until finely chopped. Stir in herbs. Refrigerate in an airtight container up to 1 week or freeze up to 3 months. Makes 24 servings.
PER 1-TBSP. SERVING *29 cal, 3 g fat, 146 mg sodium, 1 g carb.*

CHARRED JALAPEÑO-LIME AÏOLI

HANDS-ON TIME 20 min.
TOTAL TIME 1 hr 20 min.

1 bulb garlic
1 Tbsp. olive oil
4 jalapeños (tip, page 127)
1 cup mayonnaise
1 tsp. lime zest
1 Tbsp. lime juice
   Salt and black pepper

1. Cut ½ inch from top of garlic. Remove loose papery outer layers. Place cut side up on a 6-inch sheet of heavy-duty foil. Drizzle with 1½ tsp. oil. Bring up sides to enclose garlic. Brush jalapeños with remaining 1½ tsp. oil.
2. Place foil packet on grill rack. Grill, covered, directly over medium heat 10 minutes. Add peppers to grill. Grill 15 to 20 minutes more or until garlic is softened and peppers are charred, turning peppers once. Remove. Wrap peppers in foil. Let peppers and garlic cool completely. Peel blistered skin from peppers; if desired, remove stems and seeds. Chop jalapeños. Squeeze garlic cloves from papers; mash with a fork.
3. In a small bowl stir together mayonnaise, lime zest and juice, the garlic, and jalapeños. Season with salt and pepper. Refrigerate in an airtight container up to 24 hours. Makes 12 servings.
PER 2-TBSP. SERVING *141 cal, 15 g fat, 8 mg chol, 166 mg sodium, 2 g carb.*

CARAMELIZED ONIONS

TOTAL TIME 25 min.

1 Tbsp. olive oil
1 large sweet onion, such as Vidalia or Walla Walla, halved lengthwise and thinly sliced
¼ tsp. kosher salt
¼ tsp. freshly ground black pepper

In a large skillet heat oil over medium-low heat. Add onion, salt, and pepper. Cook, covered, 13 to 15 minutes or until onion slices are tender, stirring occasionally. Uncover; cook and stir over medium-high heat 3 to 5 minutes more or until golden. Makes 4 servings.
PER ⅓-CUP SERVING *39 cal, 1 g fat, 63 mg sodium, 7 g carb, 1 g fiber, 4 g sugars.*

BERRY-RED CABBAGE SLAW

TOTAL TIME 25 min.

⅓ cup white balsamic vinegar
2 Tbsp. olive oil
1 Tbsp. honey
½ tsp. salt
¼ tsp. black pepper
4 cups shredded red cabbage
1½ cups julienned strips jicama
1½ cups fresh blueberries
½ cup chopped red onion

In a large bowl whisk together vinegar, oil, honey, salt, and pepper. Add cabbage, jicama, blueberries, and onion; toss to coat. Refrigerate in an airtight container up to 24 hours. Makes 20 servings.
PER ¼-CUP SERVING *39 cal, 1 g fat, 63 mg sodium, 7 g carb, 1 g fiber, 4 g sugars.*

QUICK KIMCHI

TOTAL TIME 20 min.

½ 16-oz. pkg. shredded cabbage and carrot (coleslaw mix)
2 tsp. salt
1 cup coarsely shredded radishes
3 sliced green onions
2 Tbsp. rice vinegar
1 Tbsp. Gochujang
1 tsp. sugar
1 tsp. fish sauce
½ tsp. grated fresh ginger
1 clove garlic, minced

In a large bowl toss coleslaw mix with salt; let stand 10 minutes. Place in a colander; rinse with cold water, pressing out excess water. Return to bowl. Add radishes, green onions, vinegar, Gochujang, sugar, fish sauce, ginger, and garlic. Toss to coat. Refrigerate in an airtight container up to 3 days. Makes 10 servings.
PER ¼-CUP SERVING 15 cal, 97 mg sodium, 4 g carb, 1 g sugars, 1 g pro.

ELOTE CORN TOPPER

TOTAL TIME 15 min.

1 Tbsp. olive oil
2 cups fresh corn kernels (4 ears corn, husked, kernels cut off)
1 tsp. chili powder
2 Tbsp. lime juice
¼ cup crumbled Cotija cheese
2 Tbsp. chopped fresh cilantro

In a large skillet heat oil over medium-high heat. Add corn; cook 6 minutes or until corn starts to char, stirring occasionally. Stir in chili powder. Cook and stir 1 minute. Remove from heat. Stir in lime juice, scraping up any browned bits. Transfer to a serving bowl or container; cool slightly. Stir in cheese and cilantro. Refrigerate in an airtight container up to 3 days. Makes 8 servings.
PER ¼-CUP SERVING 158 cal, 14 g fat, 10 mg chol, 155 mg sodium, 8 g carb, 1 g fiber, 3 g sugars, 2 g pro.

BACON-SHISHITO RELISH

TOTAL TIME 20 min.

3 slices bacon
½ cup finely chopped red onion
6 oz. shishito peppers, stemmed and chopped (tip, page 127)
2 Tbsp. red wine vinegar
1 cup cherry tomatoes, quartered
2 Tbsp. chopped fresh Italian parsley
   Salt and black pepper

1. In a large skillet cook bacon until crisp. Transfer to paper towels to drain, reserving drippings in skillet. Crumble bacon when cool enough to handle.
2. Add onion to skillet. Cook over medium heat 4 minutes or until tender, stirring occasionally. Add shishito peppers. Cook 4 minutes or until browned, stirring occasionally. Stir in vinegar, scraping up any browned bits. Cook, uncovered, 30 seconds. Remove from heat. Stir in bacon, tomatoes, and parsley. Season with salt and pepper. Refrigerate in an airtight container up to 3 days. Makes 10 servings.
PER ¼-CUP SERVING 45 cal, 2 g fat, 6 mg chol, 128 mg sodium, 3 g carb, 1 g fiber, 2 g sugars, 2 g pro.

CREOLE COARSE-GROUND MUSTARD

HANDS-ON TIME 15 min.
TOTAL TIME 48 hr. 15 min., includes chilling

⅓ cup white wine vinegar
3 Tbsp. yellow mustard seeds
3 Tbsp. brown mustard seeds
¼ tsp. salt
¼ tsp. ground ginger
   Dash ground allspice
⅛ tsp. cayenne pepper
1½ tsp. honey
1 clove garlic, minced
1 to 2 tsp. prepared horseradish

1. In a medium bowl combine vinegar, mustard seeds, salt, ginger, allspice, and cayenne pepper. Cover; let stand 24 hours. (Seeds will absorb liquid.)

2. Transfer mustard seed mixture to a blender or food processor; add honey, garlic, and horseradish. Cover and blend or process 1 to 2 minutes or until desired texture and consistency (mustard will not be completely smooth). For best flavor, refrigerate in an airtight container 1 to 2 days before serving. Refrigerate up to 3 months. Makes 12 servings.
PER 1-TBSP. SERVING 25 cal, 1 g fat, 53 mg sodium, 2 g carb, 1 g sugars, 1 g pro.

QUICK PICKLED VEGGIES

HANDS-ON TIME 1 hr.
TOTAL TIME 9 hr. 30 min., includes chilling

½ lb. carrots, trimmed and thinly sliced
½ lb. radishes, trimmed and thinly sliced
1 small shallot, thinly sliced
2 Tbsp. chopped fresh cilantro
1 jalapeño, stemmed and sliced (tip, page 127)
4 tsp. whole black peppercorns
2 tsp. mustard seeds
2 tsp. cumin seeds
½ tsp. crushed red pepper (optional)
1 cup cider vinegar
2 tsp. sugar
2 tsp. salt

1. Place carrots, radishes, shallot, cilantro, and jalapeño in four clean pint canning jars. To each jar add 1 tsp. peppercorns, ½ tsp. each mustard seeds and cumin seeds, and ⅛ tsp. crushed red pepper (if using).
2. In a small nonreactive heavy saucepan combine 1¼ cups water, vinegar, sugar, and salt. Bring to boiling over medium-high heat, stirring to dissolve sugar and salt. Pour hot liquid over vegetables to cover. Cool 30 minutes. Chill 8 hours before serving. Store in the refrigerator up to 1 month. Makes 32 servings.
PER ¼-CUP SERVING 10 cal, 88 mg sodium, 2 g carb, 1 g fiber, 1 g sugars.

from top left: **CHIPOTLE KETCHUP, CUBAN MUSTARD, OLIVE TAPENADE, CHARRED JALAPEÑO-LIME AÏOLI, CARAMELIZED ONIONS, BERRY-RED CABBAGE SLAW, QUICK KIMCHI, ELOTE CORN TOPPER, BACON-SHISHITO RELISH, CREOLE COARSE-GROUND MUSTARD, QUICK PICKLED VEGGIES** *Recipes on pages 162–163*

FRUITY LAYER POPS
Recipes on page 166

FOLD FRESH BERRIES INTO LEMON CAKE MIX FOR FLAVOR BURSTS. TOP CUPCAKES WITH BUTTERCREAM AND A CITRUS TWIST.

FRUITY LAYER POPS

Berries, lemon gelatin, and vanilla yogurt flavor striped pops are reminiscent of ice cream truck treats.

HANDS-ON TIME 30 min.
TOTAL TIME 11 hr. 30 min., includes freezing

3   Tbsp. lemon-flavor gelatin
3   tsp. sugar
1   cup fresh raspberries
⅓   cup vanilla low-fat yogurt
1   cup fresh blueberries

1. In a medium bowl combine ⅓ cup boiling water, 1 Tbsp. of the gelatin, and 1 tsp. of the sugar, stirring until sugar is dissolved. In a blender combine gelatin mixture and raspberries. Blend until smooth. Strain raspberry mixture through a fine-mesh sieve; discard seeds. Divide raspberry puree among eight to ten 3-oz. ice-pop molds. Freeze 2 hours or until firm.
2. In a medium bowl combine ⅓ cup boiling water, 1 Tbsp. gelatin, and 1 tsp. sugar, stirring until sugar is dissolved. Whisk in yogurt until combined. Cool slightly. Spoon yogurt mixture over raspberry layer in molds. Freeze 1 to 2 hours or until firm.
3. In a small saucepan combine blueberries and ⅓ cup water. Bring to simmering over medium-high heat, stirring and slightly mashing berries to release juices. Simmer, uncovered, 2 minutes. In a blender combine blueberry mixture, remaining 1 Tbsp. gelatin, and remaining 1 tsp. sugar. Blend until smooth. Strain through a fine-mesh sieve; discard pulp. Let cool slightly. Spoon blueberry puree over yogurt layer in molds; insert pop sticks. Freeze pops overnight. Makes 8 to 10 pops.
PER POP *53 cal, 33 mg sodium, 12 g carb, 1 g fiber, 10 g sugars, 1 g pro.*

BERRY-LEMON CUPCAKES

HANDS-ON TIME 15 min.
TOTAL TIME 1 hr.

1   pkg. lemon-flavor cake mix (2-layer size)
1½   cups chopped fresh strawberries, fresh blueberries, or fresh raspberries
1   Tbsp. all-purpose flour
    Buttercream Frosting
    Lemon zest strips

1. Preheat oven to 350°F. Line twenty-four 2½-inch muffin cups with paper bake cups. Prepare cake mix according to package directions. Divide batter among prepared cups. In a small bowl toss berries with flour; sprinkle over batter.
2. Bake 20 minutes or until tops are light brown and spring back when lightly touched. Cool in muffin cups on a wire rack 5 minutes. Remove and cool completely on rack. Spread or pipe Buttercream Frosting onto cupcakes. Top with zest and, if desired, additional berries. Makes 24 cupcakes.
Buttercream Frosting In an extra-large bowl beat 1 cup softened butter with a mixer on medium 1 to 2 minutes or until creamy. Beat in 1 cup powdered sugar. Add 2 Tbsp. heavy cream, 1 tsp. vanilla, ¼ tsp. almond extract (if desired), and a dash salt; beat on low until combined. Gradually beat in 3 cups powdered sugar just until combined. Beat on medium 5 minutes or until fluffy, scraping bowl as needed. Add additional 1 Tbsp. heavy cream; beat on high 1 minute more.
PER CUPCAKE *243 cal, 10 g fat, 208 mg sodium, 38 g carb, 29 g sugars, 1 g pro.*

BLUEBERRY
BUNDT CAKE
Recipe on page 181

august

From stone fruit to shell beans—the bounty of summer—here are seasonal recipes for potlucks and summertime meals. Gather neighbors for an old-fashioned social with sweet treats.

171

184

189

LAVENDER

TRIPLE BERRY

SALTED MOCHA

CARAMEL

COCONUT

STRAWBERRY

BIRTHDAY CAKE

CHOCOLATE

MANGO

THYME

COFFEE

CHERRY

gatherings
SUNDAE SOCIAL

Host an ice cream social with an array of homemade flavors. This no-churn ice cream base requires only three ingredients and presents a multitude of options for flavoring.

NO-CHURN ICE CREAM

HANDS-ON TIME 10 min.
TOTAL TIME 8 hr. 20 min., includes freezing

1   14-oz. can sweetened condensed milk
    Flavoring (right)
2   cups heavy cream
2   tsp. vanilla
    Easy Fudge Sauce (recipe, right),
    Salted Bourbon Caramel Sauce
    and/or Roasted Strawberry Sauce
    (recipes, page 172) (optional)

1. Pour sweetened condensed milk into an extra-large bowl; follow directions for adding flavoring.
2. In a large bowl beat cream and vanilla until soft peaks form (tips curl); fold into condensed milk.
2. Spread into a 9×5-inch loaf pan or two one-pint freezer containers. Freeze, covered, 8 hours or until firm. If desired serve with Easy Fudge Sauce, Salted Bourbon Caramel Sauce, and/or Roasted Strawberry Sauce. Makes 8 servings.
PER SERVING *366 cal, 26 g fat, 85 mg chol, 79 mg sodium, 29 g carb, 29 g sugars, 6 g pro.*

Lavender Heat condensed milk and 3 Tbsp. dried lavender buds over low heat until bubbles begin to form along edge. Let stand, covered, 20 minutes. Strain out lavender. Cool before proceeding.
Triple Berry Stir in 3 cups pureed blackberries, blueberries, and raspberries.
Salted Mocha Whisk in ⅓ cup cocoa powder, 2 Tbsp. instant espresso coffee powder, and ½ tsp. kosher salt.
Caramel Whisk in ¼ cup caramel sauce.
Strawberry Stir in 3 cups pureed strawberries.
Coconut Whisk in ¼ cup melted coconut oil.
Birthday Cake Stir in ¼ cup sprinkles.
Chocolate Whisk in ⅓ cup cocoa powder.
Mango Stir in 3 cups pureed mango.
Thyme Heat condensed milk and 12 thyme sprigs over low heat until bubbles begin to form along edge. Let stand, covered, 10 minutes. Strain out thyme. Cool before proceeding.
Coffee Whisk in 2 Tbsp. instant espresso coffee powder.
Cherry Stir in 3 cups pureed tart pitted cherries.

EASY FUDGE SAUCE

Photo on page 173.
TOTAL TIME 10 min.

1   cup packed brown sugar
½   cup cocoa powder
½   cup butter
½   cup milk
2   tsp. vanilla

1. In a small bowl stir together brown sugar and cocoa powder.
2. In a small saucepan melt butter with milk. Cook and stir over medium heat 5 to 6 minutes or just until mixture bubbles around sides of pan. Add brown sugar mixture. Cook 1 to 2 minutes or until sugar is dissolved and sauce is smooth and slightly thickened, stirring constantly.
3. Stir in vanilla. Makes about 1½ cups.
Tip Store sauce in an airtight container in the refrigerator up to 1 week. To warm sauce, place in microwave-safe bowl. Heat on high 15 seconds; stir. Repeat until heated through.
PER 2-TBSP. SERVING *153 cal, 8 g fat, 21 mg chol, 72 mg sodium, 21 g carb, 1 g fiber, 19 g sugars, 1 g pro.*

THIS SIMPLE BASE RECIPE IS ENDLESSLY ADAPTABLE. MAKE A VARIETY OF FLAVORS AND SAUCES THEN INVITE FRIENDS TO BRING A FAVORITE BAKED GOODIE TO CRUMBLE ON TOP. LET SUNDAE FUNDAY COMMENCE!

SET THE SPREAD: THE SUNDAE BAR INCLUDES BAKED GOODS (BROWNIE POINTS IF THEY'RE HOMEMADE) FOR LAYERING AND CRUMBLING, SPRINKLES, NUTS, AND FRUIT. AND REMEMBER THE SAUCES.

SALTED BOURBON CARAMEL SAUCE

TOTAL TIME 15 min.

¾ cup packed brown sugar
½ cup heavy cream
½ cup butter
2 Tbsp. light color corn syrup
2 Tbsp. bourbon
1 tsp. vanilla
½ tsp. salt

In a medium-size heavy saucepan combine brown sugar, cream, butter, and corn syrup. Bring to boiling over medium-high heat, stirring to dissolve sugar and melt butter. Reduce heat to medium. Boil, uncovered, at a moderate, steady rate 3 minutes (do not stir). Stir in bourbon, vanilla and salt. Makes about 1¾ cups.
PER 2-TBSP. SERVING *147 cal, 10 g fat, 27 mg chol, 143 mg sodium, 14 g carb, 14 g sugars.*

ROASTED STRAWBERRY SAUCE

HANDS-ON TIME 10 min.
TOTAL TIME 30 min.

1 lb. fresh strawberries, sliced
½ cup honey
1 tsp. orange zest

1. Preheat oven to 450°F. On a foil-lined 15×10-inch baking pan toss together strawberries, honey, and orange zest. Bake 20 minutes or until cooking liquid thickens and starts to brown around edges, stirring once halfway through baking.
2. Cool slightly. Chill, covered, up to 1 week or freeze up to 1 month. Makes about 1 cup.
PER 2-TBSP. SERVING *22 cal, 6 g carb, 5 g sugars.*

MILK CHOCOLATE WAFERS

HANDS-ON TIME 45 min.
TOTAL TIME 1 hr 25 min., includes freezing

6 oz. milk chocolate, coarsely chopped
¾ cup all-purpose flour
¾ tsp. baking powder
⅛ tsp. salt
3 Tbsp. butter, softened
½ cup granulated sugar
1 egg
¾ tsp. vanilla
 Milk Chocolate-Sour Cream Frosting (optional)

1. In a small saucepan cook and stir chocolate over low heat until melted.
2. In a medium bowl stir together flour, baking powder, and salt. In a medium bowl beat butter with a mixer on medium to high 30 seconds. Beat in sugar until light and fluffy. Beat in egg, vanilla, and melted chocolate until combined. Beat in flour mixture until combined.
3. Divide dough into four portions; wrap in plastic wrap. Freeze dough 20 minutes or chill 1 hour or until easy to handle.
4. Preheat oven to 350°F. Place one dough portion on waxed paper; use paper to shape into a 10-inch log. If dough becomes too sticky, return to freezer for a few minutes. Cut each log into ¼-inch slices. Place 1 inch apart on an ungreased cookie sheet.

5. Bake 9 to 10 minutes or until edges are set. Cool on cookie sheet 2 minutes. Carefully transfer to a wire rack (cookies will be brittle); cool completely. Makes 144 cookies,
6. If desired, spread ½ tsp. Milk Chocolate-Sour Cream Frosting on half the cookie bottoms; top with remaining cookies, bottom sides down. Serve sandwich cookies the same day. Makes 72 cookie sandwiches.
Store Layer single cookies between sheets of waxed paper in an airtight container. Store, covered, at room temperature up to 3 days or freeze up to 3 months. To serve, thaw cookies if frozen. If desired, make sandwich cookies as directed in Step 6.
PER COOKIE *14 cal, 1 g fat, 2 mg chol, 8 mg sodium, 2 g carb, 1 g sugars.*
Milk Chocolate-Sour Cream Frosting In a medium saucepan melt 3 oz. chopped milk chocolate and 2 Tbsp. butter over low heat, stirring frequently. Cool 5 minutes. Stir in ¼ cup sour cream. Gradually add 1 to 1¼ cups powdered sugar, stirring until frosting is spreadable.

MISSOURI GOOEY BUTTER CAKE
Recipe on page 174

SALTED BOURBON CARAMEL SAUCE

EASY FUDGE SAUCE
Recipe on page 171

DEEP DARK CHOCOLATE BROWNIES
Recipe on page 174

MILK CHOCOLATE WAFERS

ROASTED STRAWBERRY SAUCE

SALTED BUTTERY SHORTBREAD COOKIES
Recipe on page 174

MISSOURI GOOEY BUTTER CAKE

Photo on page 173.

HANDS-ON TIME 20 min.
TOTAL TIME 2 hr. 45 min., includes cooling

2 cups all-purpose flour
1¼ cups plus 3 Tbsp. granulated sugar
⅓ cup butter
¾ cup butter, softened
1 egg
1 5-oz. can evaporated milk
¼ cup light-color corn syrup
1 tsp. vanilla
    Powdered sugar (optional)

1. Preheat oven to 350°F. Line a 9×9-inch baking pan with foil; grease foil. For crust, in a medium bowl combine 1 cup flour and 3 Tbsp. granulated sugar. Using a pastry blender, cut in ⅓ cup butter until mixture resembles fine crumbs and starts to cling. Pat crust into prepared pan.
2. For filling, in a large bowl beat 1¼ cups granulated sugar and ¾ cup softened butter with a mixer on medium until combined. Beat in egg just until combined. Alternately add 1 cup flour and evaporated milk to sugar-butter mixture, beating on low after each addition just until combined. Beat in corn syrup and vanilla until combined. Spoon over crust; spread batter to edges of pan.
3. Bake 25 to 30 minutes or until cake is puffed, lightly golden, and nearly set. Cool in pan on a wire rack. Use foil to lift uncut bars from pan. Remove foil. Cut into bars. If desired, sprinkle with powdered sugar before serving. Makes 16 servings.
PER SERVING *270 cal, 14 g fat, 47 mg chol, 116 mg sodium, 35 g carb, 23 g sugars, 3 g pro.*

DEEP DARK CHOCOLATE BROWNIES

Photo on page 173.

HANDS-ON TIME 45 min.
TOTAL TIME 2 hr. 30 min., includes cooling

1¼ cups all-purpose flour
2 Tbsp. dark or regular unsweetened cocoa powder
1 tsp. kosher salt
11 oz. quality dark chocolate (60-72% cacao), coarsely chopped
1 cup unsalted butter, cut into 1-inch pieces
1 tsp. instant espresso coffee powder
1½ cups granulated sugar
½ cup packed light brown sugar
5 eggs, room temperature
2 tsp. vanilla
    Ganache Frosting (optional)

1. Preheat oven to 350°F. Butter sides and bottom of a 13×9-inch baking pan. In a medium bowl whisk together flour, cocoa powder, and salt.
2. Place chocolate, butter, and coffee powder in a large heat-proof bowl; set bowl over a pan of barely simmering water (bottom of pan should not touch water). Heat, stirring occasionally, until chocolate and butter are completely melted and combined. Remove from heat; keep bowl over water. Add sugars; whisk until thoroughly combined. Remove bowl from water. Cool mixture to room temperature.
3. Add three eggs to cooled chocolate mixture; whisk just until combined. Add remaining two eggs and whisk just until combined. Add vanilla; stir until combined. Do not overbeat, which causes cakey brownies.
4. Sprinkle flour mixture over chocolate mixture. Use a spatula to fold batter until just a trace amount of flour is visible.
5. Pour batter into prepared pan. Bake 25 to 30 minutes, rotating pan halfway through baking, or until a toothpick inserted in center comes out with a few moist crumbs. Cool completely on a wire rack. Makes 24 brownies.
PER SERVING *240 cal, 14 g fat, 59 mg chol, 64 mg sodium, 30 g carb, 1 g fiber, 22 g sugars, 3 g pro.*

Ganache Frosting Place 6 oz. quality dark chocolate (60-72% cacao) in a medium-size heatproof bowl. In a small saucepan heat ½ cup heavy cream over medium heat just until bubbles form around edge of pan. Pour hot cream over chopped chocolate; let stand 1 minute. Whisk until smooth. Pour warm ganache over cooled brownies in pan, spread evenly with an offset spatula. Let stand 10 minutes; refrigerate 15 minutes to set completely. Freeze 30 minutes, if necessary, for easier cutting. Cut into bars.

SALTED BUTTERY SHORTBREAD COOKIES

Photo on page 173.

HANDS-ON TIME 30 min.
TOTAL TIME 1 hr. 45 min.

1 cup butter, softened
½ cup packed light brown sugar
1 egg yolk
2¼ cups all-purpose flour
2 Tbsp. cornstarch
½ tsp. salt

1. Preheat oven to 300°F. Line cookie sheets with parchment paper. In a large bowl beat butter and brown sugar 3 minutes or until light and fluffy. Add egg yolk; beat on low until combined.
2. In a medium bowl whisk together flour, cornstarch, and salt. Add half the flour mixture to butter mixture; beat on low until combined. Add remaining flour mixture; beat until dough clings together. Gather dough into a ball.
3. On a lightly floured surface, roll dough to ¼-inch thickness. Cut with 1½-inch round cookie cutter. Place 1 inch apart on prepared cookie sheets. Bake 15 to 18 minutes or until edges and bottoms are lightly browned. Transfer to a wire rack. Cool completely. Makes 60 cookies.
PER COOKIE *53 cal, 3 g fat, 11 mg chol, 44 mg sodium, 6 g carb, 2 g sugars, 1 g pro.*

great starts
SURPRISE INSIDE

Nudge waffles to the savory side by sandwiching seasonal ingredients—think BLT meets caprese salad—between spoonfuls of batter.

STUFFED WAFFLES

TOTAL TIME 35 min.

1¾ cups all-purpose flour
1   Tbsp. sugar
2   tsp. baking powder
½   tsp. salt
2   eggs, lightly beaten
1   cup buttermilk or sour milk*
½   cup milk
½   cup vegetable oil
2   Tbsp. chopped fresh basil or sage
1   cup chopped roma tomatoes
3   oz. white cheddar cheese, shredded (¾ cup)
6   slices bacon, crisp-cooked and chopped
     Black pepper
     Pepper jelly, honey-butter, or sour cream

1. In a large bowl stir together flour, sugar, baking powder, and salt. In a medium bowl combine eggs, buttermilk, milk, and oil. Add egg mixture all at once to flour mixture. Stir just until moistened. (Batter should be slightly lumpy.)

2. Lightly grease and preheat waffle baker. For each batch, spoon batter onto waffle baker according to manufacturer's directions. Sprinkle with basil, tomatoes, cheese, bacon, and pepper. Top with a small amount of batter to cover toppings. Bake until golden. If desired, top with additional basil, tomatoes, and bacon. Serve with pepper jelly, honey butter, or sour cream. Makes twelve 4-inch waffles.

*Tip For sour milk place 1 Tbsp. lemon juice or vinegar in a liquid measuring cup. Add enough milk to equal 1 cup. Stir; let stand 5 minutes before using.

PER WAFFLE *229 cal, 15 g fat, 44 mg chol, 307 mg sodium, 17 g carb, 1 g fiber, 3 g sugars, 7 g pro*

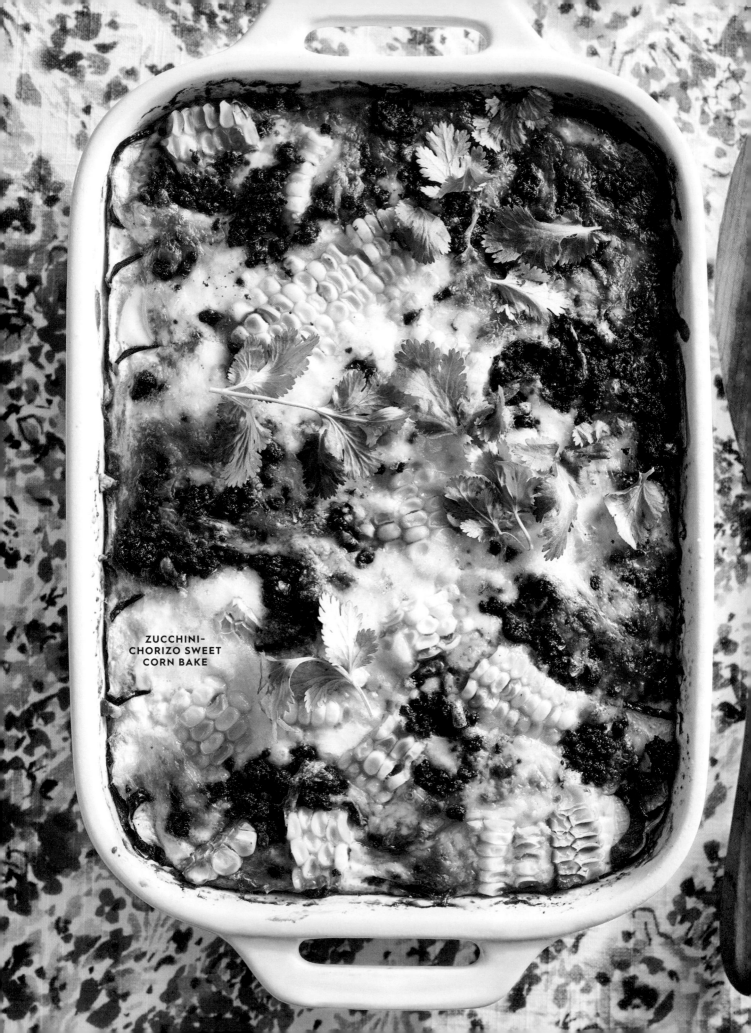

ZUCCHINI-
CHORIZO SWEET
CORN BAKE

food gatherings
BRING YOUR BEST

Looking for something new to take to a potluck? Consider one of these make-and-take recipes shared by bloggers and cookbook authors.

ZUCCHINI-CHORIZO SWEET CORN BAKE

HANDS-ON TIME 30 min.
TOTAL TIME 1 hr. 25 min.

Butter
2   large zucchini, sliced lengthwise into ⅛-inch-thick ribbons (1½ lb.)
½   tsp. kosher salt
12 oz. uncooked ground chorizo
4   eggs
2   egg yolks
1½ cups whole milk
1   tsp. garlic powder
1   tsp. onion powder
½   tsp. black pepper
1½ cups fresh corn off the cob
1½ cups shredded sharp white cheddar cheese (6 oz.)
½   cup grated Parmesan cheese

1. Preheat oven to 350°F. Lightly butter a 2-qt. baking dish. Place zucchini in a colander. Sprinkle with salt. Let stand 20 minutes. Blot dry with paper towels.
2. Meanwhile, heat a 10-inch skillet over medium heat. Add chorizo. Cook and stir 5 to 7 minutes or until cooked through. Drain in a colander. Transfer to paper towels; blot dry.
3. In a large bowl whisk together eggs, yolks, milk, garlic powder, onion powder, and pepper.
4. Evenly spread half the chorizo in prepared dish. Top with half the zucchini, corn, and cheeses. Pour half the egg mixture over top. Repeat layers. Bake, uncovered, 40 minutes or just until set and top is browned. Let stand 10 minutes before serving. Makes 12 servings.
PER SERVING *281 cal, 20 g fat, 138 mg chol, 594 mg sodium, 9 g carb, 1 g fiber, 4 g sugars, 16 g pro.*

SHRIMP IN CITRUS VINAIGRETTE

Photo on page 179.

Culantro is an herb with similar aroma and flavor as cilantro.

HANDS-ON TIME 30 min.
TOTAL TIME 1 hr. 25 min.

4   plum tomatoes, diced
6   Tbsp. fresh lemon, lime, orange, and/or grapefruit juice
¼   cup extra virgin olive oil
2   Tbsp. chopped fresh oregano
2   Tbsp. chopped fresh cilantro
1   Tbsp. chopped fresh culantro
¼   tsp. Dijon mustard
½   tsp. salt
¼   tsp. black pepper
4   Tbsp. kosher salt
8   whole black peppercorns
4   bay leaves
2   lb. shrimp, peeled and deveined
2   avocados, halved, pitted, peeled, and coarsely chopped

1. For vinaigrette: In a large serving bowl combine tomatoes, citrus juice, oil, oregano, cilantro, culantro, and mustard. Season with ½ tsp. salt and pepper.
2. In a large saucepan combine 2 qt. water, 2 Tbsp. kosher salt, the peppercorns, and bay leaves; bring to boiling. Meanwhile, prepare an ice bath with 2 Tbsp. kosher salt.
3. Add shrimp to boiling water. Turn off heat; cover. Let stand 1 to 2 minutes or until opaque; drain. Transfer shrimp to ice bath. Cool 5 minutes. Drain shrimp; blot dry with paper towels. Transfer to serving bowl. Toss with vinaigrette. Chill, covered, up to 24 hours. Add avocados just before serving. Makes 16 servings.
PER SERVING *106 cal, 6 g fat, 79 mg chol, 382 mg sodium, 3 g carb, 2 g fiber, 1 g sugars, 11 g pro.*

CROWD-PLEASER

MATT & NAOMI ROBINSON, BLOGGERS AT *REALFOODBYDAD. COM & BAKERSROYALE.COM*
Even in summer, you can't beat an indulgent cheesy casserole in the potluck mix. Matt and Naomi's is an especially good fit because it highlights peak seasonal produce (corn and zucchini) and is equally delicious served warm or at room temperature. A bit of chorizo spices it and tilts the dish in a hearty direction for those who come hungry. "Know your audience," Naomi says. "Beyond that, your dish shouldn't be too fussy or require any major last-minute prep. This dish checks all those boxes."

QUICK AND SIMPLE

VON DIAZ, AUTHOR OF *COCONUTS & COLLARDS*
Von poaches shrimp then tosses it with tomatoes and a citrus-herb vinaigrette for a bright dish inspired by the cooking of her native Puerto Rico. It takes only a few minutes to throw together—most of which you can do ahead of time. "I like to make this dish in the morning or the night before; the flavors continue to meld as it sits," Von says. "But wait until party time to add the avocado." The recipe works as a blueprint to adapt as you please: Stir in a little minced shallot, chopped red onion, or sliced green onion; switch up the citrus; or try with any number of fresh herbs.

AUGUST

"COUNTERBALANCE INDULGENT COOKOUT FARE WITH A REALLY LIGHT AND FRESH DISH." — VON DIAZ

A BETTER-FOR-YOU DISH

LIZ MOODY, AUTHOR OF *HEALTHIER TOGETHER* "Most basic salads won't hold up to the heat at your average summer potluck, but this one holds up perfectly," says Liz, who contributes healthier options to the spread. Her version of tabbouleh trades bulgur for broccoli rice and includes avocado for extra appeal.

CLASSIC WITH A TWIST

JESSICA MERCHANT, AUTHOR OF *THE PRETTY DISH* AND BLOGGER AT *HOWSWEETEATS.COM* For Jessica, deviled eggs are mandatory for a potluck. For her take, she whirls sun-dried tomatoes into the filling along with Greek yogurt then tops with assorted fresh herbs.

BROCCOLI RICE TABBOULEH WITH LEMON AND DILL

HANDS-ON TIME 20 min.
TOTAL TIME 1 hr.

- 2 Tbsp. avocado oil or olive oil
- 4 cups broccoli rice
- 2 tsp. sea salt
- 1 cup walnuts, coarsely chopped and toasted (tip, page 37)
- 2 English cucumbers, diced
- 1 cup chopped flat-leaf parsley
- 1 cup chopped fresh mint
- 1 cup chopped fresh dill
- ½ cup chopped red onion
- ¼ cup extra virgin olive oil
- ¼ cup fresh lemon juice
- 2 Tbsp. white wine vinegar
- 1 tsp. black pepper
- 1 avocado, halved, pitted, peeled, and diced

1. In a large skillet heat avocado oil over medium heat. Add broccoli rice and sea salt. Cook and stir 4 to 6 minutes or until softened. Cool slightly. Transfer to a serving bowl.
2. Add walnuts, cucumbers, parsley, mint, dill, onion, oil, juice, vinegar, and pepper to bowl. Toss to combine. Chill, covered, up to 24 hours. Add avocado just before serving. Makes 12 servings.
PER SERVING *168 cal, 15 g fat, 391 mg sodium, 8 g carb, 3 g fiber, 2 g sugars, 3 g pro.*

SUN-DRIED TOMATO DEVILED EGGS

HANDS-ON TIME 15 min.
TOTAL TIME 25 min.

- 12 hard-boiled eggs
- ½ cup sun-dried tomatoes packed in oil, drained, patted dry, and finely chopped
- ⅓ cup mayonnaise
- ¼ cup plain Greek yogurt
- 1 Tbsp. white wine vinegar
- 1 Tbsp. Dijon mustard
- ¼ tsp. garlic powder
- ¼ tsp. salt
- ¼ tsp. black pepper
- 2 Tbsp. chopped fresh herbs, such as chives, oregano, basil, and/or dill

1. Peel eggs, halve lengthwise, and remove yolks. In a food processor combine yolks, all but 2 Tbsp. chopped tomatoes, the mayonnaise, yogurt, vinegar, mustard, garlic powder, salt, and pepper. Process until smooth. Spoon or pipe filling into egg whites.
2. Top with remaining tomatoes, the herbs, and additional black pepper. Chill, covered, up to 24 hours before serving. Makes 24 servings.
PER SERVING *63 cal, 5 g fat, 94 mg chol, 94 mg sodium, 1 g carb, 4 g pro.*

SUN-DRIED TOMATO
DEVILED EGGS

BROCCOLI RICE
TABBOULEH WITH
LEMON AND DILL

SHRIMP IN CITRUS
VINAIGRETTE
Recipe on page 177

If your contribution
includes any common
allergens—tree nuts,
shellfish, dairy, or
gluten—consider
placing a small sign
next to the dish to let
people know.

BLUEBERRY BUNDT CAKE

HANDS-ON TIME 15 min.
TOTAL TIME 3 hr. 30 min., includes cooling

CAKE

2   cups all-purpose flour, plus more for dusting pan
1   cup rye flour or whole wheat flour
1½ tsp. baking powder
1½ tsp. kosher salt
½   tsp. baking soda
½   cup unsalted butter, softened
¼   cup neutral oil, such as canola
1¾ cups granulated sugar
1   lemon, zested and juiced
2   tsp. ground cardamom
3   eggs, room temperature
1¼ cups plain whole milk yogurt
2   tsp. vanilla
2   cups fresh blueberries

BLUEBERRY GLAZE

½   cup fresh blueberries
¾   cup powdered sugar

1. Preheat oven to 325°F. Grease and flour a 10-inch fluted tube pan.
2. In a medium bowl whisk together flours. Reserve 2 Tbsp. flour mixture in another medium bowl. Whisk baking powder, salt, and baking soda into remaining flour mixture.
3. In a large mixing bowl beat butter, oil, sugar, lemon zest (reserve juice for glaze), and cardamom on medium-high 5 minutes or until light and fluffy.

4. Add eggs one at a time, completely incorporating each egg before adding the next. Stir in yogurt and vanilla. Add flour mixture all at once. Beat on low until almost completely combined.
5. Add 2 cups blueberries to reserved flour mixture; toss to combine. Using a rubber spatula, gently fold berries into batter, scraping bowl for even mixing. (Batter will be thick.)
6. Spoon batter into prepared pan. Smooth top; tap pan on counter a few times to release any large air bubbles. Bake 60 minutes or until top is golden and a skewer inserted in center comes out clean. Cool in pan on a wire rack 15 minutes. Invert cake onto rack. Cool completely.
7. For glaze: In a small saucepan combine ½ cup blueberries and 2 Tbsp. lemon juice. Using a fork, crush berries. Cook over medium 5 minutes or until berries have softened and released their juices. Cook 3 minutes more or until mixture has reduced to ¼ cup, stirring occasionally. Cool slightly. Whisk in powdered sugar until smooth. Add additional lemon juice, if necessary, for drizzling consistency. Drizzle glaze over cake just before serving. Makes 10 to 12 servings.
PER SERVING *502 cal, 18 g fat, 84 mg chol, 334 mg sodium, 78 g carb, 3 g fiber, 49 g sugars, 9 g pro.*

A STELLAR DESSERT

YOSSY AREFI, AUTHOR OF *SWEETER OFF THE VINE* AND BLOGGER AT *APT2BBAKINGCO.COM*
"A Bundt cake is easy to love," says Yossy, who adds rye flour, which lends a bit of tang to mellow the sweetness to the all-purpose flour. "This cake is sturdy and travels well. Because I live in New York, it has to be able to withstand a subway transfer and a few blocks' walk. It would certainly hold up to a bumpy car ride too," she says. Tote the blueberry glaze in a separate container then pour it over the cake immediately before serving.

'LAZY
WIFE
GOLDEN'

'AUNTIE
WILDER'

'ELSIE
CHURCH'

'BIG
BROWN'

the not-so-humble
BEAN

Grown in your backyard and eaten fresh,
shelling beans go from staple to sensational.

Vine-ripened tomatoes, fresh-picked basil, corn snapped right off the stalk—these crops get all the summer glory. Shelling beans? They're typically the kind of thing you buy dried and stash in the pantry. But these beans deserve to join the ranks of the popular warm-weather garden crops. That's in part because of a late-summer moment in their life cycle: the shelling stage, when beans can be pulled from their pods and eaten before they've dried. "They have so much flavor at that moment," says Philip Kauth, director of preservation at Seed Savers Exchange, a nonprofit that grows and sells heirloom and rare seeds. You won't find many fresh shelling beans in the supermarket (the exception is cranberry beans), to enjoy them, you have to grow your own. You'll be rewarded with creamy texture and sweet, earthy flavor. Plus, while dried beans need soaking and hours on the stove, fresh ones cook in about 30 minutes, at which point they can be pureed into a spread, tossed into a salad or soup, or eaten by the bowlful with a little olive oil and salt. "I always thought a bean was a bean was a bean," Kauth says. "Then I tried a fresh shelling bean."

GROW HEIRLOOM BEANS TO TRY A TYPE YOU'D NEVER TASTE OTHERWISE. ANY BEAN YOU THINK OF AS DRIED CAN BE HARVESTED EARLIER IN THE SEASON AND EATEN AT THE FRESH SHELLING STAGE. LOOK FOR TYPES LABELED SHELL BEAN ON SEED PACKETS FOR THE BEST FLAVOR.

COOL BEANS

These unusual types that look like little jewels have full flavor. Find them at seedsavers.org or exchange.seedsavers.org.

'FAGY UTAN'

'PAINTED PONY'

'CALYPSO'

'CHRISTMAS' LIMA

'LINA SISCO'S BIRD EGG'

'BLACKSNAKE'

'CHARLEVOIX' DARK RED KIDNEY

MEDITERRANEAN THREE-BEAN SALAD

HANDS-ON TIME 15 min.
TOTAL TIME 4 hr. 30 min., includes chilling

- 2 cups assorted fresh shelling beans, washed*
- 8 oz. fresh wax and/or green beans, trimmed and cut into bite-size pieces
- ½ cup red wine vinegar
- ¼ cup olive oil
- 2 Tbsp. sugar
- 2 Tbsp. Dijon mustard
- 1 tsp. salt
- ½ tsp. black pepper
- 1 cup sliced red onion
- ¼ cup chopped flat-leaf parsley
- ¼ cup chopped fresh mint
  Crumbled feta cheese

1. In a 4- to 5-qt. pot place shelling beans and water to cover by 2 inches. Bring to boiling; reduce heat. Simmer, covered, 15 minutes. Add wax and/or green beans. Cook 10 minutes more or until tender. Drain; rinse with cold water; drain again.
2. In a large bowl whisk together vinegar, olive oil, sugar, mustard, salt, and pepper. Add beans, onion, parsley, and mint; toss. Chill, covered, 4 to 24 hours. Top with feta. Makes 12 servings.
*Tip Or substitute fully cooked dried beans for fresh beans. One cup of most types of dried beans yields 2½ to 3 cups cooked.
PER SERVING *58 cal, 1 g fat, 3 mg chol, 59 mg sodium, 9 g carb, 2 g fiber, 2 g sugars, 3 g pro.*

SMASHED BEAN SPREAD

HANDS-ON TIME 10 min.
TOTAL TIME 45 min.

- 2 cups shelled fresh lima or butter beans, washed
- 1 lemon
- 3 Tbsp. olive oil
- 2 Tbsp. chopped fresh thyme
- 3 cloves garlic, minced
- ½ tsp. salt
- ¼ tsp. freshly ground black pepper
  Toasted baguette slices

In a large pot place beans and enough water to cover by 2 inches. Bring to boiling; reduce heat. Cover and simmer 35 minutes or until tender. Drain and add to a food processor. Remove ½ tsp. zest and 1½ Tbsp. juice from lemon. Add lemon juice and zest, oil, thyme, garlic, salt, and pepper. Process until smooth. Spread on baguette slices; top with additional thyme and lemon zest, then drizzle with additional oil. Makes 16 servings.
PER SERVING *118 cal, 5 g fat, 213 mg sodium, 16 g carb, 1 g fiber, 3 g pro.*

SUMMER BEAN SOUP

Photo on page 186.
HANDS-ON TIME 15 min.
TOTAL TIME 55 min.

- 1 Tbsp. olive oil
- 2 cups thinly sliced leeks
- 4 cloves garlic, minced
- 6 cups reduced-sodium chicken broth
- 2 cups assorted fresh shelling beans, washed*
- 1 medium zucchini or yellow summer squash, halved and sliced
- 2 medium fresh tomatoes, chopped
- ½ tsp. salt
- ½ tsp. black pepper
- 2 cups chopped Swiss chard
- ½ cup chopped fresh basil
- 1 lemon, juiced

In a 5-qt. pot heat oil over medium heat. Add leeks and garlic. Cook and stir 4 to 5 minutes or until tender. Stir in broth and shelling beans. Bring to boiling; reduce heat. Simmer, covered, 25 minutes or until beans are tender. Stir in zucchini, tomatoes, salt, and pepper. Simmer, uncovered, 10 minutes. Stir in Swiss chard and basil; cook just until chard is wilted. Stir in lemon juice. Makes 6 servings.
*Tip To substitute soaked dried beans for fresh beans, increase initial simmering time to 50 minutes and increase broth as necessary for desired consistency.
PER SERVING *138 cal, 5 g fat, 787 mg sodium, 14 g carb, 4 g fiber, 5 g sugars, 11 g pro.*

SMASHED BEAN
SPREAD

MEDITERRANEAN
THREE-BEAN
SALAD

SUMMER BEAN SOUP
Recipe on page 184

PIT CREW

It's peak season for peaches, plums, and apricots, and they work equally well in sweet and savory recipes. Bake them, blend them, or grill them—these juicy beauties make everything taste like summer.

Apricots, peaches, plums, and nectarines hit their stride mid- to late-summer, and each bite of the pitted fruits can send juices dripping down your arm. Now let's talk a little science and strategy before you shop. Unlike berries and melons, stone fruits are climacteric. Because they convert starch to sugars as they age, they continue to ripen after being picked. Grocery store produce sections tend to stock underripe fruit because it travels better than ripe does and has a longer shelf life, which is fine when it has time to ripen. If you crave immediate satisfaction of juice-dripping fruit, a farmers market is apt to have bushels of nearly ripe to fully ripe stone fruits. (Select varying degrees of ripeness when you buy fruit to last a few days.) Look for fruits that are fragrant, firm, and yield under slight pressure from your thumb. Plums should feel heavy when you hold them. Apricots ripen more quickly than peaches and plums, so purchase only what you can eat within a couple days. Store stone fruits at room temperature. (Chilling slows ripening but results in mealy texture.) To expedite ripening, place fruit in a paper bag, remembering to check daily.

SMASHED PEACH AND POBLANO GRILLED CHEESE

SMASHED PEACH AND POBLANO GRILLED CHEESE

For this grown-up grilled cheese sandwich, dust a peach half with ancho chile powder and smash with a potato masher before layering with sharp cheddar, poblano, and bacon.

HANDS-ON TIME 15 min.
TOTAL TIME 25 min.

- 2 medium peaches, halved and pitted
- ½ tsp. ground ancho chile pepper (optional)
- 4 slices sourdough bread
- 3 oz. sliced sharp white cheddar cheese
- 1 large fresh poblano pepper, roasted* and cut into strips (tip, page 127)
- 4 slices bacon, crisp-cooked
- 2 Tbsp. softened butter

1. If desired, sprinkle cut sides of peach halves with ground ancho chile. Using a potato masher or the flat side of a meat mallet, gently smash peach halves to ½-inch thickness.
2. Top two bread slices with cheese slices. Add two peach halves, poblano strips, and bacon. Top with remaining bread slices. Butter both sides of each sandwich.
3. Cook sandwiches in a hot skillet over medium 2 to 3 minutes or until toasted. Turn; cook on opposite side until cheese is melted. Makes 2 servings.
*Tip Preheat oven to 425°F. Cut poblano pepper in half lengthwise; remove stems and seeds. Place cut sides down on a foil-lined baking sheet. Roast 20 to 25 minutes or until tender. Wrap in foil. When cool enough to handle, peel and discard skin. Chill up to 3 days.
PER SERVING *680 cal, 30 g fat, 75 mg chol, 1,220 mg sodium, 78 g carb, 5 g fiber, 18 g sugars, 27 g pro.*

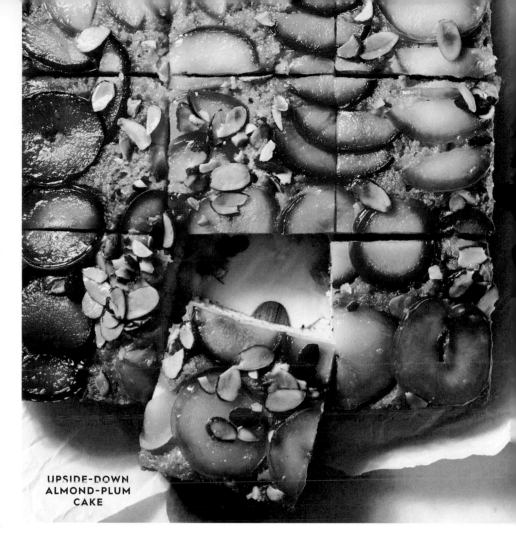

UPSIDE-DOWN ALMOND-PLUM CAKE

UPSIDE-DOWN ALMOND-PLUM CAKE

If you're a fan of almonds, this might be your new favorite dessert of the season.

HANDS-ON TIME 20 min.
TOTAL TIME 1 hr. 30 min., includes cooling

- 6 Tbsp. butter
- ¾ cup packed brown sugar
- 1 Tbsp. honey
- 4 to 5 plums, halved and pitted
- ¼ cup sliced almonds, toasted
- 1½ cups all-purpose flour
- ½ cup almond meal
- 1 tsp. baking powder
- ¾ tsp. baking soda
- ½ tsp. salt
- ½ cup butter, softened
- 1 cup granulated sugar
- 2 eggs
- 1 cup sour cream
- 1 tsp. vanilla
- ½ tsp. almond extract

1. Preheat oven to 350°F. In a small saucepan melt 6 Tbsp. butter over medium heat. Stir in brown sugar and honey; bring just to boiling, stirring until sugar is dissolved. Spread in a 9-inch square baking pan.
2. Thinly slice plum halves; arrange on sauce in pan. Sprinkle almonds over plums.
3. In a bowl stir together flour, almond meal, baking powder, baking soda, and salt. In a large bowl beat ½ cup butter on medium 30 seconds. Gradually add granulated sugar, ¼ cup at a time, beating on medium until combined. Scrape bowl; beat 2 minutes more. Add eggs one at a time, beating after each until combined. Beat in sour cream, vanilla, and almond extract. Add flour mixture; beat just until combined. Spread batter over plums in pan.
4. Bake 40 minutes or until a toothpick inserted near center comes out clean and center is set. Cool in pan 15 minutes. Loosen sides of cake; invert onto serving plate. Cool 15 minutes. Serve warm. Makes 9 servings.
PER SERVING *523 cal, 28 g fat, 101 mg chol, 459 mg sodium, 65 g carb, 2 g fiber, 46 g sugars, 6 g pro.*

BOTANICALLY SPEAKING, STONE FRUITS ARE A TYPE OF DRUPE: THIN-SKIN FRUITS WITH SOFT FLESH AROUND A HARD STONE OR PIT ENCASING SEEDS.

APRICOT SKILLET PIE

Apricots and cherries (smallest of the stone fruits) get equal billing in this ginger-scented dessert. Strips of puff pastry crust—some doubled back to expose filling—keep the cast-iron pie practically effortless.

HANDS-ON TIME 20 min.
TOTAL TIME 1 hr. 15 min.

⅓ cup packed brown sugar
2 Tbsp. all-purpose flour
1 tsp. ground ginger
½ tsp. ground cinnamon
⅛ tsp. salt
2 Tbsp. butter
1¾ lb. fresh apricots, pitted and quartered (4½ cups)
1½ cups fresh tart red cherries, pitted, or frozen pitted tart red cherries, thawed and drained
1 tsp. vanilla
½ 17.3-oz. pkg. frozen puff pastry sheets (1 sheet), thawed
1 egg, slightly beaten
   Coarse sugar
   Ice cream or whipped cream (optional)

1. Preheat oven to 400°F. In a small bowl stir together brown sugar, flour, ginger, cinnamon, and salt. In a 9- or 10-inch cast-iron skillet melt butter over medium. Add apricots; cook 2 to 3 minutes or until apricots start to release juice, stirring occasionally. Remove from heat. Stir in cherries, vanilla, and brown sugar mixture.

2. On a lightly floured surface, unfold pastry. Roll to a 10-inch square. Using a sharp knife, cut 1-inch-wide strips, cutting from the center of the square to one edge. Fold cut strips over uncut side of pastry. Place on filling, fold at center. Unfold every other strip over filling. Trim pastry even with edge of skillet. (Or roll pastry to a 10-inch square. Lay over filling in skillet. Trim pastry even with edge of skillet. Cut slits in center.) Brush pastry with beaten egg. Sprinkle with coarse sugar.

3. Bake 25 minutes or until golden and bubbly. Let stand 30 minutes before serving. If desired, top with ice cream or whipped cream. Makes 8 servings.

PER SERVING *272 cal, 11 g fat, 31 mg chol, 177 mg sodium, 40 g carb, 3 g fiber, 24 g sugars, 5 g pro.*

STONE FRUIT HYBRIDS

Stone fruits are easily crossbred and many hybrids can be found in the grocery store. Interchange these new fruits with their parent fruits in these recipes.

PLUOT Mostly plum with a bit of apricot mixed in. Firm plumlike texture and a decidedly apricot flavor.

APRIUM More apricot than plum (approximately 75:25). The fruit is smaller and sweeter than both its parent fruits.

PLUMCOT These 50:50 combos are first-generation hybrids of plums and apricots. The parent varietals determine the color.

PEACHARINE This practically fuzzless fruit is a 50:50 genetic split between a peach and a nectarine. It gets firm texture from the nectarine and sweetness from the peach.

PEACH CRUMBLE BARS
Recipe on page 194

**APRICOT-THYME-
GLAZED CHICKEN**
Recipe on page 194

PEACH CRUMBLE BARS

Photo on page 192.

This recipe has the best features of peach crumble in bar form.

HANDS-ON TIME 20 min.
TOTAL TIME 1 hr.

CRUST
    Nonstick cooking spray
2¼ cups all-purpose flour
¼ cup plus 2 Tbsp. packed brown sugar
¼ cup plus 2 Tbsp. powdered sugar
¼ tsp. salt
1 cup plus 2 Tbsp. cold butter, chopped

FILLING
1 cup granulated sugar
1 Tbsp. plus 1 tsp. cornstarch
6 large peaches, peeled and chopped (about 6 cups)
2 Tbsp. lemon juice

TOPPING
1 cup all-purpose flour
⅔ cup packed brown sugar
⅔ cup cold butter, cut into pieces
⅔ cup chopped toasted hazelnuts (tip, page 37)
½ cup shredded coconut
    Ice cream (optional)

1. For crust: Preheat oven to 350°F. Line a 13×9-inch baking pan with foil, extending foil over edges; coat with cooking spray. In a bowl stir together flour, brown sugar, powdered sugar, and salt. Cut in butter until mixture resembles coarse crumbs; press into pan. Bake 15 minutes.
2. For filling: In a medium saucepan combine granulated sugar and cornstarch. Stir in peaches and lemon juice. Cook over medium until thickened and bubbly, stirring occasionally. Spoon over partially baked crust.
3. For topping: In a bowl stir together flour and brown sugar. Cut in butter until mixture resembles coarse crumbs. Stir in nuts and coconut.
4. Crumble topping over filling. Bake 20 to 25 minutes or until golden brown and filling is bubbly. Cool in pan 10 minutes. Use foil to lift uncut bars from pan. Cut into bars and, if desired, serve with ice cream. Makes 20 servings.
PER SERVING *363 cal, 20 g fat, 44 mg chol, 164 mg sodium, 45 g carb, 2 g fiber, 28 g sugars, 3 g pro.*

APRICOT-THYME-GLAZED CHICKEN

Photo on page 193.

Chopped apricots are the base of the glaze. Halved apricots and shallots are grilled alongside chicken for just a few minutes.

HANDS-ON TIME 20 min.
TOTAL TIME 1 hr. 35 min.

13 fresh apricots, halved and pitted
1 Tbsp. butter
2 Tbsp. minced shallot
1 clove garlic, minced
3 Tbsp. honey
1 Tbsp. cider vinegar
2 tsp. snipped fresh thyme leaves
1¼ tsp. salt
3 to 3½ lb. chicken pieces (breast halves, thighs, drumsticks)
¼ tsp. black pepper
3 large shallots, peeled and halved
2 Tbsp. melted butter
    Fresh thyme sprigs

1. Chop seven apricots (1½ cups); set aside. For glaze: In a medium saucepan melt 1 Tbsp. butter over medium heat. Add minced shallot and garlic; cook and stir 2 minutes. Stir in chopped apricots, ½ cup water, the honey, and vinegar. Bring to boiling; reduce heat. Simmer, uncovered, 10 minutes or until apricots are softened, stirring occasionally. Cool slightly. Transfer to a blender; blend until smooth. Stir in thyme leaves and 1 tsp. salt. Set 1 cup glaze aside for serving.
2. Prepare grill for medium indirect heat. Sprinkle chicken with ¼ tsp. salt and pepper. Place chicken, skin sides down, over drip pan. Grill, covered, 25 minutes. Turn chicken. Brush some of the glaze on chicken. Grill 25 minutes more or until done (170°F breast halves, 175°F thighs and drumsticks), brushing occasionally with glaze (discard any remaining glaze). If desired, for crispier chicken, grill over direct heat, skin-sides, down the last 5 minutes.
3. Brush apricot and shallot halves with 2 Tbsp. melted butter. Grill, covered, directly over medium 4 to 5 minutes or until lightly charred, turning once. Serve apricots, shallots, reserved 1 cup glaze, and thyme sprigs with chicken. Makes 4 to 6 servings.
PER SERVING *597 cal, 28 g fat, 178 mg chol, 938 mg sodium, 33 g carb, 4 g fiber, 28 g sugars, 53 g pro.*

PLUM-PORK NOODLE BOWL

Use a portion of the marinade to make a punchy plum relish for this fresh noodle bowl.

HANDS-ON TIME 20 min.
TOTAL TIME 45 min., plus marinating

⅓ cup reduced-sodium soy sauce
¼ cup rice vinegar
2 Tbsp. lime juice
2 Tbsp. honey
¼ cup chopped shallots
1½ tsp. grated fresh ginger
3 cloves garlic, minced
¼ tsp. crushed red pepper
1 tsp. Asian chili-garlic sauce
1 lb. pork tenderloin
8 plums, pitted (about 2 lb.)
¼ cup chopped fresh cilantro
4 cups shredded cabbage
4 oz. dried wide rice noodles, cooked and drained
1 cup bias-sliced snow peas
1 cup coarsely shredded carrots
    Chopped peanuts or cashews

1. For marinade: In a medium bowl combine soy sauce, vinegar, lime juice, honey, shallots, ginger, garlic, and crushed red pepper. Place half the marinade in a resealable plastic bag with chili-garlic sauce; knead to combine. Add pork to bag and seal; turn to coat. Chill up to 24 hours.
2. For plum salsa: Chop four plums; place in a bowl. Add remaining marinade and cilantro. Chill, covered, up to 24 hours.
3. Prepare grill for medium indirect grilling. Remove pork from marinade (discard marinade); grill pork over a drip pan 25 to 30 minutes or until 145°F. Remove; let stand 5 minutes. Slice pork.
4. Slice remaining plums. Arrange cabbage, noodles, pork, plums, peas, and carrots in four bowls with plum salsa; top with peanuts. Makes 4 servings.
PER SERVING *424 cal, 8 g fat, 385 mg sodium, 62 g carb, 7 g fiber, 30 g sugars, 31 g pro.*

PLUM-PORK
NOODLE BOWL

HIBISCUS PUNCH
Recipe on page 212

september

Cooking lessons from the pros: Mark Bittman shares updated classics; Nik Sharma invigorates recipes with turmeric; and recipes from Julia Turshen reflect her relaxed entertaining style.

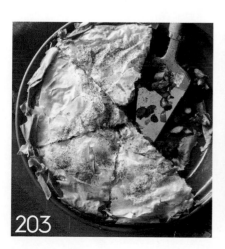

203

207

214

MIRACLE
MOUSSAKA

MUSHROOM-
SWEET POTATO
MOUSSAKA

what's for DINNER?

Cookbook author Mark Bittman answers that question with recipes for three iconic dishes—a quick version for hurried weeknights and a plant-based one that will please vegans and nonvegans.

MIRACLE MOUSSAKA

Mark streamlines this classic Greek dish by baking eggplant, onion, tomatoes, and lamb together—rather than precook each separately and assemble the layers. After he stirs in a cinnamon- and oregano-spiced sauce he returns the dish to the oven.

TOTAL TIME 40 min.

4	Tbsp. olive oil
12	oz. eggplant, unpeeled, cut into 1-inch cubes (4½ cups)
	Salt
	Black pepper
1½	cups chopped red onion
1	Tbsp. chopped garlic cloves
1	14.5-oz. can diced tomatoes, drained
1	lb. ground lamb or ground chuck
2	Tbsp. all-purpose flour
1	tsp. ground cinnamon
1	tsp. dried oregano
⅔	cup milk
2	egg yolks
¼	cup chopped flat-leaf parsley

1. Preheat oven to 425°F. Coat a large ovenproof skillet with 2 Tbsp. oil. Add eggplant. Sprinkle with ¼ tsp. each salt and pepper. Toss to coat. Scatter onion and garlic then tomatoes over eggplant.
2. Gently mix lamb with ¼ tsp. each salt and pepper. Dot tomatoes with ground lamb; sprinkle with ¼ tsp. each salt and pepper. Bake 10 to 15 minutes, undisturbed, until mixture sizzles and browns in spots.
3. In a small saucepan stir together remaining 2 Tbsp. oil and the flour over medium-low. Cook 8 to 12 minutes or until flour turns golden and forms a paste, whisking almost constantly. Stir in cinnamon, oregano, and ⅛ tsp. each salt and pepper. Cook and whisk until

fragrant, less than 1 minute. Remove from heat. Add milk, whisking constantly until smooth. Whisk in egg yolks.
4. Drizzle sauce over meat and vegetables in skillet; shake to distribute liquid. Bake 7 to 10 minutes more or until bubbly and sauce is still a little loose. Let stand 10 minutes. Sprinkle with parsley. Makes 4 servings.
PER SERVING *534 cal, 38 g fat, 173 mg chol, 761 mg sodium, 23 g carb, 5 g fiber, 9 g sugars, 24 g pro.*

MUSHROOM-SWEET POTATO MOUSSAKA

Mushrooms replace traditional lamb in this shepherd's pie take on moussaka. Mark tops the dish with mashed sweet potatoes and a cashew cream sauce.

HANDS-ON TIME 25 min.
TOTAL TIME 2 hr. 25 min., plus soaking

1	cup raw cashews
2	lb. assorted mushrooms, sliced
¼	cup olive oil
	Salt and black pepper
1	Tbsp. chopped garlic
2	Tbsp. chopped fresh oregano
1	cup chopped onion
2	tsp. ground cinnamon
½	tsp. ground nutmeg
1	28-oz. can crushed tomatoes
2	lb. sweet potatoes, peeled and cut into chunks

1. For cashew cream: Soak cashews in 2 cups water at least 4 hours. Drain, reserving liquid. Transfer cashews to a blender. Blend, adding reserved liquid 2 Tbsp. at a time, 6 to 8 Tbsp. total, until the consistency of buttercream frosting.
2. Preheat oven to 400°F. Line a baking pan with parchment paper. Add mushrooms and 2 Tbsp. oil. Sprinkle with

salt and pepper; toss to coat. Bake 20 to 25 minutes or until mushrooms are crisp and pan is dry, stirring every 5 minutes. Stir in garlic and oregano; season to taste. Reduce oven to 350°F.
3. For tomato sauce: In a large pot heat remaining 2 Tbsp. oil over medium heat. Add onion; sprinkle with salt and pepper. Cook 5 to 8 minutes or until onion softens and starts to turn golden, stirring occasionally. Add cinnamon and nutmeg. Cook and stir 30 seconds or until fragrant. Add tomatoes. Bring to boiling; reduce heat. Simmer 30 to 35 minutes or until thickened, stirring occasionally; season to taste.
4. For mashed potatoes: Place potatoes in a large pot with enough cold water to cover by 1 inch. Add a generous pinch salt. Bring to boiling. Keep water bubbling steadily until potatoes are fork-tender, 10 to 25 minutes depending on size of pieces. Drain, reserving some liquid.
5. Using a potato masher, mash sweet potatoes in pot. Add two-thirds of the cashew cream and about ¼ cup reserved cooking liquid; sprinkle with salt and pepper. If potatoes are stiff, add cooking liquid, 1 Tbsp. at a time, until creamy. Season to taste.
6. Spread tomato sauce in a 2-qt. baking dish. Add mushrooms in an even layer. Carefully spread mashed potatoes to completely cover. Spread remaining cashew cream. Place a foil-lined baking sheet on oven rack below dish. Bake 45 to 50 minutes or until sauce is bubbling and top is browned. Let stand a few minutes before serving. If desired, sprinkle with additional oregano. Makes 4 to 6 servings.
PER SERVING *595 cal, 29 g fat, 1,641 mg sodium, 75 g carb, 15 g fiber, 25 g sugars, 20 g pro.*

COOKING MUSTS

Mark's long-running column in *The New York Times* was called "The Minimalist" for a reason. A few of his basic tips for home-cooking success:

BUY THE BEST Always start with quality ingredients. He says, "I let what I find at the market determine what I'll make for dinner instead of the other way around."

TASTE AS YOU GO Often all you need is salt and pepper to make good ingredients taste delicious. For Mark that means kosher salt and freshly ground black peppercorns.

STOCK UP When you have a well-stocked pantry, adapting a recipe or experimenting with flavor is easy. Use recipes as a blueprint; play with spices and seasonings to keep them interesting.

HEARTY VEGETABLE CACCIATORE

"This is the kitchen-sink version of cacciatore," Mark says. His vegan spin includes mushrooms, onion, bell pepper, potatoes, and fava beans, but you could use almost any vegetable you have on hand.

HANDS–ON TIME 35 min.
TOTAL TIME 1 hr.

¼ cup olive oil, plus more as needed
1 lb. portobello mushrooms, sliced
   Salt and black pepper
1 large red onion, halved and sliced
1 red bell pepper, cored and sliced
1 cup green olives, pitted if desired
1 Tbsp. chopped garlic
½ tsp. crushed red pepper or to taste
1 28-oz. can whole tomatoes, undrained
1 cup dry white wine or water
1 lb. fingerling potatoes, halved if large
1 Tbsp. chopped fresh oregano or 1 tsp. dried oregano, crushed
1 cup frozen fava beans, lima beans, or edamame

1. In an extra-large skillet heat ¼ cup oil over medium-high heat. Add mushrooms. Sprinkle with salt and pepper. Reduce heat to medium-low. Cook, covered, 5 minutes (do not stir). Uncover. (If mushrooms haven't released liquid, cover and cook 1 to 2 minutes more.) Increase heat to medium-high. Cook, uncovered, 10 minutes or until skillet is dry and mushrooms are crisp. Remove mushrooms from skillet; set aside.
2. Add onion and bell pepper to skillet with additional oil if needed; season with salt and pepper. Cook over medium 3 to 5 minutes or until vegetables begin to soften, stirring occasionally. Add olives, garlic, and crushed red pepper. Cook until fragrant, less than 1 minute. Add tomatoes, wine, potatoes, and oregano. Bring to boiling; reduce heat. Simmer, covered, 20 to 30 minutes or until potatoes are tender.
3. Add mushrooms and beans to skillet. Stir to combine. Simmer 5 to 10 minutes or until beans are tender. Makes 4 servings.
PER SERVING *408 cal, 20 g fat, 42 mg chol, 1,270 mg sodium, 42 g carb, 11 g fiber, 13 g sugars, 8 g pro.*

DRUMSTICK CACCIATORE

Italian hunter stew typically involves hours of simmering meaty bone-in chicken pieces in a tomato-based sauce. On a weeknight, Mark builds flavor fast by searing quick-cooking drumsticks, then braises them in a sauce of tomato, balsamic, and dried herbs.

HANDS–ON TIME 20 min.
TOTAL TIME 40 min.

2 Tbsp. olive oil
8 chicken drumsticks (about 2 lb.)
   Salt and black pepper
¼ cup tomato paste
¼ cup balsamic vinegar
1 tsp. dried sage, oregano, or thyme
¼ tsp. crushed red pepper or to taste
1 lb. small whole button mushrooms
1 Tbsp. chopped garlic

1. In a large skillet heat oil over medium heat. Add chicken; sprinkle with salt and pepper. Adjust heat so chicken sizzles but doesn't burn. Cook 5 to 8 minutes, undisturbed, until browned and releases easily from pan.
2. Meanwhile, for sauce, in a medium bowl combine tomato paste and vinegar. Add 1½ cups water, the sage, and crushed red pepper. Season with salt and pepper. Whisk until sauce is smooth.
3. Turn chicken. Cook 5 minutes more or until browned and releases easily from pan. Scatter mushrooms and garlic in skillet. Pour sauce over chicken and mushrooms. Shake pan once or twice to combine. Bring to boiling; reduce heat. Simmer 20 minutes, uncovered, or until chicken is done (175°F), carefully shaking pan a couple of times. Season to taste with salt and pepper. Makes 4 servings.
PER SERVING *238 cal, 14 g fat, 71 mg chol, 568 mg sodium, 10 g carb, 2 g fiber, 7 g sugars, 18 g pro.*

HEARTY
VEGETABLE
CACCIATORE

DRUMSTICK
CACCIATORE

MOROCCAN
PASTILLA

CHICKEN-AND-BISCUIT
POT PIE

"THINK OF THIS AS THE POT PIE VERSION OF COBBLER," MARK SAYS. TOPPING CREAMY CHICKEN-AND-VEGETABLE FILLING WITH STIR-TOGETHER BISCUIT DOUGH MAKES IT POSSIBLE TO WHIP UP HOMEMADE POT PIE IN ABOUT AN HOUR.

CHICKEN-AND-BISCUIT POT PIE

HANDS-ON TIME 50 min.
TOTAL TIME 1 hr. 5 min.

2½ cups milk, plus more as needed
2½ cups plus 2 Tbsp. all-purpose flour, plus more as needed
2 tsp. baking powder
1 tsp. salt
⅓ cup olive oil
2 Tbsp. unsalted butter
1½ lb. skinless, boneless chicken thighs
1 cup chopped onion
1 cup chopped carrots
½ cup chopped celery
   Black pepper
1 cup fresh or frozen peas

1. Preheat oven to 450°F. In a saucepan heat 2½ cups milk over medium heat just until steaming.
2. In a large bowl stir together 2½ cups flour, the baking powder, and salt. Add oil and 1 cup warm milk. Stir just until dough is mixed (dough will be lumpy). If it's too dry and hasn't come together, stir in additional milk, 1 Tbsp. at a time. If dough is too wet, add 1 Tbsp. flour and stir once. Dough should drop like biscuit batter from a spoon.
3. Meanwhile, in an extra-large oven-safe skillet melt butter over medium heat. Add chicken, onion, carrots, and celery; sprinkle with salt and pepper. Cook 10 to 15 minutes or until chicken is cooked through (175°F) but not browned, turning occasionally. Cut into bite-size pieces.
4. Return chicken to skillet. Sprinkle with remaining 2 Tbsp. flour. Reduce heat to medium-low. Cook just until flour turns golden. Slowly pour in remaining 1½ cups milk. Simmer, stirring occasionally, until sauce coats the back of a spoon. Stir in peas; season to taste with salt and pepper.

5. One at a time, drop a heaping tablespoon dough onto hot chicken mixture, spacing mounds evenly. Bake 15 to 20 minutes or until mixture is bubbling and crust is golden. Makes 4 to 6 servings.
PER SERVING *795 cal, 33 g fat, 147 chol, 1,359 mg sodium, 83 g carb, 6 g fiber, 13 g sugars, 41 g pro*

MOROCCAN PASTILLA

Mark's riff on pastilla—a North African sweet-savory chicken pie—features a hearty Moroccan-spiced filling of parsnips, dried fruit, nuts, and olives beneath a flaky phyllo crust.

HANDS-ON TIME 40 min.
TOTAL TIME 1 hr. 10 min.

1 lb. parsnips, peeled and cut into 1-inch chunks
1 red onion, quartered
1 cup pitted green olives
½ cup dried apricots
½ cup pitted dates
½ cup raw almonds
4 cloves garlic, smashed
3 Tbsp. olive oil, plus more for pie plate and brushing onto phyllo
   Salt and black pepper
1 Tbsp. ras el hanout*
1 cup fresh cilantro, thicker stems removed, chopped
1 lemon (zest and, if desired, juice)
½ 16-oz. pkg. phyllo dough, thawed in refrigerator 8 hours ahead
1 Tbsp. powdered sugar
1 tsp. ground cinnamon

1. Preheat oven to 400°F. In a food processor combine parsnips, onion, olives, apricots, dates, almonds, and garlic. Pulse until pieces are pea size, working in batches if necessary and scraping down sides as needed.

2. In a large skillet heat 3 Tbsp. oil over medium-high. Add parsnip mixture and 1 cup water. Sprinkle with salt and black pepper. Cook 10 to 15 minutes or until parsnips soften and pan is mostly dry, stirring occasionally and adjusting heat so mixture sizzles without burning. Add ras el hanout. Cook 1 minute or until fragrant. Turn off heat. Stir in cilantro and lemon zest. Season to taste, adding a little lemon juice if desired.
3. Oil a 9-inch pie plate. Cut eight sheets phyllo into 9-inch squares. (Discard scraps.) Place one square in bottom of pie plate, allowing corners to extend over rim. Brush phyllo with oil. Top with a phyllo sheet at a 45-degree angle. Brush with oil. Repeat with two more sheets, fanning to evenly cover sides of pie plate.
4. Spread vegetable mixture evenly over phyllo. Top with four phyllo squares, brushing each with a little olive oil and offsetting corners. Fold down edges of all phyllo into sides of pie plate to enclose. Brush top with oil. Cut a few small slits in top to allow steam to escape. Cover with foil.
5. Bake 15 minutes. Remove foil. Bake 5 to 10 minutes more or until golden brown and crisp. In a small sieve combine sugar and cinnamon. Shake over pie to dust. Serve warm or at room temperature. Makes 4 servings.
*Tip Ras el hanout is a distinctive Moroccan spice blend. In a pinch, substitute garam masala.
PER SERVING *620 cal, 37 g fat, 908 mg sodium, 69 g carb, 13 g fiber, 32 g sugars, 9 g pro.*

Nik Sharma on
TURMERIC

Turmeric, a nubby root closely related to ginger, adds herbaceous, peppery notes and rich, buttery color to whatever it touches. Thanks to rising popularity of the roots on the health and wellness scene, fresh turmeric can be found in most larger grocery stores. Cookbook author and blogger Nik Sharma shares recipes for using the rhizome in dishes for grilled pork, chicken soup, and granola.

TURMERIC-PINEAPPLE SIPPER

Fresh turmeric simple syrup meets fruit juice and sparkling water in this tropical mocktail. (A splash of gin or vodka pushes the drink squarely into happy hour territory.) Leftover turmeric syrup? Nik suggests adding fresh fruit juice and a squeeze of lime then freezing it into granita or ice pops.

HANDS-ON TIME 5 min.
TOTAL TIME 35 min.

- ½ cup sugar
- 2 2-inch pieces fresh turmeric, thinly sliced
- 2 cups chilled fresh pineapple juice
  Chilled sparkling water

1. For turmeric simple syrup: In a small saucepan bring sugar, ½ cup water, and turmeric slices to boiling over medium-high, stirring until sugar is dissolved. Steep 30 minutes. Discard turmeric. Transfer syrup to a storage container; chill up to 1 week.
2. In a pitcher combine turmeric syrup and pineapple juice. For each serving, pour ⅔ cup turmeric mixture over ice. Top with sparkling water. Makes 4 servings.
PER SERVING *164 cal, 14 mg sodium, 41 g carb, 38 g sugars*

**PORK KABOBS
WITH COUSCOUS
SALAD**

**TURMERIC,
GINGER, AND
HONEY AFFOGATO**
Recipe on page 208

**SPICED PAPAYA-
CRANBERRY
GRANOLA**

PORK KABOBS WITH COUSCOUS SALAD

These marinated kabobs are served over turmeric-scented couscous salad.

HANDS-ON TIME 25 min.

TOTAL TIME 1 hr. 30 min., includes marinating

- 1 lb. pork tenderloin, trimmed of fat and cut into 1-inch cubes
- 1 shallot, peeled and chopped
- 2 cloves garlic, peeled and halved
- ¼ cup lime juice (2 limes)
- 1 tsp. purchased garam masala or Garam Masala (recipe, page 208)
- 1 tsp. chili powder
- 1½ tsp. ground turmeric
- 1 tsp. fine sea salt
- 1 cup low-sodium vegetable or chicken stock
- 2 Tbsp. olive oil
- 1 cup couscous
- 2 shallots, thinly sliced
- 2 Tbsp. cashews
- ¼ cup dried tart cherries
- 1 1-inch piece fresh ginger, peeled and julienned
- 1 cup packed arugula leaves
- ½ cup crumbled feta
  Black pepper
  Lime wedges

1. Place pork in a bowl. In a small food processor pulse shallot, garlic, 2 Tbsp. lime juice, the garam masala, chili powder, and ½ tsp. each turmeric and salt; pour over pork. Toss to coat. Marinate in the refrigerator, covered, 1 hour.

2. Thread pork onto eight bamboo skewers* or metal skewers. Grill, covered, over medium heat 4 to 6 minutes or until meat is still slightly pink in center, turning once.

3. Meanwhile, in a medium saucepan bring stock to a rolling boil with remaining salt and 1 tsp. oil. Stir in couscous; remove from heat. Let stand, covered, 8 to 10 minutes or until couscous is tender. Fluff with a fork.

4. In a medium saucepan heat 2 tsp. oil over medium-high heat. Add sliced shallots; cook and stir 3 to 4 minutes or until light brown. Add cashews, cherries, ginger, and remaining turmeric. Cook 2 to 3 minutes more or until cashews are golden brown and slightly seared.

5. Place couscous in a large bowl; fold in arugula and feta. Add remaining lime juice. Season to taste with salt and pepper. Transfer to a platter. Top with pork kabobs. Drizzle with remaining 1 Tbsp. oil. Serve with lime wedges. Makes 4 servings.

*Tip Soak wooden skewers in water to cover at least 30 minutes before grilling.

PER SERVING *503 cal, 17 g fat, 90 mg chol, 1,060 mg sodium, 53 g carb, 4 g fiber, 10 g sugars, 34 g pro.*

SPICED PAPAYA-CRANBERRY GRANOLA

Leave purchased granola on the shelf. Nik's version includes two dried fruits, nuts, and a splash of apple cider vinegar for subtle zip.

HANDS-ON TIME 15 min.

TOTAL TIME 1 hr. 50 min.

- 2 cups regular rolled oats
- ½ cup dried cranberries
- ½ cup dried papaya
- ½ cup chopped pistachios
- ½ cup chopped walnuts or cashews
- 1½ tsp. ground ginger
- 1 tsp. ground turmeric
- ½ tsp. fine sea salt
- ½ cup maple syrup
- ¼ cup olive oil
- 1 Tbsp. apple cider vinegar

1. Line a baking sheet with parchment paper. In a large bowl mix together oats, cranberries, papaya, pistachios, walnuts, ginger, turmeric, and salt. In a small bowl whisk together maple syrup, oil, and vinegar. Drizzle over oat mixture; stir to coat.

2. Preheat oven to 300°F. Spread granola on prepared pan in a single layer. Let stand 20 minutes. Bake 45 minutes or until toasted, stirring every 10 minutes. Cool. Store in an airtight container up to 2 weeks. Makes 16 servings.

PER SERVING *192 cal, 12 g fat, 74 mg sodium, 21 g carb, 2 g fiber, 11 g sugars, 3 g pro.*

NIK SHARMA

Nik is the author and photographer behind the award-winning book *Season* and the blog *A Brown Table*. Born and raised in present-day Mumbai, Nik immigrated to the Midwest for grad school and worked as a molecular geneticist in Washington, D.C., before moving to the Bay Area and pursuing a food career full time.

TURMERIC TIPS

High levels of the antioxidant compound curcumin give the root sunny color and reputation to halt inflammation. Although many health claims are unsubstantiated as of yet, the flavorful perks of including turmeric in cooking are undeniable. Here's how:

BUYING Look for fresh turmeric in large grocery stores near fresh ginger and garlic or in specialty stores and Indian markets.

STORING Refrigerate fresh roots, unpeeled, up to 2 weeks. Keep ground spice in a cool, dark cabinet up to 6 months.

PREPPING To peel fresh turmeric, scrape away its thin, tender skin using a vegetable scrubber or a small metal spoon.

FIGHTING STAINS "Turmeric binds to alkaline ingredients, such as baking soda," Nik says. "Try mixing baking soda and soap to scrub out stains." Nik also suggests treating wooden spoons and utensils with mineral oil to seal the wood.

TOASTED NAAN AND CHICKEN SOUP

"If Indians had a version of chicken tortilla soup, this would be it," Nik says. Spice up the familiar with cardamom, cloves, turmeric, and garam masala (a spice blend that varies region to region—even cook to cook—in India).

TOTAL TIME 50 min.

	Seeds of 2 green cardamom pods
4	Tbsp. olive oil
1	cup finely diced red onion
2	cloves garlic, minced
1	tsp. ground Kashmiri chile*
1	tsp. Garam Masala (right)
½	tsp. ground turmeric
1	14.5-oz. can diced tomatoes, undrained
2	cups shredded cooked chicken
4	cups low-sodium chicken broth
1	cup fresh or frozen whole kernel corn, thawed
3	Tbsp. fresh lime juice
½	tsp. fine sea salt
2	naan
4	hard-boiled eggs, halved
3	Tbsp. fresh cilantro leaves
2	Tbsp. thinly sliced green onion
1	serrano pepper, seeded (if desired) and thinly sliced (tip, page 127)

1. Preheat oven to 350°F. Using a mortar and pestle or spice grinder, grind cardamom seeds. Heat 2 Tbsp. oil in a 4- to 5-qt. stockpot or Dutch oven over medium-high heat. Add onion; cook and stir 4 to 5 minutes or until translucent. Reduce heat to medium-low. Add cardamom, garlic, ground chile, Garam Masala, and turmeric. Cook 30 to 45 seconds or until fragrant.
2. Add tomatoes and juices. Cook 3 to 4 minutes, stirring occasionally. Stir in chicken. Cook 2 minutes. Add broth, corn, and lime juice. Increase heat to high; bring to boiling. Reduce heat; simmer gently, covered, 10 to 12 minutes or until corn is tender. Stir in salt. Let stand, covered, 10 minutes.
3. Meanwhile, cut naan into ¼-inch-wide strips; spread on a baking sheet. Drizzle remaining 2 Tbsp. oil. Bake 10 to 13 minutes or until golden brown. Cool (naan will crisp as it cools).
4. Garnish soup with toasted naan, hard-boiled eggs, cilantro, green onion, and serrano pepper. Makes 4 servings.

*Tip Mild Kashmiri chile colors this soup deep red. If you can't find ground Kashmiri, substitute ½ tsp. each smoked paprika and ground ancho chile powder.
PER SERVING *593 cal, 29 g fat, 248 g chol, 1,076 mg sodium, 46 g carb, 3 g fiber, 9 g sugars, 38 g pro.*

GARAM MASALA

Garam masala is a ground spice blend commonly used in Indian cuisines.

TOTAL TIME 10 min.

2	Tbsp. cumin seeds
2	Tbsp. coriander seeds
1	Tbsp. black peppercorns
2	dried bay leaves
1	2-inch cinnamon stick
12	whole cloves
1	tsp. black cardamom pods
1	tsp. green cardamom pods
1	tsp. freshly grated nutmeg
1	tsp. ground mace

Heat a small dry skillet over medium-high heat. Reduce heat and add cumin and coriander seeds, peppercorns, bay leaves, cinnamon stick, cloves, and black and green cardamom pods. Toast 30 to 45 seconds or until the spices become fragrant, shaking the pan. (If spices burn, discard and start fresh.) Transfer toasted spices to a mortar and pestle or spice grinder. Add nutmeg and mace; grind to a fine powder. Store in an airtight container in a cool, dark place up to 6 months.

GARAM MASALA

TURMERIC, GINGER, AND HONEY AFFOGATO

Photo on page 206.

"As a kid, whenever I got a cold, my dad would recommend a glass of hot milk with turmeric and honey," Nik says. "This is a playful take on those flavors—in ice cream form." Traditional affogato involves pouring espresso over ice cream or gelato, but Nik recommends coffee to avoid overwhelming the ice cream flavors.

HANDS-ON TIME 20 min.
TOTAL TIME 6 hr., includes chilling

2	cups whole milk
2	cups half-and-half
½	cup superfine granulated sugar
¼	cup honey
1	tsp. ground turmeric
½	tsp. fine sea salt
1½	Tbsp. cornstarch
3	oz. cream cheese, softened
1½	Tbsp. freshly grated ginger
	Strong freshly brewed coffee

1. In a Dutch oven or large saucepan combine milk, half-and-half, sugar, honey, turmeric, and salt. Cook and stir constantly over medium-high heat until milk starts to boil vigorously. In a small bowl whisk together cornstarch and 2 Tbsp. water. Whisk into milk mixture. (Reduce heat to medium if milk bubbles up too fast.) Boil 4 minutes, stirring constantly, or until mixture resembles custard and coats the back of a spoon.
2. Strain hot mixture through a sieve to remove solids if necessary. In a large bowl whisk hot mixture into cream cheese; chill 1 hour.
3. Using a garlic press or a piece of cheesecloth, squeeze and collect juice from grated ginger. Stir juice into ice cream base. Pour mixture into ice cream maker. Churn according to manufacturer's instructions. Transfer to a container. Freeze at least 4 hours.
4. To serve, scoop ice cream into dishes or mugs. Top with hot coffee. Makes 8 servings.
PER SERVING *249 cal, 12 g fat, 38 g chol, 239 mg sodium, 32 g carb, 30 g sugars, 5 g pro.*

TOASTED NAAN
AND CHICKEN
SOUP

"I RECOMMEND
COOKING TURMERIC
TO MELLOW
ITS FLAVOR. IT'S
PUNGENT RAW."

great starts
SIDE-DISH REVAMP

Turn a breakfast side into a filling meal with smoked Gouda, white cheddar, and savory mushrooms. This bowl may be humble grits' highest calling.

CHEESY GRITS BOWL

HANDS-ON TIME 15 min.
TOTAL TIME 25 min.

- 2 Tbsp. butter
- 4 cloves garlic, minced
- 3½ cups reduced-sodium chicken broth
- 1⅓ cups milk
- ¼ tsp. black pepper
- 1¼ cups quick-cooking grits
- 1 cup shredded smoked Gouda cheese (4 oz.)
- 1 cup shredded white cheddar cheese (4 oz.)
  Sautéed mushrooms, crème fraîche, and/or snipped fresh rosemary (optional)

1. In a large saucepan heat butter over medium heat. Add garlic; cook and stir 2 minutes. Stir in chicken broth, milk, and pepper. Bring to a simmer.

2. Add grits in a steady stream, stirring constantly. Reduce heat to medium-low. Cook and stir 6 to 8 minutes or until mixture thickens. Stir in cheeses until melted. If desired, top with sautéed mushrooms, crème fraîche, and/or rosemary. Makes 8 servings.

PER SERVING *253 cal, 13 g fat, 40 mg chol, 463 mg sodium, 23 g carb, 1 g fiber, 3 g sugars, 12 g pro.*

Chorizo Bowl Prepare as directed, except substitute Monterey Jack cheese for Gouda and add 1 finely chopped jalapeño (tip, page 59) with cheeses. Top with cooked chorizo or breakfast sausage, avocado, cilantro, and salsa.

Bacon and Eggs Prepare as directed, stirring chopped cooked bacon into grits with cheeses. Top each serving with an egg and bacon strips.

Spinach and Tomato Prepare as directed, except substitute mozzarella cheese for Gouda and stir 3 cups fresh baby spinach and 2 chopped roma tomatoes into grits with cheeses. Top with fresh basil and roasted tomatoes.

QUICK-COOKING GRITS ARE FINELY GROUND FOR A SPEEDY BOIL. (DON'T USE INSTANT HERE; PRECOOKED DEHYDRATED GRAINS WOULD TURN TO MUSH.)

gatherings
TABLE TALK

When cookbook author Julia Turshen hosts her culinary podcast *Keep Calm and Cook On*, she has a relaxed, comfortable style that sets her listeners at ease. She takes the same approach when she throws a party. Keep calm and host on.

Julia Turshen started cooking at such a young age that her family nickname was "Julia the Child." Before she was old enough to hold a chef's knife, she was hosting parties. Her first, a Valentine's Day soiree for her grandparents and assorted relatives, had a strict black-tie dress code and featured little sandwiches that 6-year-old Julia fancied up with a heart-shape cookie cutter. "It was all

very extra," Julia says with a laugh. "My entertaining style has gotten a whole lot more relaxed."

These days, Julia—who writes best-selling cookbooks and runs Equity at the Table, a database connecting underrepresented minorities in the food world—is much more likely to greet her guests in an untucked shirt and jeans.

Her enthusiasm for bringing people together, however, still flourishes. Most of Julia's gatherings are spontaneous and happen at the 150-year-old farmhouse in upstate New York that she shares with wife Grace Bonney, founder of the blog DesignSponge. "Because we live in a rural area without many restaurants, I cook at home every day," Julia says. "That makes it really easy to text friends and say, 'Hey, I bought too much chicken. Do you want to come over?'"

Julia believes good food can be uncomplicated. She serves simple dishes that are delicious hot or at room temperature, eliminating the stress of last-minute cooking. "I don't want to be stuck in the kitchen wondering if everyone is talking out there." She also makes sure to prepare meals that everyone will enjoy. So when inviting guests for the first time, she asks about food restrictions. "I don't want anyone to feel on the outside of my table, and that translates to what we're eating."

It's about more than delicious food, though. "What's most important to me is the quality of our time together," she says. "I want people to leave my home thinking, that was such a great night!" To that end, she loves to bring together friends from different circles whom she predicts will hit it off, then encourages them to get to know one another and hash out solutions to the dilemmas of the day. "I love that meaningful conversations start around my table, and my goal is to make sure they don't end there."

HIBISCUS PUNCH
Recipe on page 212

JULIA SETS UP A DRINK AND APPETIZER STATION TO ENCOURAGE INTERACTION— LOTS OF MIXING AND TASTING. "IT'S AN OPPORTUNITY FOR GUESTS TO GET TO KNOW EACH OTHER RIGHT AWAY."

OLD BAY BAGEL CHIPS

ROASTED GREEN ONION DIP

HIBISCUS PUNCH

Photo on pages 196 and 211.

A friend from the West Indies introduced Julia to this tea steeped with Caribbean spices—clove and ginger—then mixed with fresh citrus juices. It's a regular at her gatherings.

HANDS-ON TIME 10 min.
TOTAL TIME 55 min., includes cooling

¼ cup sugar
2 Tbsp. minced fresh ginger
6 whole cloves
4 hibiscus tea bags
1½ cups orange juice
1½ cups grapefruit juice
    Ice cubes
2 limes, thinly sliced

In a small pot combine sugar, ginger, cloves, and 2 cups water. Bring to boiling over high; cook and stir 1 minute or until sugar dissolves. Add tea bags. Cool to room temperature. Strain through a sieve into a large pitcher. Stir in citrus juices. If desired, chill up to 24 hours. Serve over ice with lime slices. Makes 8 servings.

Tip Serve alongside rum, sparkling wine, seltzer water, ginger ale, or other desired mixers.

PER SERVING *68 cal, 4 mg sodium, 17 g carb, 1 g fiber, 14 g sugars, 1 g pro.*

ROASTED GREEN ONION DIP

Two classics inspired this dip: green onion-cream cheese spread and French onion dip.

HANDS-ON TIME 10 min.
TOTAL TIME 1 hr.

24 green onions, trimmed and coarsely chopped
2 Tbsp. olive oil
    Kosher salt and black pepper
1 8-oz. pkg. cream cheese, cut up and softened
1 8-oz. carton sour cream
1 lemon, zested and juiced

1. Preheat oven to 425°F. Place green onions in a shallow baking pan. Drizzle with oil. Sprinkle with ½ tsp. salt; toss to coat. Spread in an even layer. Roast 15 to 20 minutes or until softened and browned in spots, stirring once. Cool.
2. Transfer onions to a food processor. Add cream cheese, sour cream, lemon zest and juice, and ½ tsp. salt; process until smooth. Or finely chop the onions; stir into remaining ingredients. Season to taste with salt and pepper. Chill up to 3 days. Makes 10 servings (2½ cups).
PER ¼-CUP SERVING *201 cal, 19 g fat, 45 mg chol, 175 mg sodium, 7 g carb, 1 g fiber, 3 g sugars, 3 g pro.*

OLD BAY BAGEL CHIPS

Toasted bagels and cream cheese— Julia's favorite childhood snack—get a grown-up makeover. The familiar seafood seasoning gives the bagels distinctive flavor.

HANDS-ON TIME 15 min.
TOTAL TIME 40 min.

4 plain unsliced bagels
¼ cup olive oil
2 Tbsp. Old Bay seasoning

1. Preheat oven to 300°F. Cut bagels in half crosswise, then cut each half into thin half-moons. Place slices on two baking sheets in a single layer. Drizzle bagel slices with 2 Tbsp. oil; sprinkle with 1 Tbsp. Old Bay seasoning. Turn slices over and repeat.
2. Bake 25 minutes or until golden brown, rotating baking sheets and turning chips once halfway through baking. Cool completely. (Chips will crisp as they cool.) Makes 8 servings.
Tip Store toasted bagel chips in an airtight container up to 24 hours.
PER SERVING *154 cal, 631 mg sodium, 19 g carb, 1 g fiber, 3 g sugars, 4 g pro.*

SHEET-PAN CHICKEN WITH PEACHES AND TOMATOES

Julia says this dish is as delicious at room temperature as it is hot out of the oven. Relax. Let the chicken stand for a bit while guests gather at the table.

HANDS-ON TIME 20 min.
TOTAL TIME 55 min.

- 1   lb. on-vine small tomatoes or cherry tomatoes
- 1   lb. peaches, cut into wedges
- 1   large red onion, cut into thin half-moons (2½ cups)
- 4   Tbsp. olive oil
- 1   tsp. salt
- 2   cloves garlic, minced
- 3   Tbsp. Dijon mustard
- 2   Tbsp. red wine vinegar
- 2   Tbsp. honey
- ½   tsp. freshly ground black pepper
- 8   8-oz. skinless, boneless chicken breast halves

1. Preheat oven to 450°F. Arrange tomatoes, peaches, and onion in a shallow baking pan. Drizzle with 2 Tbsp. oil; sprinkle with ½ tsp. salt. Toss to coat; spread in a single layer.
2. In a large bowl combine remaining 2 Tbsp. oil, the garlic, mustard, vinegar, honey, ½ tsp. salt, and pepper. Whisk to combine. Add chicken; turn to coat.*
3. Arrange chicken in a second baking pan. Drizzle with remaining mustard mixture. Place pans in oven on separate racks. Roast 20 to 25 minutes or until chicken is done (165°F), stirring tomato mixture halfway and rotating pans top to bottom. Transfer chicken to a cutting board. Let rest 10 minutes. Continue roasting tomatoes and peaches just until starting to brown.
4. Cut chicken into thick slices; transfer to a platter and top with tomato and peaches. Makes 8 servings.
*Tip If desired, brown chicken after coating with mustard mixture. In a 12-inch skillet heat 1 Tbsp. olive oil over medium-high heat. Cook half the chicken 2 minutes on each side or until browned. Transfer to a shallow baking pan. Repeat with remaining chicken and additional oil. Continue as directed in Step 3.
PER SERVING *414 cal, 14 g fat, 165 mg chol, 231 mg sodium, 17 g carb, 2 g fiber, 13 g sugars, 53 g pro.*

SHEET-PAN CHICKEN WITH PEACHES AND TOMATOES

AROMATIC RICE PILAF
Recipe on page 214

ZUCCHINI WITH PISTACHIOS AND MINT

Cook zucchini in two batches for the best browning.

TOTAL TIME 25 min.

3   lb. zucchini (4 to 6), trimmed and sliced into ½-inch-thick rounds
½   tsp. salt
¼   cup olive oil
2   Tbsp. red wine vinegar
½   cup roasted, salted pistachios, coarsely chopped
½   cup coarsely chopped fresh mint

Season zucchini with salt. In a 12-inch skillet heat 2 Tbsp. oil over medium-high heat. Add half the zucchini. Cook 5 minutes or until browned and crisp-tender, turning once. Transfer zucchini to a serving bowl. Repeat with remaining 2 Tbsp. oil and zucchini; add to serving bowl. Drizzle with vinegar. Sprinkle with half the pistachios and mint; gently toss. Top with remaining chopped pistachios and mint. Serve immediately or at room temperature. Makes 8 servings.

PER SERVING *136 cal, 11 g fat, 119 mg sodium, 8 g carb, 3 g fiber, 5 g sugars, 4 g pro.*

ZUCCHINI WITH PISTACHIOS AND MINT

AROMATIC RICE PILAF

Photo on page 213.

For a simple side dish Julia cooks fragrant basmati rice with fresh aromatics like garlic, onion, and ginger.

HANDS-ON TIME 15 min.
TOTAL TIME 35 min.

2   Tbsp. unsalted butter
2   Tbsp. olive oil
1½ cups minced yellow onion
4   cloves garlic, minced
2   Tbsp. minced fresh ginger
2   tsp. ground cinnamon
1½ cups basmati rice
3   Tbsp. tomato paste
3   cups chicken or vegetable stock
2   tsp. salt
½   cup golden raisins
½   cup unsalted roasted almonds, coarsely chopped
½   cup finely chopped flat-leaf parsley

1. In a large heavy pot melt butter and oil over medium-high heat. Add onion, garlic, ginger, and cinnamon. Cook and stir 5 minutes or until onion begins to soften. Stir in rice and tomato paste. Cook and stir 3 minutes or until rice is well-coated and smells nutty. Stir in stock and salt. Bring to boiling; reduce heat to low. Simmer, covered, 10 to 15 minutes or until rice is tender and liquid has evaporated.
2. Place a kitchen towel or paper towel between pot and lid to absorb liquid from steam (to keep rice fluffy). Let stand 10 minutes. Fluff with a fork. Stir in raisins, almonds, and parsley. Serve immediately or at room temperature. Makes 8 servings.
Make Ahead Prepare rice through Step 1. Cover as directed in Step 2; refrigerate up to 2 days. To reheat, spread rice on a baking pan. Bake at 425°F 10 minutes. Stir in raisins, almonds, and parsley.
PER SERVING *287 cal, 11 g fat, 8 mg chol, 514 mg sodium, 43 g carb, 3 g fiber, 9 g sugars, 6 g pro.*

ALMOND CAKE WITH FRUIT AND ROSÉ DRIZZLE

Bake this cake year-round and top it with any peak-season fruit. If rosé isn't your first pick, chose a dry red wine. The syrup color will be deeper.

HANDS-ON TIME 20 min.
TOTAL TIME 1 hr. 45 min., includes cooling

1   cup all-purpose flour
½   cup almond meal or flour*
1½ tsp. baking powder
½   tsp. kosher salt
2   large eggs
½   cup extra virgin olive oil
¼   cup buttermilk
½   cup plus 2 Tbsp. granulated sugar
½   tsp. almond extract
¾   cup dry rosé wine
2   cups assorted fresh fruit
    Powdered sugar

1. For cake: Preheat oven to 350°F. Coat an 8-inch cake pan with nonstick baking spray. In a bowl whisk together flours, baking powder, and salt.
2. In a large bowl whisk together eggs, oil, buttermilk, ½ cup sugar, and almond extract. Whisk until sugar is dissolved. (Test by rubbing the mixture between two fingers.) Stir in the flour mixture.
3. Pour batter into prepared cake pan. Bake 25 to 30 minutes or until golden brown and a toothpick inserted near center comes out clean. Cool completely in pan on wire rack. Transfer to a serving platter.
4. Meanwhile, for rosé syrup: In a small saucepan combine wine and remaining 2 Tbsp. sugar. Bring to boiling, stirring to dissolve sugar. Boil gently, uncovered, 8 to 10 minutes or until syrupy and reduced to about ½ cup; cool.
5. Top cake with fruit; drizzle with syrup. Sift powdered sugar on top. Makes 8 servings.
***Tip** Almond meal includes skins and is coarsely ground. Almond flour is finely ground blanched (no skins) almonds.
Make Ahead Prepare cake through Step 3. Wrap in plastic and store up to 3 days.
PER SERVING *339 cal, 19 g fat, 47 mg chol, 198 mg sodium, 36 g carb, 3 g fiber, 20 g sugars, 5 g pro.*

ALMOND CAKE
WITH FRUIT AND
ROSÉ DRIZZLE

**CARAMEL APPLE
POKE CAKE**
Recipe on page 232

october

Cool weather brings fall sports and plentiful apples—and we have inventive recipes for both. Pan-searing 101 is a cooking class to take in the comfort of your own kitchen.

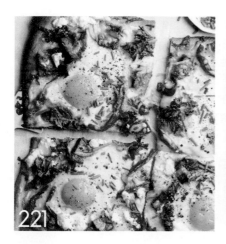
221

225

232

Pipe icing "laces" onto purchased mini ice cream sandwiches then insert crafts sticks.

GINGER-INFUSED
APPLE CIDER
Recipe on page 220

ITALIAN
PRESSED
SANDWICHES

TEAM SPIRIT
COOKIES
Recipe on page 220

ROASTED RED PEPPER
AND FETA DIP

TANGY SOUR CREAM
AND ONION DIP
Recipe on page 220

gatherings
PARTY GOALS

On game day, super fans get together to watch the play-by-play. The rest of the party is there for the socializing—and snacks. These no-stress concessions, easy serving ideas, and crafty touches tee up your winningest watch party yet. All sports fans (and snacks fans) welcome.

ITALIAN PRESSED SANDWICHES

Customize these sandwiches to your preference and stock your pantry. For crispy sandwiches, pat nearly dry any moist foods.

HANDS-ON TIME 10 min.
TOTAL TIME 20 min.

- 1 ciabatta or focaccia loaf (approximately 1 lb.), halved horizontally
- 8 oz. thinly sliced salami, prosciutto, and/or capicola
- 1 6-oz. jar marinated artichoke hearts, drained and chopped
- 4 oz. thinly sliced provolone
- ½ cup fresh basil leaves
- 2 to 3 Tbsp. green or black olive tapenade

1. On loaf bottom layer meat, artichoke hearts, provolone cheese, and basil. Spread top half with tapenade; place on bottom half. Wrap in heavy foil. (To tote, store wrapped sandwiches in an insulated cooler until ready to grill.)
2. Place foil-wrapped sandwich on grill rack; place a foil-covered brick on top to weight it down. Grill, covered, over medium heat 10 to 15 minutes or until cheese is melted, turning once. Makes 8 to 10 servings.
PER SERVING *334 cal, 16 g fat, 40 mg chol, 1,127 mg sodium, 30 g carb, 1 g fiber, 1 g sugars, 15 g pro.*

Veggie Pressed Sandwiches Layer loaf bottom with 6 oz. thin lengthwise slices of zucchini; ½ cup roasted red bell peppers (patted dry); ¼ cup thin red onion wedges; and 8 oz. fresh mozzarella slices. Top with ¼ cup bruschetta topping. Spread 2 to 3 Tbsp. basil pesto on top half; place on bottom half. Wrap in heavy foil. Continue as directed in Step 2.

ROASTED RED PEPPER AND FETA DIP

HANDS-ON TIME 25 min.
TOTAL TIME 1 hr. 10 min.

- 1 onion, cut into ½-inch wedges
- 4 cloves garlic (unpeeled)
- 2 Tbsp. olive oil
- 1 cup bottled roasted red bell peppers, drained (or see "How to Roast Peppers," right)
- 1 cup crumbled feta cheese (4 oz.)
- 2 Tbsp. fresh oregano leaves
- 2 Tbsp. lemon juice
- ¼ tsp. salt
- ⅛ to ¼ tsp. crushed red pepper Chopped roasted peppers, feta, and/or fresh oregano (optional)

1. Preheat oven to 425°F. Line a baking sheet with foil. Add onion and garlic. Brush with some of the oil. Roast 30 to 35 minutes or until onion wedges and garlic are tender.
2. In a food processor combine peppers and onion. Squeeze garlic cloves from paper husks into processor. Add remaining oil, feta, oregano, lemon juice, salt, and crushed red pepper. Cover; pulse until nearly smooth.
3. Transfer dip to a serving bowl. If desired, top with additional chopped roasted peppers, feta, and/or oregano. Makes 12 servings (1½ cups).
PER 2-TBSP. SERVING *118 cal, 9 g fat, 17 mg chol, 223 mg sodium, 7 g carb, 1 g fiber, 4 g sugars, 4 g pro.*

HOW TO ROAST PEPPERS

To roast bell peppers for Roasted Red Pepper and Feta Dip, place two peppers on the baking sheet with onion and garlic. Brush with olive oil. Roast as directed in Step 1 until pepper skins are blistered. Enclose peppers in foil; let stand 15 minutes. Peel and discard skins, stems, seeds, and membranes. Cut peppers in strips.

A MIX OF PURCHASED AND MAKE-AHEAD SNACKS MEANS THE ONLY PARTY-TIME STRESSOR IS GUESSING WHO WILL WIN THE BIG GAME.

TANGY SOUR CREAM AND ONION DIP

Photo on page 218.

HANDS-ON TIME 30 min.
TOTAL TIME 2 hr. 30 min., includes chilling

2   Tbsp. olive oil
1   cup chopped onion
    Pinch sugar
    Pinch salt
1   clove garlic, minced
½   cup sour cream
½   cup mayonnaise
½   cup plain Greek yogurt
    Black pepper
    Crisp bacon, crumbled, and/or
    fresh snipped chives (optional)

1. In an 8-inch skillet heat oil over medium-low heat. Add onion, sugar, and salt. Cook 15 minutes or until lightly browned, stirring occasionally. Add garlic; cook 3 to 5 minutes or until onion is golden and caramelized.

2. Transfer onion mixture to a bowl; cool 5 minutes. Stir in sour cream, mayonnaise, and yogurt. Season with pepper. Chill at least 2 hours before serving or up to 24 hours. If desired, top with crumbled bacon and/or snipped chives. Makes 12 servings (1½ cups).
PER 2-TBSP. SERVING *113 cal, 11 g fat, 10 mg chol, 113 mg sodium, 2 g carb, 1 g sugars, 1 g pro.*

GINGER BOURBON COCKTAIL

TOTAL TIME 10 minutes

1   tsp. grated fresh ginger
     Few dashes orange bitters
     Ice cubes
⅔   cup apple cider
1½   oz. (3 Tbsp.) bourbon
     Thinly sliced fresh ginger and thinly
     sliced apple (optional)

In a cocktail shaker combine grated ginger and bitters. Mash together with a cocktail muddler or wooden spoon. Add ice cubes, apple cider, and bourbon. Cover and shake until well chilled. Strain through a small fine-mesh sieve into an ice-filled glass. If desired, garnish with ginger and apple slices. Makes 1 serving.
PER SERVING *185 cal, 18 mg sodium, 21 g carb, 18 g sugar.*

Ginger-Infused Apple Cider In a small saucepan combine ⅔ cup apple cider and three thin slices fresh ginger. Bring to boiling. Transfer cider and ginger to a small bowl. Chill, covered, 1 hour or until cold. Makes 1 serving.

**GINGER-INFUSED
APPLE CIDER**

TEAM SPIRIT COOKIES

Photo on page 218.

Use letter shape cutters to cut dough, then frost with Royal Icing tinted in team colors. This recipe stands in for holiday cutouts too.

HANDS-ON TIME 30 min.
TOTAL TIME 2 hr., includes chilling

1⅓   cups butter, softened
⅔   cup sugar
1   tsp. baking powder
½   tsp. salt
2   eggs
2   tsp. vanilla
3   cups all-purpose flour
     Royal Icing
     Sprinkles

1. Preheat oven to 375°F. In a large bowl beat butter with an electric mixer on medium 30 seconds. Add sugar, baking powder, and salt; beat until combined. Beat in eggs and vanilla. Beat in as much flour as you can; stir in remaining flour. Divide dough in half; wrap each half in plastic wrap. Chill 30 to 60 minutes or until dough is easy to handle.
2. On a lightly floured surface, roll one dough portion to ¼-inch thickness. Using 2½-inch round or letter cutters, cut out dough. Arrange 2 inches apart on ungreased cookie sheets. Reroll and cut scraps. Bake 7 minutes or until edges are firm and lightly browned. Cool on a wire rack. Repeat with remaining dough. Decorate with Royal Icing and sprinkles. Makes about 48 cookies.

Royal Icing In a large bowl stir together 4 cups powdered sugar, 3 Tbsp. meringue powder, and ½ tsp. cream of tartar. Add ½ cup warm water and 1 tsp. vanilla. Beat with an electric mixer on low until combined. Beat on high 7 to 10 minutes or until icing is very stiff. Stir in food coloring. If not using immediately, cover bowl with a damp paper towel then cover tightly with plastic wrap. (Icing will dry out quickly when exposed to air.) Chill up to 48 hours. Stir before using.
PER COOKIE *88 cal, 5 g fat, 21 mg chol, 78 mg sodium, 9 g carb, 3 g sugars, 1 g pro.*

great starts
BLUE PLATE SPECIAL

Reimagine a good ol' diner mainstay—steak and eggs—as a breakfast pizza. Made with purchased dough and leftover steak, it's simple enough to pull off while your coffee kicks in.

STEAK AND EGG BREAKFAST PIZZA

HANDS-ON TIME 25 min.
TOTAL TIME 50 min.

1   **13.8-oz. pkg. refrigerated pizza dough**
     Olive oil
4   **oz. cooked steak, thinly sliced**
3   **cloves garlic, thinly sliced**
1½ **cups shredded mozzarella cheese (6 oz.)**
½   **cup torn kale leaves**
¼   **cup roasted red bell pepper strips**
½   **cup crumbled goat cheese (2 oz.)**
6   **eggs**
     Black pepper
1   **Tbsp. chopped fresh chives**

1. Preheat oven to 400°F. On a large lightly greased baking sheet stretch pizza dough into a 15×12-inch rectangle. Bake 6 minutes or just until set; cool slightly.
2. Brush dough with olive oil. Top with steak, garlic, mozzarella, kale, red pepper, and goat cheese. Break eggs onto pizza (or break eggs, individually, into a measuring cup and slide onto the pizza), 2 inches apart. Sprinkle pizza with black pepper.
3. Bake 18 minutes or until crust is golden, egg whites are set, and yolks begin to thicken. Top with chives. Makes 6 servings.
PER SERVING *397 cal, 18 g fat, 224 mg chol, 663 mg sodium, 34 g carb, 1 g fiber, 1 g sugars, 25 g pro.*

how to cook
PAN-SEARING

Mastering this simple technique results in meltingly tender meat with silky pan sauce to spoon over.

The basics of pan-searing meat, fish, or poultry are straightforward. Heat a pan, cook the meat until it has a char on both sides, then let it rest on a plate while stirring browned bits in the skillet into a quick sauce. It's the kind of one-pan dish that'll wow company yet is easy enough to pull off any night. We tasked our Test Kitchen with pinpointing the crucial steps to get a richly caramelized crust, juicy and flavorful interior, and a sauce so irresistible you'll be tempted to eat it straight from the skillet.

WHAT'S LEFT FROM THE SEAR IS THE FLAVORFUL START FOR A QUICK PAN SAUCE.

SECRETS TO THE SEAR

SEASON AND CHILL Rub kosher salt onto the meat and chill 2 hours for the seasoning to penetrate the meat. Salt initially draws out some moisture, and as muscle fibers break down, the meat reabsorbs that moisture to ensure juiciness.

CHOOSE THE RIGHT PAN For best results, pull out your heaviest pan that heats evenly. Cast iron is always a sure bet. So is carbon steel or stainless steel with a copper or aluminum layer. Skip nonstick; most don't retain heat evenly.

TURN UP THE BURNER Medium-high ensures an even char without smoking up your kitchen. Heat the skillet 2 to 3 minutes, then flick in a large drop of water. If it rolls around like a bead, the pan is ready. (Note: The water won't bead in cast iron, but it should immediately evaporate.) Add 2 Tbsp. oil and swirl to coat pan bottom. Opt for a neutral oil with a high smoke point (vegetable, grapeseed, or canola). Avoid butter and olive oil, which can burn at high heat.

BE PATIENT After adding meat to the pan, exhibit restraint with your tongs: Flipping too often or too soon prevents a crust from forming. If the meat sticks a bit when you try to flip it, let it cook a few more minutes. The meat will easily release once it has developed a crust.

THE PAN SAUCE BLUEPRINT

DEGLAZE THE PAN While the meat rests (to lock in prized juices), make the pan sauce. Remove the pan from the burner to prevent splatters. Pour in a flavorful liquid like wine, vinegar, or citrus juice to deglaze the pan (loosen browned bits on the bottom). If you want to toss in aromatics like garlic or shallots for extra flavor, add them with the liquid. Return the pan to the heat and scrape up the browned bits with a wooden spoon.

CONCENTRATE THE FLAVOR Bring the sauce to boiling and cook 5 to 10 minutes or until reduced by about half, stirring constantly.

FINISH THE SAUCE A little fat from butter or cream yields rich, velvety texture. Remove the pan from the heat and whisk in the fat to emulsify. If you want to add fresh herbs, do so at this point.

MEAT NEEDS ROOM IN THE PAN—TOO LITTLE AND IT WILL STEAM INSTEAD OF SEAR. IF NEEDED, COOK IN BATCHES FOR THE BEST CHAR.

**MUSTARD-
SHALLOT PORK**
Recipe on page 226

CHIPOTLE CHICKEN

ONCE YOU MASTER THE BASICS, APPLY THE TECHNIQUE TO ANY NUMBER OF MEATS, POULTRY, FISH, OR EVEN HEARTY VEGETABLES. TRY ONE OF OUR FAVORITE COMBINATIONS OR EXPERIMENT WITH THE LIQUIDS, AROMATICS, AND HERBS.

CHIPOTLE CHICKEN

HANDS-ON TIME 15 min.
TOTAL TIME 3 hr. includes chilling time

1   to 1½ lb. skinless, boneless chicken breast halves
    Kosher salt
    Freshly ground black pepper
2   Tbsp. vegetable oil
¾   cup reduced-sodium chicken broth
3   Tbsp. lime juice
4   cloves garlic, minced
2   Tbsp. butter
1   chipotle chile pepper in adobo sauce, finely chopped
    Chopped fresh cilantro

1. Season chicken generously with salt and pepper. Place on a plate. Chill, uncovered, 2 hours. Remove from refrigerator; let stand at room temperature 30 minutes. Heat a heavy 12-inch skillet over medium-high heat 2 to 3 minutes or until very hot.
2. Remove skillet from heat; add oil. Swirl to coat bottom of skillet. Return to medium-high heat. Add chicken (don't crowd skillet). Cook 5 minutes or until a browned crust forms on bottom. Turn; cook 5 to 7 minutes more or until chicken is done (170°F).
3. Transfer chicken to a plate; cover loosely. Remove skillet from heat. Carefully add broth, lime juice, and garlic to skillet; return to heat. Bring to boiling, scraping up browned bits in skillet. Boil gently, uncovered, 5 minutes or until reduced by about half. Remove from heat. Whisk in butter, chipotle, and any juices from the chicken.
4. Spoon sauce over chicken. Sprinkle with cilantro. Makes 4 servings.
PER SERVING *259 cal, 15 g fat, 98 mg chol, 361 mg sodium, 3 g carb, 1 g sugars, 26 g pro.*

LEMON SCALLOPS

Photo on page 228.
HANDS-ON TIME 15 min.
TOTAL TIME 2 hr. 50 min.

1   to 1½ lb. sea scallops
    Kosher salt
    Freshly ground black pepper
2   Tbsp. vegetable oil
½   cup dry white wine
¼   cup reduced-sodium chicken broth
3   Tbsp. lemon juice
2   cloves garlic, minced
2   Tbsp. butter
    Chopped fresh mint

1. Pat scallops dry. Generously season scallops with salt and pepper. Place on a plate. Chill, uncovered, 2 hours. Remove from refrigerator and let stand at room temperature 30 minutes.
2. Heat a heavy 12-inch skillet over medium-high heat 2 to 3 minutes or until very hot.
3. Remove skillet from heat; add oil. Swirl to coat bottom of skillet. Return to medium-high heat. Add scallops, half at a time. Cook 2 minutes or until browned and a crust forms on bottom. Turn and cook 2 minutes more or until opaque.
4. Transfer scallops to a plate; cover loosely. Remove skillet from heat. Carefully add wine, broth, lemon juice, and garlic. Return to heat. Bring to boiling, scraping up browned bits in skillet. Boil gently, uncovered, 5 minutes or until reduced by about half. Remove from heat. Whisk in the butter.
5. Spoon sauce over scallops. Sprinkle with mint. Makes 4 servings.
PER SERVING *220 cal, 13 g fat, 42 mg chol, 807 mg sodium, 6 g carb, 1 g sugars, 14 g pro.*

ORANGE SQUASH

Photo on page 229.

TOTAL TIME 30 min.

1   2- to 2½-lb. butternut squash,
     peeled, seeds removed, and cut
     into ½-inch-thick slices
     Kosher salt
     Freshly ground black pepper
2   Tbsp. vegetable oil, plus more as
     needed
½   cup vegetable broth
½   cup orange juice
4   cloves garlic, minced
2   Tbsp. butter
1   Tbsp. chopped fresh sage

1. Season squash with salt and pepper.
Heat a heavy 12-inch skillet over medium-
high heat 2 to 3 minutes or until very hot.
2. Remove skillet from heat; add oil.
Swirl to coat bottom of skillet. Return to
medium-high heat. Add half the squash;
cook 2½ to 3 minutes or until browned
and a crust forms on bottom. Turn and
cook 4 to 5 minutes more or until tender,
reducing heat to medium, if necessary, to
prevent overbrowning.
3. Transfer squash to a serving platter;
cover loosely and keep warm. Repeat with
remaining squash, adding additional oil if
needed. Remove skillet from heat. Carefully
add broth, juice, and garlic. Return to
heat. Bring to boiling, stirring to scrape
up browned bits. Boil gently, uncovered,
5 minutes or until reduced by about
half. Remove from heat. Whisk in butter
and sage.
4. Spoon sauce over squash. Top
with additional sage if desired. Makes
4 servings.
PER SERVING *218 cal, 13 g fat, 15 mg chol,
276 mg sodium, 27 g carb, 4 g fiber, 7 g
sugars, 2 g pro.*

MUSTARD-SHALLOT PORK

Photo on page 223.

HANDS-ON TIME 25 min.
TOTAL TIME 2 hr. 50 min.

4   bone-in pork loin chops, 1¼ to
     1½ inches thick
     Kosher salt
     Freshly ground black pepper
2   Tbsp. vegetable oil
1   cup dry white wine
¼   cup finely chopped shallot
2   Tbsp. butter
1   Tbsp. Dijon mustard
     Chopped flat-leaf parsley

1. Generously season pork with salt
and pepper. Place on a plate. Chill,
uncovered, 2 hours. Remove from
refrigerator and let stand 30 minutes.
Heat a heavy 12-inch skillet over
medium-high heat 2 to 3 minutes. (To
check when skillet is hot, add a large
drop of water [⅛ tsp.] to skillet. When it
rolls around the pan it is ready.)
2. Remove from heat; add oil. Swirl
to coat bottom of skillet. Return to
medium-high heat. Add two pork chops.
Cook 5 to 7 minutes or until a crust forms
(be patient; the pork will release when it's
ready to be turned). Turn and cook 5 to
7 minutes more or until done (145°F).
3. Transfer meat to a plate; cover loosely
and keep warm. Repeat with remaining
two pork chops. Remove skillet from
heat. Carefully add wine and shallot to
skillet. Return to heat. Bring to boiling,
scraping up browned bits in skillet. Boil
gently, uncovered, 8 to 10 minutes or
until reduced by about half and slightly
thickened. Remove from heat. Whisk in
butter and mustard.
4. Spoon sauce over pork. Sprinkle with
parsley. Makes 8 servings.
PER SERVING *719 cal, 28 g fat, 267 mg
chol, 689 mg sodium, 3 g carb, 1 g
sugars, 103 g pro.*

GINGER-MISO BEEF

HANDS-ON TIME 10 min.
TOTAL TIME 2 hr. 50 min.

4   beef tenderloin steaks (filet
     mignon), cut 1 to 1¼ inches thick
     Kosher salt
     Freshly ground black pepper
2   Tbsp. vegetable oil
⅔   cup rice wine
2   Tbsp. white miso paste
2   Tbsp. reduced-sodium soy sauce
2   Tbsp. butter
¼   cup thinly sliced green onion
1   tsp. grated fresh ginger
     Toasted sesame seeds

1. Generously season beef with salt
and pepper. Place on a plate. Chill,
uncovered, 2 hours. Remove and let
stand 30 minutes. Heat a heavy 12-inch
skillet over medium-high heat 2 to
3 minutes or until very hot.
2. Remove from heat; add oil. Swirl to
coat bottom of skillet. Return to medium-
high heat. Add beef. Cook 5 minutes or
until browned and a crust forms. Turn
and cook 2 to 4 minutes more or until
done (135°F).
3. Transfer beef to a clean plate; cover
loosely. Remove skillet from heat.
Carefully add wine, miso, and soy sauce.
Return to heat. Bring to boiling, scraping
up browned bits in skillet. Remove from
heat. Whisk in butter, green onions,
and ginger.
4. Spoon sauce over beef. Sprinkle with
sesame seeds. Makes 4 servings.
PER SERVING *369 cal, 21 g fat, 89 mg
chol, 878 mg sodium, 7 g carb, 1 g fiber,
1 g sugars, 27 g pro.*

GINGER-MISO
BEEF

LEMON SCALLOPS
Recipe on page 225

ORANGE SQUASH
Recipe on page 226

FALL'S FAVORITE FRUIT

Sure, you can find apples in the grocery store year-round, but fall marks their heyday—when they're the juiciest and most flavorful. With these sweet and savory recipes, "an apple a day" is an easy goal.

SPICED CIDER DONUTS

*Dough is spiced with smoky
ancho chile powder heat or a hit
of cardamom, then fried, baked,
or air-fried.*

HANDS-ON TIME 45 min.
TOTAL TIME 3 hr.

3¼ to 3¾ cups all-purpose flour
2 pkg. active dry yeast (4½ tsp.)
1½ tsp. ancho chile powder or ground
   cardamom
¾ cup peeled, cored, and finely
   chopped apple (1 small)
½ cup butter
½ cup apple cider or apple juice
¼ cup milk
¼ cup sugar
1 tsp. salt
2 eggs, lightly beaten
   Vegetable oil for deep-fat frying
   Spiced Glaze

1. In a large bowl stir together 1¾ cups
flour, the yeast, and chile powder. In a
medium saucepan heat and stir apple,
butter, cider, milk, sugar, and salt just
until warm (120°F to 130°F) and butter is
almost melted. Add cider mixture and
eggs to flour mixture. Stir to combine. Stir
in as much remaining flour as you can.
2. Turn dough out onto a lightly floured
surface. Knead in enough remaining
flour to make a moderately soft dough
that is smooth and elastic (3 to 5 minutes
total; dough will be slightly sticky). Shape
into a ball. Place in a lightly greased
bowl, turning once to grease surface of
dough. Cover; let rise in a warm place
until double in size (1 to 1½ hours).
3. Punch dough down. Turn out onto
a lightly floured surface. Divide in half.
Cover; let rest 10 minutes. Line a large
baking sheet with parchment paper;
lightly dust with flour.
4. Roll each dough half to ½-inch
thickness. Cut dough with a floured
2½-inch donut cutter, dipping it into flour
between cuts. Reroll scraps as necessary.
Place donuts and donut holes on
prepared baking sheet. Cover with a light
kitchen towel; let rise in a warm place
until double in size (45 to 60 minutes).

5. Choose an option to cook donuts:
fry, bake, or air-fry. **To fry donuts:** In a
3-qt. heavy saucepan heat 1½ inches
oil over medium heat to 365°F. (If
using an electric deep-fat fryer, follow
manufacturer's directions.) Fry donuts,
two or three at a time, 2 minutes or until
golden brown, turning once. (To prevent
donuts from absorbing too much oil, use
a deep-fry thermometer to maintain oil
temperature at 365°F.) Remove donuts
with a slotted spoon. Drain on paper
towels. **To bake donuts:** Preheat oven to
350°F. Bake 12 to 15 minutes or just until
bottoms are golden. **To air-fry donuts:**
Spritz donuts with vegetable oil spray.

Air-fry, in batches, 4 to 5 minutes or just
until bottoms are golden.
6. Dip tops of donuts and holes in Spiced
Glaze. Let stand until glaze is set. Makes
21 donuts plus holes.

Spiced Glaze In a small bowl combine
2 cups powdered sugar and ¼ tsp. ancho
chile powder or ground cardamom. Stir
in enough milk (2 to 3 Tbsp.) to make a
thin icing consistency.
PER DONUT *319 cal, 21 g fat, 30 mg chol,
156 mg sodium, 31 g carb, 1 g fiber, 15 g
sugars, 3 g pro.*

CARAMEL APPLE POKE CAKE

Photo on page 216.

This recipe, a take on popular poke cakes from the '70s, calls for dulce de leche in place of gelatin. Even the whipped cream topping gets an update.

HANDS-ON TIME 25 min.
TOTAL TIME 3 hr.

2 cups all-purpose flour
2 tsp. baking powder
½ tsp. baking soda
½ tsp. salt
⅔ cup butter, softened
1 cup sugar
2 eggs, room temperature
1 tsp. vanilla
½ cup apple butter (no added pectin)
3 cups finely chopped apples (about 3 medium)
¼ cup milk
1 14-oz. can dulce de leche
1 cup heavy cream
1 tsp. vanilla

1. Preheat oven to 350°F. Grease and flour two 8×4-inch or 9×5-inch loaf pans.
2. In a medium bowl whisk together flour, baking powder, baking soda, and salt.
3. In a large bowl beat butter with an electric mixer on medium 30 seconds. Gradually add sugar, ¼ cup at a time, beating until combined. Scrape bowl; beat 2 minutes more. Add eggs, one at a time, beating after each addition. Beat in 1 tsp. vanilla. Alternately add flour mixture and apple butter, beating on low after each addition until well combined. Fold in apples. Divide batter between pans; smooth tops.
4. Bake 40 minutes or until tops are golden and a toothpick inserted in center comes out clean. Cool cakes in pans on a wire rack 10 minutes. Remove cakes from pans. Place top sides up on wire racks. Using the handle of a wooden spoon, poke ¼- to ½-inch holes about 1½ to 2 inches apart and three-fourths through cakes.
5. In a bowl whisk milk into dulce de leche until smooth. Reserve 2 Tbsp. for whipped topping, and ½ cup for serving.

6. Slowly spread remaining ¾ cup dulce de leche mixture over cakes, seeping into holes. Cool completely. In a large chilled bowl beat heavy cream, the 2 Tbsp. reserved dulce de leche mixture, and 1 tsp. vanilla on medium until stiff peaks form (tips stand straight). Before serving, top cakes with whipped cream and drizzle with reserved ½ cup dulce de leche mixture. Makes 16 servings.
PER SERVING *374 cal, 16 g fat, 68 mg chol, 286 mg sodium, 53 g carb, 1 g fiber, 37 g sugars, 5 g pro.*

MARBLED CARAMEL APPLES

What's better than a caramel apple? A caramel apple finished with a layer of marbled chocolate. A quick dip and twist creates delicious edible spin art.

HANDS-ON TIME 30 min.
TOTAL TIME 2 hr.

8 small apples (3 to 4 oz. each)
16 oz. vanilla caramels, unwrapped
1½ Tbsp. heavy cream
12 oz. chocolate-flavor candy coating, chopped, or chocolate candy melts
8 oz. vanilla-flavor candy coating, chopped, or white candy melts

1. Line a large baking sheet with parchment paper. Insert candy apple sticks or skewers into stem ends of apples. Place caramels and cream in a 2-cup microwave-safe glass measuring cup. Microwave on high 1 to 1½ minutes or until smooth and flowing freely, stirring every 30 seconds. Dip apples into caramel mixture to coat, allowing excess to drip back into cup. Place coated apples on prepared baking sheet. Let stand 1 hour or until set.
2. Place chocolate candy coating in a medium microwave-safe bowl. Microwave on high 1 to 2 minutes or until coating is melted and smooth, stirring

every 30 seconds. In a separate bowl melt vanilla candy coating. Transfer three-quarters of the chocolate candy coating to a microwave-safe 2-cup glass measuring cup. Place remaining melted chocolate candy coating in a small resealable plastic bag. Transfer all the vanilla candy coating to a resealable plastic bag. Snip a small hole in a corner of each bag.
3. Heavily drizzle white candy coating over chocolate candy coating in the 2-cup glass measuring cup, lines in one direction. Lightly drizzle chocolate candy coating over white drizzles perpendicular to white lines. Drizzle more white candy coating over chocolate drizzles, lines perpendicular to previous layer. Dip each caramel apple half to two-thirds into mixture. As you lift the apple, twist it to swirl and marble the coating. Return apple to parchment. Scrape down candy coating from sides of measuring cup, but do not stir. Redo drizzles on surface of candy coating between dipping apple. Let apples stand 30 minutes or until set. Makes 8 caramel apples.
PER APPLE *590 cal, 26 g fat, 3 mg chol, 167 mg sodium, 86 g carb, 2 g fiber, 65 g sugars, 3 g pro.*

MARBLED
CARAMEL
APPLES

APPLES AND PORK ARE OLD PALS, AND THIS STUFFED PORK LOIN PLAYS ON THE CLASSIC COMBO IN A SURPRISINGLY MANAGEABLE ROLLED PRESENTATION THAT'S IMPRESSIVE ENOUGH FOR A FALL DINNER PARTY.

FRUIT-STUFFED PORK ROAST

We plumped dried fruit with balsamic vinegar and tossed it with onions and thyme to nudge this stuffing more savory, less sweet. If you don't have mixed dried fruit bits, substitute 1½ cups snipped dried apricots, sweetened dried cranberries, and/or golden raisins.

HANDS-ON TIME 25 min.
TOTAL TIME 2 hr. 40 min.

1½	cups mixed dried fruit bits
⅓	cup apple juice
¼	cup plus 1 Tbsp. white balsamic or cider vinegar
½	cup finely chopped onion
1	tsp. fresh chopped thyme leaves
¼	tsp. salt
¼	tsp. black pepper
1	3- to 4-lb. boneless pork top loin roast
2	medium onions, cut into wedges
2	Tbsp. butter, melted
1	Tbsp. olive oil
⅓	cup red currant jelly
2	medium apples, cored and cut into wedges
	Fresh thyme leaves (optional)

1. For stuffing: In a small saucepan combine dried fruit, apple juice, and ¼ cup vinegar. Bring to boiling over medium-high. Boil gently, uncovered, 2 minutes. Remove from heat. Let stand 30 minutes. Stir in chopped onion, chopped thyme, salt, and pepper.

2. Preheat oven to 425°F. Butterfly pork loin (see "How to Butterfly," right). If some areas are thicker than others, lay a piece of plastic wrap on top and pound thick areas with the flat side of a meat mallet.

3. Season meat lightly with additional salt and pepper. Spoon stuffing onto meat. Starting from a short side, roll into a spiral. Tie securely with 100-percent-cotton kitchen string.

4. Place onion wedges in a shallow roasting pan. Drizzle with 1 Tbsp. melted butter and the olive oil; toss to coat. Arrange onion wedges in an even layer. Place meat on onions. Season roast with additional salt and pepper.

5. Roast, uncovered, 30 minutes. Reduce oven temperature to 325°F; roast 30 minutes more.

6. Meanwhile, in a small saucepan melt jelly over low. Remove from heat. Stir in remaining 1 Tbsp. vinegar.

7. Place apple wedges in a medium bowl. Drizzle with remaining 1 Tbsp. melted butter; toss to coat. Arrange apples in roasting pan around roast. Brush meat, onions, and apples with jelly mixture. Roast 30 to 45 minutes more or until a thermometer inserted in meat registers 145°F. Remove from oven. Cover meat with foil; let stand 15 minutes before slicing. If desired, top with additional thyme. Serve with onions and apples. Makes 10 servings.

PER SERVING *318 cal, 7 g fat, 80 mg chol, 360 mg sodium, 36 g carb, 3 g fiber, 27 g sugars, 27 g pro.*

HOW TO BUTTERFLY

SLICE ALONG CENTER Place pork loin fat side down on a large cutting board. Using a long sharp knife, cut lengthwise along the center, leaving ½ inch intact, to open like a book.

CUT AND UNROLL Place knife at the base of the V, blade perpendicular to first cut. Using shallow slices and the cutting board as a guide, cut through the left side, maintaining a ½- to ¾-inch thickness and opening loin.

REPEAT ON OPPOSITE SIDE Make shallow slices and unroll to a flat surface and relatively even thickness across the entire piece of meat.

CHICKEN-APPLE BURGERS

The internal color of a burger is not a reliable doneness indicator. A chicken patty cooked to 165°F is safe, regardless of color.

HANDS-ON TIME 40 min.
TOTAL TIME 55 min.

- 4 slices bacon, chopped
- ½ cup finely chopped onion
- 1 Tbsp. minced garlic
- ½ tsp. black pepper
- ¼ tsp. salt
- ¼ cup apple brandy, apple juice, or dry white wine
- ⅔ cup cored and finely chopped Granny Smith apple (1 medium)
- 2 Tbsp. snipped fresh flat-leaf parsley
- 1 tsp. snipped fresh sage
- 2 lb. uncooked ground chicken
- 1 cup soft bread crumbs
- 6 pretzel buns or hamburger buns, split and toasted
- 6 grilled apple slices (optional) Toppings, such as whole grain mustard, applewood-smoked bacon, grilled red onion slices, lettuce, and/or cheese (optional)

1. For apple mixture: In a large skillet cook chopped bacon until crisp. Drain bacon on paper towels, reserving 1 tsp. drippings in skillet. Add onion, garlic, pepper, and salt to skillet. Cook 3 minutes or until onion is tender, stirring occasionally. Carefully add apple brandy. Simmer, uncovered, until nearly all the brandy evaporates. Remove from heat. Stir in bacon, chopped apple, parsley, and sage; cool.

2. In a large bowl combine ground chicken, bread crumbs, and apple mixture. Divide mixture into six portions; shape each portion into a 4-inch diameter patty.

3. Grill patties, covered, over medium heat 14 to 18 minutes or until done (165°F), turning once halfway through. Serve burgers on buns with grilled apple slices and/or toppings. Makes 6 servings.

PER SERVING *558 cal, 21 g fat, 136 mg chol, 696 mg sodium, 56 g carb, 3 g fiber, 7 g sugars, 37 g pro.*

CHICKEN-APPLE BURGERS

SPICED APPLESAUCE

HANDS-ON TIME 1 hr.
TOTAL TIME 1 hr. 25 min.

8   lb. cooking apples, cored and quartered
¼   cup fresh-squeezed lemon juice, strained
10 inches stick cinnamon
1½ tsp. apple pie spice
¾   to 1¼ cups packed brown sugar

1. In an 8- to 10-qt. heavy pot or Dutch oven combine apples, 2 cups water, the lemon juice, cinnamon, and apple pie spice. Bring to boiling; reduce heat. Simmer, covered, 25 to 30 minutes or until apples are very tender, stirring often. Discard stick cinnamon.
2. Press apples through a food mill or sieve. Return pulp to pot; discard skins. Stir in brown sugar to taste. If necessary, add ½ to 1 cup water to reach desired consistency. Bring to boiling, stirring until sugar is dissolved.
3. Place pot of applesauce in a sink filled with ice water; stir to cool. Ladle into clean wide-mouth pint or quart freezer containers, leaving ½-inch headspace. Seal and label. Store in refrigerator up to 2 weeks or freeze up to 8 months. Makes 6 pints or 3 quarts.
PER ½-CUP SERVING 81 cal, 1 mg sodium, 21 g carb, 2 g fiber, 18 g sugars.

Very Berry Applesauce Prepare as directed, except in Step 1 replace 1 lb. (4 cups) apples with 1 lb. (4 cups) fresh or frozen raspberries and/or strawberries and decrease water to 1½ cups.

APPLE-PEAR BUTTER

HANDS-ON TIME 45 min.
TOTAL TIME 2 hr. 45 min.

2½ lb. tart cooking apples, cored and quartered (about 7 medium)
2   lb. ripe pears, cored and quartered (about 4 medium)
3   cups apple cider or apple juice
2   cups sugar
2   Tbsp. fresh-squeezed lemon juice, strained
½   tsp. ground cinnamon

1. In an 8- to 10-qt. heavy pot or Dutch oven combine apples, pears, and cider. Bring to boiling; reduce heat. Simmer, covered, 30 minutes, stirring occasionally.

Press apple mixture through a food mill or sieve. (Should have 7½ to 8 cups.) Return pulp to pot; discard skins.
2. Stir in sugar, lemon juice, and cinnamon. Bring to boiling; reduce heat. Cook, uncovered, over very low heat 1½ to 1¾ hours or until thick enough that mixture mounds on a spoon, stirring often.
3. Place pot of apple butter in a sink filled with ice water; stir to cool. Ladle into clean wide-mouth half-pint freezer containers, leaving ½-inch headspace. Seal and label. Store in refrigerator up to 2 weeks or freeze up to 6 months. Apple butter may darken slightly on freezing. Makes 5 to 6 half-pints.
PER 1-TBSP. SERVING 28 cal, 7 g carb, 7 g sugars.

Classic Apple Butter Prepare as directed, except omit pears and increase apples to 4½ lb.
Caramel Apple Butter Prepare as directed, except omit pears, increase apples to 4½ lb., decrease granulated sugar to ½ cup, and add 1½ cups packed brown sugar.

FALL SURPLUS

When a trip to the farmers market or orchard yields a mountain of fresh apples, here's how to preserve them.

APPLESAUCE Spiced Applesauce and Very Berry Applesauce recipes use up to 8 pounds of apples.

APPLE BUTTER Our spins on Classic Apple Butter, Apple-Pear Butter, and Caramel Apple Butter use 4½ pounds of apples and keep in the freezer up to 6 months.

DRIED APPLES For apple chips, arrange 2 large apples cut into ⅛-inch-thick slices in a single layer on parchment paper lined baking sheets. Brush lightly with apple juice. Bake 2 to 2½ hours at 200°F or until crisp, turning apple slices and rotating pans every 30 minutes. Let cool. Store in an airtight container up to 3 days or freeze up to 3 months.

THESE BARS ARE THE BEST OF APPLE PIE AND APPLE TART: LAYERS OF SLICED APPLES, AS IN PIE, AND A TART-INSPIRED STURDY SHORTBREAD CRUST. WE ADDED A CREAMY FILLING AND DRIZZLE OF SPICED BROWN BUTTER TO CREATE A NEW FALL FAVORITE.

APPLE-BROWN BUTTER BARS

HANDS-ON TIME 20 min.
TOTAL TIME 2 hr. 30 min.

Nonstick cooking spray
1½ cups all-purpose flour
½ 8-oz. pkg. almond paste, crumbled
½ cup packed brown sugar
¼ cup almonds
½ cup cold butter, cut up
¼ cup butter
¼ tsp. ground cinnamon
¼ tsp. ground allspice
2 eggs, lightly beaten
⅔ cup granulated sugar
⅓ cup apple juice
2 Tbsp. all-purpose flour
2 Tbsp. heavy cream
2 to 3 medium apples (6 oz. each), such as Honeycrisp, Gala, and/or Granny Smith, cored, halved, and very thinly sliced
2 Tbsp. apple jelly (optional)
Sea salt flakes

1. Preheat oven to 350°F. Line a 9-inch square baking pan with foil; coat foil with nonstick cooking spray. In a food processor combine 1½ cups flour, the almond paste, brown sugar, and almonds. Cover and pulse until finely chopped. Add ½ cup butter. Cover and pulse until crumbly. Pat mixture into bottom of prepared pan. Bake 15 minutes or until edges are light brown.
2. Meanwhile, for spiced brown butter, place ¼ cup butter in a small saucepan. Heat over medium-low 15 minutes or until browned. Remove from heat. Stir in spices; set aside.
3. For filling: In a small bowl whisk together eggs, granulated sugar, apple juice, 2 Tbsp. flour, and the cream. Pour over hot crust. Bake 15 minutes. (Filling will not be completely set.) Arrange apple slices on filling, overlapping as necessary. Brush with half the brown butter mixture. Bake 10 to 15 minutes or until apples are tender. Cool on a wire rack. Drizzle with remaining brown butter. If desired, brush with apple jelly. Sprinkle with sea salt flakes. Makes 16 bars.
PER BAR *257 cal, 13 g fat, 48 mg chol, 118 mg sodium, 32 g carb, 1 g fiber, 21 g sugars, 3 g pro.*

CRANBERRY PIE WITH HONEY MERINGUE
Recipe on page 262

november

Let the holiday season begin! These recipes—from make-ahead appetizers to luscious desserts—are designed for carefree entertaining and will receive oohs and aahs.

244

253

266

IMPROVED
BLOOD ORANGE
PUNCH

POMEGRANATE-
CITRUS
SANS-GRIA

holiday hosting guide
BATCH THE BEVERAGES

Mixologist and author Maggie Hoffman tapped her bartender buddies for their best make-ahead pitcher drinks. Now hosts can spend more time mingling.

POMEGRANATE-CITRUS SANS-GRIA

A bit of cayenne gives Pomegranate-Citrus Sans-Gria a little kick.

HANDS-ON TIME 10 min.
TOTAL TIME 2 hr. 50 min., includes chilling

- 2 Tbsp. raspberry jam
- 2 chai tea bags
- 2 English breakfast tea bags
- 8 thin orange slices, plus more for garnish
- 2¼ cups chilled unsweetened 100% pomegranate juice
- 1½ cups grapefruit juice
- 1 cup fresh orange juice
- 6 Tbsp. fresh lemon juice
- ⅛ to ¼ tsp. cayenne pepper
- 4 thin lemon slices
- ¾ cup chilled club soda, plus more as needed
  Pomegranate seeds
  Orange slices

1. In a 1-qt. saucepan combine raspberry jam and 1 cup water. Bring to a simmer over medium-high, stirring to dissolve jam completely. Remove from heat. Fully submerge chai and English breakfast tea bags. Let steep 40 minutes; discard bags. Chill, covered, up to 24 hours.
2. In a 2-qt. pitcher combine four orange slices and tea mixture. Using a wooden spoon, gently press orange slices about 10 times to release juices and bruise peel (don't pulverize). Stir in pomegranate, grapefruit, orange, lemon juices, and the cayenne. Gently stir in lemon slices and remaining orange slices. Chill, covered, up to 2 hours.
3. To serve: Stir mixture well. Add club soda. Stir. Pour into ice-filled glasses. Garnish with pomegranate seeds and orange slices. Makes 8 servings.
PER SERVING *96 cal, 14 mg sodium, 24 g carb, 1 g fiber, 19 g sugars, 1 g pro.*

IMPROVED BLOOD ORANGE PUNCH

A splash of Prosecco tops off Improved Blood Orange Punch made with fresh blood orange juice and maraschino liqueur.

HANDS-ON TIME 20 min.
TOTAL TIME 2 hr. 20 min., includes chilling

- 1½ cups vodka, chilled
- ¾ cup maraschino cherry liqueur (such as Luxardo)
- 3 cups fresh blood orange juice
- 1½ cups fresh lemon juice
- 1 750-ml bottle chilled Prosecco
- 12 blood orange half-moons
  Maraschino cherries

1. For punch mix: In a 2-qt. pitcher combine vodka, maraschino liqueur, blood orange juice, and lemon juice. Chill, covered, up to 2 hours.
2. For each drink: Fill collins glass to top with ice. Pour in ¼ cup chilled Prosecco. Top with ½ cup punch mix. Garnish with blood orange half-moons and maraschino cherries. Serve immediately. Makes 12 servings.
PER SERVING *165 cal, 4 mg sodium, 9 g carb, 12 g sugars, 1 g pro.*

"IT'S HARD TO HOLD A CONVERSATION WHILE SEARCHING FOR BITTERS, MEASURING WITH JIGGERS, AND RATTLING A SHAKER FULL OF ICE."
—MAGGIE HOFFMAN

holiday hosting guide
FREEZE SOME APPETIZERS

Your freezer is a party hero. Stock it with ready-to-heat appetizers (homemade or from the grocery), and you'll be ready to serve a selection of nibbles—whether the party is planned or impromptu.

POT STICKERS

HANDS-ON TIME 35 min.
TOTAL TIME 1 hr. 20 min., plus freezing

- 2 cups chopped napa cabbage
- 1 tsp. salt
- 2 Tbsp. thinly sliced green onion
- 1 Tbsp. chopped fresh cilantro
- 2 tsp. toasted sesame oil
- 2 tsp. soy sauce
- 2 tsp. rice wine
- 1 small fresh serrano pepper, seeded and finely chopped (tip, page 127)
- 1 tsp. grated fresh ginger
- 8 oz. ground turkey breast
- 28 to 30 3½-inch round wonton wrappers (gyoza)
  Nonstick cooking spray
  Asian sweet chili sauce (optional)

1. For filling: In a small bowl toss together cabbage and salt. Let stand at room temperature 30 minutes. Transfer cabbage to a fine-mesh sieve; press firmly to remove excess moisture. Place cabbage in a medium bowl. Add green onion, cilantro, sesame oil, soy sauce, rice wine, pepper, and ginger; toss to combine. Stir in turkey.
2. Line a baking sheet with parchment paper. For each pot sticker: Spoon a scant 1 Tbsp. filling onto center of a wonton wrapper. (Cover remaining wrappers with a damp cloth to prevent drying out.) Lightly brush edge of wrapper with water. Fold wrapper in half; pinch edges together. Place pot sticker, sealed side up, on prepared baking sheet. (Cover filled pot stickers while working.) Freeze 1 to 2 hours or until firm. Transfer to freezer containers. Freeze up to 1 month.
3. To serve: Line a bamboo steamer basket or steamer insert with parchment

paper; coat lightly with nonstick cooking spray. Arrange frozen pot stickers in a single layer, not touching, in basket. (Work in batches, if necessary.)
4. Place steamer basket in a wok or large pot over, but not touching, boiling water. Steam, covered, 16 minutes or until filling in pot stickers is no longer pink (165°F). If desired, serve with Asian sweet chili sauce. Makes 28 to 30 pot stickers.
PER POT STICKER *37 cal, 6 mg chol, 157 mg sodium, 5 g carb, 3 g pro.*

MINI CHEESE BALLS

HANDS-ON TIME 35 min.
TOTAL TIME 5 hr. 20 min., plus freezing

- 1 8-oz. pkg. cream cheese, softened
- 1 cup finely shredded Gouda cheese (4 oz.)
- ¼ cup butter, softened
- 1 Tbsp. milk
- ½ tsp. Worcestershire sauce
- 2 Tbsp. thinly sliced green onion
- 2 Tbsp. chopped fresh dill or 2 tsp. dried dill
- ½ cup Toppings

1. Place cream cheese, Gouda, and butter in a large bowl; let stand at room temperature 30 minutes. Add milk and Worcestershire. Beat with a mixer on medium until light and fluffy. Stir in green onion and dill. Chill, covered, 4 to 24 hours.
2. Shape cheese mixture into 12 balls, using 2 Tbsp. for each. Place in a single layer in a freezer container. Freeze up to 3 months.
3. To serve: Thaw in refrigerator overnight. Roll each cheese ball in desired Toppings; let stand at room temperature 15 minutes. Serve with crackers. Makes 12 cheese balls.

Topping Ideas (pick one or more)
Poppy seeds, sesame seeds, or everything bagel seasoning; finely chopped fresh herbs; toasted chopped nuts; citrus zest; finely crushed crackers and/or chips; snipped dried cranberries; finely shredded cheese and/or crumbled crisp-cooked bacon; finely chopped fresh jalapeño peppers
PER CHEESE BALL *164 cal, 15 g fat, 40 mg chol, 172 mg sodium, 3 g carb, 1 g fiber, 1 g sugars, 5 g pro.*

SPANAKOPITA

HANDS-ON TIME 50 min.
TOTAL TIME 1 hr. 5 min., plus freezing

- 2 Tbsp. butter
- ½ cup finely chopped onion
- 1 clove garlic, minced
- 1 10-oz. pkg. frozen chopped spinach, thawed and well drained
- 1½ cups crumbled feta cheese (6 oz.)
- ½ tsp. dried oregano, crushed
- 24 sheets frozen phyllo dough (14×9-inch rectangles), thawed
- ½ cup butter, melted

1. For filling: In a large skillet melt butter over medium. Add onion and garlic. Cook and stir 5 minutes or until onion is tender. In a medium bowl combine onion mixture, spinach, feta, and oregano.
2. Line a large baking sheet with waxed paper. Unfold phyllo; remove a sheet. (Cover remaining phyllo with plastic wrap to prevent drying out.) Lightly brush sheet with some of the melted butter. Place another phyllo sheet on top; brush with butter.
3. Cut the two layered sheets lengthwise into three strips. Spoon one rounded teaspoon of filling 1 inch from one end of each strip. To fold into a triangle, bring

POT STICKERS

SPANAKOPITA

MINI CHEESE BALLS

GOUGÈRES

one a corner over filling so the short edge lines up with a long side edge. Continue folding the length of strip in a triangle that encloses filling. Place on prepared baking sheet. Repeat with remaining phyllo, melted butter, and filling. Freeze 1 hour or until firm. Transfer to freezer containers. Freeze up to 2 months.

4. To serve: Preheat oven to 375°F. Place frozen triangles on a baking sheet; brush with additional melted butter. Bake 15 minutes or until golden. Serve warm. Makes 36 spanakopita.

PER SPANAKOPITA *87 cal, 5 g fat, 14 mg chol, 161 mg sodium, 8 g carb, 2 g pro.*

GOUGÈRES

HANDS-ON TIME 30 min.
TOTAL TIME 1 hr. 5 min., plus freezing

- ½ cup butter, cut into pieces
- ¼ tsp. salt
- 1½ cups all-purpose flour
- 5 eggs
- 1½ cups shredded Gruyère cheese (6 oz.)
- 1 Tbsp. Dijon mustard
- ⅛ tsp. cayenne pepper

1. Line two baking sheets with parchment paper. In a large saucepan combine 1½ cups water, the butter, and salt. Bring to boiling. Immediately add flour all at once; stir vigorously using a large wooden spoon. Cook and stir until

mixture forms a ball. Remove from heat. Let cool 10 minutes. Add eggs, one at a time, stirring after each until smooth. Stir in cheese, mustard, and cayenne pepper.

2. Using a pastry bag fitted with a ½-inch star tip, pipe batter into 1-inch mounds close together on prepared baking sheets. (Or use a small cookie scoop to drop batter into 1¼-inch mounds.) Freeze 1 to 2 hours or until firm. Transfer to freezer containers. Freeze up to 1 month.

3. To serve: Preheat oven to 400°F. Line a baking sheet with parchment paper. Place desired number of mounds 1 inch apart on prepared baking sheet. Bake 25 minutes or until puffed and golden. Serve warm. Makes 72 gougères.

PER GOUGÈRE *37 cal, 3 g fat, 19 mg chol, 48 mg sodium, 2 g carb, 2 g pro.*

holiday baking
SWEET FINISHES

Grab your oven mitts. Baking season has arrived. We turned to Grandbaby Cakes blogger and cookbook author Jocelyn Delk Adams for a lineup of delicious desserts that don't require an all-nighter in the kitchen or a certificate in cake decorating.

WHY IT'S EASY

Traditional cheesecakes bake in a springform pan in a water bath to ensure even baking and to prevent the filling from sinking. Jocelyn uses a 13×9 pan for a thinner cake, which means it bakes evenly without the cumbersome water bath.

MAPLE CHEESECAKE WITH VANILLA BEAN WHIPPED CREAM

Bright-tasting pomegranate and orange compote dresses up the bars and contrasts the indulgent cheesecake.

HANDS-ON TIME 30 min.
TOTAL TIME 6 hr., includes chilling

        Nonstick cooking spray
2   cups graham cracker crumbs
⅓   cup sugar
¼   tsp. salt
½   cup butter, melted
4   8-oz. pkg. cream cheese, softened
⅔   cup maple syrup
½   cup sugar
⅓   cup heavy cream
4   eggs
½   cup sour cream
2   Tbsp. all-purpose flour
2   tsp. vanilla
        Vanilla Bean Whipped Cream
        Pomegranate Compote

1. Preheat oven to 350°F. Line a 13×9-inch baking pan with foil, extending foil over pan edges; coat foil with nonstick cooking spray.
2. For crust: In a medium bowl combine cracker crumbs, the ⅓ cup sugar, and the salt. Add melted butter; stir to combine. Press crumb mixture into bottom of pan. Bake 10 minutes. Remove from oven.

3. Meanwhile, for filling: In an extra-large mixing bowl beat cream cheese, maple syrup, and ½ cup sugar 2 minutes on medium until smooth. Add heavy cream; beat until combined. Beat in eggs, one at a time, beating on low after each until combined. Add sour cream, flour, and vanilla; beat until combined. Pour filling over crust.
4. Bake 40 minutes or just until center is set. Cool in pan on a wire rack 1 hour. Cover. Chill in pan 4 hours or overnight.
5. Use foil to lift uncut cheesecake from pan; transfer to a cutting board. Cut into bars. Top with Vanilla Bean Whipped Cream and Pomegranate Compote. Makes 24 bars.
Vanilla Bean Whipped Cream Halve a vanilla bean lengthwise; scrape seeds into a large bowl. Add 1 cup heavy cream and 2 tsp. powdered sugar. Beat on medium until stiff peaks form (peaks stand straight).
Pomegranate Compote In a small saucepan combine ⅓ cup dry red wine or pomegranate juice and ⅓ cup sugar. Bring to boiling, stirring to dissolve sugar. Reduce heat. Simmer, uncovered, about 3 minutes or until slightly reduced and syrupy. Remove from heat; let cool completely. In a small bowl combine ½ cup pomegranate seeds and ¼ cup chopped fresh orange sections. Pour syrup over pomegranate seed mixture. Stir in 2 tsp. lemon juice.
PER BAR 340 cal, 24 g fat, 97 mg chol, 212 mg sodium, 27 g carb, 21 g sugars, 5 g pro.

MAPLE CHEESECAKE
WITH VANILLA BEAN
WHIPPED CREAM

FOR JOCELYN DELK ADAMS, BAKING IS ALL ABOUT LOVE. "SHARING A HOMEMADE CAKE, COOKIE, OR PIE IS LIKE GIVING SOMEONE A WARM HUG," SHE SAYS.

CARAMELIZED PEAR SKILLET CAKE

"This upside-down cake is deceptively easy even though its impressive appearance might indicate otherwise," Jocelyn says. *She tops the spice-laden molasses cake with a quick bourbon hard sauce. "Expect oohs and aahs when you flip this one out of the skillet. A scoop of vanilla ice cream served over the warm cake takes it over the top."*

HANDS-ON TIME 20 min.
TOTAL TIME 1 hr. 20 min.

- ½ cup butter
- ⅔ cup packed light brown sugar
- 4 Bosc pears, peeled, halved lengthwise, and cored
- 2 cups all-purpose flour
- 1 tsp. baking powder
- 1 tsp. ground ginger
- ¼ tsp. salt
- ¼ tsp. baking soda
- ¼ tsp. ground nutmeg
- ¼ tsp. ground cloves
- ½ cup butter, softened
- 2 eggs
- ½ cup molasses
- ¾ cup water
  Bourbon Sauce

1. Place ½ cup butter in a 10-inch cast-iron skillet. Place in cold oven; preheat oven to 350°F. Once butter has melted, whisk ⅓ cup brown sugar into melted butter in skillet. Arrange pears cut sides down in skillet. Roast 20 to 25 minutes or just until tender and starting to brown. Meanwhile, in a medium bowl whisk together flour, baking powder, ginger, salt, baking soda, nutmeg, and cloves.
2. In a large mixing bowl beat the ½ cup softened butter on medium 30 seconds. Add remaining ⅓ cup brown sugar; beat until combined. Beat in eggs and molasses. Alternately add flour mixture and the water to mixing bowl, beating on low after each addition just until combined. Pour batter over pears.
3. Bake 30 to 35 minutes or until a toothpick inserted near center comes out clean. Cool in skillet 10 minutes. Invert onto a serving plate. Drizzle with Bourbon Sauce. Makes 8 servings.
Bourbon Sauce In a small saucepan melt ¼ cup butter over medium. Stir in ½ cup sugar, 1 egg yolk, and 2 Tbsp. water. Cook and stir 6 to 8 minutes or just until boiling. Remove from heat. Stir in 2 Tbsp. bourbon. Let cool slightly. Makes ¾ cup.
PER SERVING *640 cal, 31 g fat, 146 mg chol, 435 mg sodium, 85 g carb, 4 g fiber, 55 g sugars, 6 g pro.*

WHY IT'S EASY

Jocelyn places pear halves cut sides down in a cast-iron skillet to caramelize in a mixture of brown sugar and melted butter while she mixes the cake batter. "This cake is inherently gorgeous—you need zero decorating skills. Arrange the fruit however you please; when you invert the skillet, you get a magical surprise."

JOCELYN'S BEST BAKING PRACTICES

A few pointers before heating the oven.

1 "Read the recipe top to bottom before you start. You don't want an unexpected overnight chilling step to derail your plans to take a homemade tart to a holiday party."

2 "Salt is the most crucial ingredient for a well-balanced and flavorful dessert. I personally love finely ground sea salt, but if iodized table salt is all you have, go for it."

3 "I use unsalted butter and add salt separately; it gives me more control. But if a cake craving calls and salted butter is what you have, omit the salt in the recipe."

4 "All ovens are different, so temperatures and baking times may vary. Check your baked goods a few minutes before time is up to ensure you don't overbake."

JOCELYN SAYS: "DIFFICULT ISN'T SYNONYMOUS WITH DELICIOUS. KEEP YOUR DESSERTS SIMPLE AND DO WHAT YOU CAN AHEAD OF TIME."

WHY IT'S EASY

These dainty cups get a gold star for presentation. Spoon the frosting directly into the baked cookie cups or place the frosting in a resealable plastic bag, snip off an end, and squeeze to fill.

BROWN BUTTER SNICKERDOODLE COOKIE CUPS

Jocelyn reinvented the snickerdoodle cookie with the addition of brown butter. "The toasted nuttiness and caramelization amplifies the yum factor," she says. She stirs half the brown butter into the cookie dough, which she pats into mini muffin tins to create tassie cups. The rest of the brown butter is beaten with milk and powdered sugar for a sweet filling.

HANDS-ON TIME 30 min.
TOTAL TIME 2 hr. 15 min.

- 1 cup butter
- 1⅓ cups all-purpose flour
- 1 tsp. cream of tartar
- ½ tsp. baking soda
- ¼ tsp. salt
- ⅛ tsp. apple pie spice
- ⅓ cup granulated sugar
- ⅓ cup packed brown sugar
- 1 egg
- 2 tsp. vanilla
- 2 Tbsp. finely chopped toasted almonds
  Nonstick cooking spray
- ¼ cup granulated sugar
- 1 tsp. ground cinnamon
- 2 cups powdered sugar
- 1 to 2 Tbsp. milk
  Dried cranberries and/or finely chopped toasted almonds (optional)

1. For brown butter: In a medium saucepan melt butter over medium. Cook 15 to 18 minutes or until dark golden brown with specks throughout. Transfer to a small bowl. Freeze 1 hour or until firm.
2. For cookie cups: In a medium bowl whisk together flour, cream of tartar, baking soda,. salt, and apple pie spice.

3. In a large bowl beat ½ cup of the firm brown butter and ⅓ cup each granulated and brown sugar on medium until fluffy. (Set aside remaining brown butter to soften.) Add egg; beat until combined. Beat in 1 tsp. vanilla. Gradually add flour mixture, beating until combined. Stir in the finely chopped almonds.
4. Preheat oven to 350°F. Coat thirty-six 1¾-inch muffin cups with nonstick cooking spray. In a small bowl stir together ¼ cup granulated sugar and the cinnamon; set aside. Shape dough into 36 balls, about 1 inch in diameter. Roll in sugar mixture to coat. Place a ball in each prepared muffin cup. Press into bottom and up sides of cups.
5. Bake 8 minutes or until lightly browned. Use the rounded side of a measuring spoon to press down centers of cookie cups. Cool in muffin cups on a wire rack 5 minutes. Loosen and remove. Cool completely.
6. For filling: In a large bowl beat the remaining brown butter on medium 1 minute or until creamy. Beat in ½ cup powdered sugar until combined. Beat in 1 Tbsp. milk and remaining 1 tsp. vanilla until combined. Beat in remaining 1½ cups powdered sugar until combined. Beat 1 to 2 minutes or until fluffy, adding additional milk if necessary. Spoon or pipe filling into each cookie cup. If desired, sprinkle with cranberries and/or additional almonds. Makes 36 cookie cups.
PER COOKIE CUP *114 cal, 5 g fat, 19 mg chol, 37 mg sodium, 16 g carb, 12 g sugars, 1 g pro.*

IF YOU'RE A FAN OF PUMPKIN-SPICE EVERYTHING, THIS SWEET POTATO CAKE WILL DOUBLE YOUR DELIGHT. "I HAVE SOUTHERN ROOTS, SO SWEET POTATOES HAVE ALWAYS BEEN A BAKING STAPLE— MORE SO THAN PUMPKIN," JOCELYN SAYS.

SWEET POTATO- CHOCOLATE POUND CAKE

We baked our cake in a couple of loaf pans. Bundt pans would contribute fancier results.

HANDS-ON TIME 35 min.
TOTAL TIME 2 hr.

1   10- to 12-oz. sweet potato, scrubbed
8   oz. semisweet or bittersweet chocolate, chopped
3   cups all-purpose flour
2   tsp. pumpkin pie spice
1½ tsp. baking powder
1½ tsp. salt
1   cup butter, softened
2   cups sugar
5   eggs
1   cup sour cream
1   Tbsp. vanilla
⅔   cup heavy cream
    Flaked sea salt

1. Pierce potato several times with a fork. Microwave on high 5 minutes or until tender. Let cool.
2. Halve potato lengthwise. Scrape pulp into a medium bowl. Mash until smooth. Measure ¾ cup; set aside any remaining for another use. In a small microwave-safe bowl melt 2 oz. chocolate in microwave on high 30 to 45 seconds, stirring once.

3. Preheat oven to 350°F. Grease and flour two 8-inch loaf pans or coat with nonstick spray for baking. In a medium bowl whisk together flour, pumpkin pie spice, baking powder, and salt. In an extra-large bowl beat butter and sugar on medium-high 2 to 3 minutes or until light and fluffy. Add eggs, one at a time, beating after each until combined. Gradually add flour mixture, beating until combined. Beat in sour cream, mashed sweet potato, and vanilla until combined. Remove 3 cups batter to a medium bowl and stir in melted chocolate.
4. Alternately spoon mounds of each cake batter into prepared pans. Using a knife, lightly swirl batters together. Bake 50 minutes* or until a toothpick inserted near centers comes out clean. Let cool in pans on a wire rack 10 minutes. Remove from pans; let cool completely.
5. For ganache: In a small saucepan bring cream just to boiling over medium-high. Remove from heat. Add remaining chopped chocolate (do not stir). Let stand 5 minutes. Stir until smooth. Spoon ganache over cakes. Sprinkle with flaked sea salt. Makes 16 servings.
*Tip For one 10-inch fluted tube pan, bake 50 minutes or until a toothpick inserted near center comes out clean; for two 9-inch loaf pans, bake 45 minutes or until a toothpick inserted near centers comes out clean.
PER SERVING *447 cal, 23 g fat, 110 mg chol, 376 mg sodium, 56 g carb, 2 g fiber, 27 g sugars, 6 g pro.*

WHY IT'S EASY

"There's an endearing simplicity to pound cake," Jocelyn says. "The batter is super forgiving, so it's a great dessert for a novice baker." Pound cakes freeze well too. Bake a few extra and freeze them so you have dessert ready for impromptu get-togethers and potlucks throughout the season. Simply thaw and top with warm ganache to serve.

FAST & FRESH

Easy, delicious recipes for a better dinner tonight.

CREAMY PASTA WITH TURKEY AND CRISPY CRUMBS

Think of this quick skillet pasta as a cross between Tetrazzini and piccata.

TOTAL TIME 35 min.

- 2   Tbsp. butter
- 3   cloves garlic, minced
- ⅓   cup coarse fresh bread crumbs
     Kosher salt
- 2   Tbsp. coarsely chopped flat-leaf parsley
- ¾   cup chopped celery
- 1   cup heavy cream
- 3   cups shredded cooked turkey
- 1   tsp. fresh thyme or sage leaves
- 8   oz. dry linguine
- ½   cup grated Parmesan cheese
- 2   to 3 tsp. drained capers
- ¼   tsp. black pepper

1. In a large skillet heat 1 Tbsp. butter over medium heat. Add half the garlic; cook 30 seconds. Add bread crumbs and a pinch of salt. Cook and stir 2 minutes or until bread crumbs are golden brown and aromatic. Transfer to a small bowl. Wipe out pan. Stir parsley into bread crumbs.

2. Bring a large pot of salted water to boiling. Meanwhile, melt remaining 1 Tbsp. butter in skillet. Add celery and remaining garlic; cook and stir over medium 5 minutes. Stir in cream; simmer, uncovered, 3 minutes. Add turkey and thyme; cook and stir until heated through.

3. Cook pasta according to package directions. Drain, reserving ¼ cup cooking liquid. Stir cooking liquid into turkey mixture; toss all with pasta. Stir in cheese, capers, ½ tsp. salt, and pepper. Top servings with bread crumbs. Makes 4 servings.

PER SERVING *730 cal, 37 g fat, 204 mg chol, 710 mg sodium, 51 g carb, 3 g fiber, 4 g sugars, 46 g pro.*

RED CURRY-LIME SWEET POTATO SOUP

This is the easiest way we've found to clean leeks: After chopping, place them in a bowl of cold water and swirl with your hand. The dirt will sink to the bottom of the bowl. Remove the leeks and pat dry with paper towels.

TOTAL TIME 35 min.

2   Tbsp. vegetable oil
2   leeks, white and light green parts chopped and washed
    Kosher salt
2   Tbsp. Thai red curry paste

4   cups mashed sweet potatoes
1   13- to 14-oz. can unsweetened coconut milk
3   cups water
1   lime, zested and juiced
    Olive oil (optional)
    Freshly ground coarse black pepper (optional)
    Cilantro (optional

1. In a 4- to 5-qt. saucepan heat vegetable oil over medium heat. Add leeks and a pinch of salt. Cover and cook until tender, about 8 minutes. Stir in red curry paste. Increase heat to medium-high. Cook and stir 1 minute; stir in sweet potatoes, coconut milk, 3 cups water, and 1 tsp. salt. Bring to boiling; reduce heat. Simmer, covered, 10 minutes or until heated through, stirring occasionally. Remove from heat. Cool slightly.

2. Using an immersion blender, blend until smooth. Stir in lime zest and juice; heat through. If desired, drizzle with olive oil, sprinkle with black pepper, and top with cilantro. Makes 6 servings.

PER SERVING *330 cal, 15 g fat, 540 mg sodium, 44 g carb, 6 g fiber, 14 g sugars, 4 g pro.*

SAUSAGE, BEANS, AND OLIVES SKILLET

To easily chop canned plum tomatoes, use kitchen shears to cut them up in the can, then pour the whole can into the skillet.

TOTAL TIME 30 min.

1   Tbsp. olive oil
1½ lb. spicy or sweet Italian sausage, casings removed and cut into 1-inch pieces
1   cup thinly sliced and halved red onion
4   cloves garlic, thinly sliced
1   28-oz. can plum tomatoes, coarsely chopped
1   15-oz. can cannellini beans, rinsed and drained
¼   tsp. salt
2   cups cooked green beans, halved crosswise
¼   cup pitted Kalamata olives
½   cup lightly packed fresh basil leaves

1. In a 12-inch skillet heat olive oil over medium-high heat. Add sausage in a single layer. Cook 5 minutes or until browned, stirring occasionally. Drain sausage, reserving 2 Tbsp. drippings. Return sausage to skillet. Stir in onion and garlic. Reduce heat to medium. Cook 6 minutes or until onion is tender, stirring occasionally. Add undrained tomatoes and the cannellini beans. Season with salt. Bring to boiling; reduce heat. Simmer, covered, 10 minutes, stirring occasionally.

2. Stir in green beans and olives. Cover; simmer 3 to 4 minutes or until heated through. Top with fresh basil. Makes 6 servings.

PER SERVING *394 cal, 16 g fat, 34 mg chol, 1,293 mg sodium, 40 g carb, 8 g fiber, 7 g sugars, 27 g pro.*

MUSHROOM PATTIES WITH SOUR CREAM AND HERBS

Chopping the stuffing and mushrooms in a food processor ensures uniform texture regardless of the stuffing you start with. Try a variety of mushrooms, including button, baby bella, or shiitake.

TOTAL TIME 40 min.

3   Tbsp. olive oil
2   Tbsp. butter
2   cups mushrooms
1   clove garlic, minced
    Salt
3   cups bread stuffing
1   egg
2   tsp. fresh thyme or sage leaves
¼   tsp. black pepper
⅓   cup flour
1   head Bibb lettuce, coarsely torn
½   cup lightly packed flat-leaf parsley
½   cup lightly packed fresh dill
⅓   cup sour cream
2   Tbsp. lemon juice

1. In a large skillet heat 2 Tbsp. olive oil and butter over medium heat; add mushrooms, garlic, and a pinch of salt. Cook 4 to 6 minutes or until mushrooms are browned and liquid is evaporated, stirring occasionally. Transfer to a food processor.

2. Add stuffing, egg, thyme, ½ tsp. salt, and pepper to mushroom mixture. Cover; process until finely chopped. Spoon mixture into 12 mounds on a parchment paper-lined baking sheet. Flatten each to ¼ inch thick. If desired, cover and chill up to 4 hours.

3. Place flour in a shallow dish. Coat both sides of patties with flour. In a large skillet heat 1 Tbsp. olive oil over medium. Add patties to skillet in batches (do not crowd). Cook 2 to 3 minutes on each side or until browned and heated through. Place on a baking sheet. Keep warm in a 200°F oven. Repeat with remaining patties, adding additional oil to skillet if necessary.

4. In a large bowl toss together lettuce and herbs. Divide among four plates. For dressing: In a small bowl whisk together sour cream, lemon juice, 1 tsp. water, and a pinch of salt and black pepper. Top greens with patties. Drizzle with dressing. Makes 4 servings.

PER SERVING *532 cal, 39 g fat, 71 mg chol, 954 mg sodium, 39 g carb, 2 g fiber, 5 g sugars, 9 g pro.*

SIDES & PIES

Bird is still the word on the Thanksgiving table, yet add-ons are always the surprising attractions. We tapped two favorite cookbook authors to help us shake up turkey's supporting cast. Add one of these dishes to the buffet or try them all.

SIDES Cookbook author Alison Roman can roast a Thanksgiving turkey with the best of them, and she keeps guests happy with new takes on popular sides. In this batch of recipes, Alison takes the usual suspects—green beans, potatoes, carrots—and applies a fresh, modern filter.

SPICY GREEN BEANS WITH HERB SALAD

This recipe is an excellent excuse to buy a tube of anchovy paste (ground anchovies, salt, and oil) to keep on hand for adding salty-savory umami to sauces and dressings.

TOTAL TIME 45 min.

- 2 Tbsp. olive oil, plus more for drizzling
- 4 small shallots, cut into ½-inch wedges
- 4 cloves garlic, thinly sliced
  Kosher salt and black pepper
- 2 to 4 anchovy fillets or 2 tsp. anchovy paste (optional)
- ¼ to ½ tsp. crushed red pepper
- 2 Tbsp. apple cider vinegar or white wine vinegar, plus more to finish
- 1½ lb. green beans, trimmed
- 1 cup flat-leaf parsley leaves and tender stems
- ½ cup fresh dill leaves
- ½ cup fresh mint and/or cilantro (leaves and tender stems)

1. In a large Dutch oven heat the 2 Tbsp. oil over medium-high heat. Add shallots and garlic. Season with salt and black pepper. Cook, without stirring, 4 to 5 minutes or until golden brown on one side. Stir and let them brown a bit more, another 4 to 5 minutes. If desired, add anchovies and let them sizzle and dissolve. Stir in crushed red pepper.

2. Add vinegar; simmer 1 to 2 minutes. Stir in green beans and ½ cup water. Season with salt and black pepper. Simmer, covered, 10 to 12 minutes or until tender. Remove from heat. Season with salt, black pepper, and, if desired, additional crushed red pepper.

3. For herb salad: Toss parsley, dill, and mint with a splash of vinegar and a drizzle of olive oil; season with salt and black pepper.

4. Transfer bean mixture to a large shallow bowl. Scatter herb salad over beans before serving. Makes 6 servings.
PER SERVING *146 cal, 10 g fat, 2 mg chol, 303 mg sodium, 13 g carb, 4 g fiber, 5 g sugars, 4 g pro.*

BUTTERED STUFFING WITH MUSHROOMS

Photo on page 260.
HANDS-ON TIME 40 min.
TOTAL TIME 1 hr. 25 min.

- 1 loaf crusty bread (about 1 lb.), such as ciabatta or sourdough, torn into 1½-inch pieces
- 8 Tbsp. unsalted butter
- 2 Tbsp. olive oil
- 2 large leeks, white and light green parts thinly sliced
  Salt and black pepper
- 1½ lb. mushrooms, such as cremini, maitake, shiitake, and/or oyster, cut into bite-size pieces
- ¼ cup fresh oregano, thyme, or marjoram, coarsely chopped
- ½ cup dry white wine, such as Sauvignon Blanc or Pinot Gris
- 2 to 2½ cups chicken or vegetable broth
- 1 large egg
- 1 cup flat-leaf parsley leaves and tender stems, finely chopped

1. If possible, dry bread pieces overnight on a rimmed baking sheet. If not, toast in a 300°F oven 15 to 20 minutes until just lightly toasted, tossing once or twice.

2. Heat 6 Tbsp. butter and the olive oil in a large skillet over medium. Add leeks. Season with salt and black pepper. Cook 10 to 12 minutes or until leeks are totally softened and starting to brown, stirring occasionally.

3. Add mushrooms. Season with salt and pepper. Increase heat to medium-high. Cook 12 to 15 minutes more or until mushrooms and leeks are completely softened and deeply browned, stirring occasionally.

4. Add oregano and wine. Using a wooden spoon, scrape up any browned bits from bottom of skillet. Simmer 3 to 4 minutes or until wine is mostly evaporated. Remove from heat.

5. Preheat oven to 425°F. In a large bowl whisk together chicken broth and egg. Season with salt and pepper. Add dried bread, parsley, and mushroom mixture. Toss to coat evenly. (It should look a bit like uncooked bread pudding.)

6. Transfer mixture to a 2-qt. baking dish. Cover with foil. Bake 15 to 20 minutes.

7. Remove foil. Dot top of stuffing with remaining 2 Tbsp. butter. Return to oven. Bake about 20 minutes more or until edges and top are crispy and golden brown. Makes 8 servings.
PER SERVING *310 cal, 16 g fat, 55 mg chol, 633 mg sodium, 32 g carb, 3 g fiber, 3 g sugars, 8 g pro.*

ROASTED SQUASH WITH SPICED PISTACHIOS

Photo on page 261.

This recipe also works with butternut or honeynut squash, cut into 1-inch-thick slices instead of wedges. Roast as directed, about 30 minutes.

HANDS-ON TIME 25 min.
TOTAL TIME 1 hr. 5 min.

1   (1½ to 2 lb.) winter squash, such as kabocha, acorn, or red kuri, washed and sliced into 1½-inch-thick wedges
3   Tbsp. olive oil
    Kosher salt and black pepper
6   Tbsp. unsalted butter
¼   cup raw pistachios, finely chopped
½   tsp. ground cumin
½   tsp. ground turmeric
    Pinch ground cinnamon
    Pinch crushed red pepper (optional)
    Flaked sea salt
1   cup full-fat plain Greek yogurt

1. Preheat oven to 425°F. If desired, remove seeds from squash. On a rimmed baking sheet toss squash with olive oil. Season with salt and black pepper. Roast 40 to 50 minutes or until totally tender, golden brown, and caramelized.
2. Meanwhile, in a small saucepan melt butter over medium heat. Cook 3 to 5 minutes or until butter has browned and started to foam, swirling occasionally. Remove from heat. Add pistachios, cumin, turmeric, cinnamon, and, if desired, crushed red pepper. Season with flaked sea salt.
3. Spoon yogurt onto a serving platter; arrange squash on yogurt then spoon pistachio mixture on top. Sprinkle with additional flaked sea salt, black pepper, and/or a pinch of crushed red pepper. Makes 4 servings.
Make Ahead Roast squash, cover loosely, store up to 4 hours at room temperature, then continue with Step 2.
PER SERVING *395 cal, 34 g fat, 53 mg chol, 597 mg sodium, 18 g carb, 3 g fiber, 3 g sugars, 8 g pro.*

SPICY GREEN BEANS WITH HERB SALAD

CRUSHED POTATOES WITH LEMONY BROWN BUTTER

Photo on page 260.

TOTAL TIME 35 min.

1½ lb. small round and/or fingerling potatoes
2   lemons
6   Tbsp. unsalted butter
2   Tbsp. olive oil
    Kosher salt and black pepper
½   cup finely chopped chives
    Flaked sea salt
    Sour cream (optional)

1. In a 4- to 5-qt. saucepan cook potatoes in enough salted boiling water to cover 12 to 15 minutes or until tender. Drain. When cool enough to handle, lightly crush potatoes.
2. Meanwhile, thinly slice one lemon; remove and discard seeds. Cut remaining lemon in half. Reserve one half for zesting and juicing; cut remaining half into wedges.
3. In a large skillet heat butter over medium heat. Cook, swirling occasionally, until butter begins to brown, 5 to 7 minutes. Add olive oil and lemon slices. Season with salt and pepper. Cook 3 to 4 minutes or until lemon edges start to brown. Remove; reserve lemon slices.
4. Add crushed potatoes to skillet. Season with salt and pepper. Cook 6 minutes or until potatoes start to brown slightly around edges, turning once. Remove from heat. Zest and juice reserved lemon half over potatoes.
5. Transfer to a serving platter with lemon slices. Scatter with chives, flaked sea salt, and additional pepper. Serve with lemon wedges and, if desired, sour cream. Makes 6 to 8 servings.
PER SERVING *229 cal, 16 g fat, 31 mg chol, 386 mg sodium, 22 g carb, 3 g fiber, 2 g sugars, 2 g pro.*

STICKY ROASTED
CARROTS WITH
CITRUS

CRUSHED
POTATOES WITH
LEMONY BROWN
BUTTER

CREAMED
CAULIFLOWER
AND GREENS

BUTTERED
STUFFING WITH
MUSHROOMS
Recipe on page 258

ROASTED SQUASH WITH SPICED PISTACHIOS
Recipe on page 259

STICKY ROASTED CARROTS WITH CITRUS

HANDS-ON TIME 15 min.
TOTAL TIME 40 min.

1   small or ½ medium red onion, cut into ½-inch wedges
2   Tbsp. fresh lemon or lime juice
    Kosher salt and black pepper
2   bunches small carrots (about 1 lb.), tops trimmed, scrubbed, and halved lengthwise
2   small blood oranges and/or clementines, thinly sliced and seeded
4   whole chiles de arbol or ½ tsp. crushed red pepper
2   Tbsp. pure maple syrup or honey
¼   cup olive oil, plus more for drizzling
¼   cup tahini
1½ Tbsp. orange or clementine juice

1. Preheat oven to 425°F. In a small bowl toss together onion and lemon juice. Season with salt and black pepper. Let stand 8 to 10 minutes to lightly pickle.
2. Drain onion, reserving liquid. On a rimmed baking sheet toss onion with carrots, orange slices, chiles, maple syrup, and ¼ cup olive oil.
3. Roast, tossing occasionally, 25 to 30 minutes or until carrots and citrus are totally tender and caramelized at the tips. Drizzle with reserved liquid.
4. In a small bowl combine tahini and orange juice. If necessary, gradually whisk in 1 to 2 Tbsp. water until smooth; season with salt and pepper.
5. Spoon some of the tahini sauce on a large serving platter or plate. Top with carrots, onion, and citrus. Serve remaining tahini sauce alongside. If desired, finish with additional lemon juice, maple syrup, and/or olive oil. Makes 4 servings.
Make Ahead Carrots and citrus can be roasted a few hours ahead and kept loosely wrapped until ready to serve (no need to reheat). Tahini sauce can be made 1 week ahead and kept refrigerated in a sealed container.
PER SERVING *327 cal, 22 g fat, 288 mg sodium, 32 g carb, 6 g fiber, 20 g sugars, 5 g pro.*

CREAMED CAULIFLOWER AND GREENS

TOTAL TIME 40 min.

6   Tbsp. olive oil
¾   cup coarse fresh bread crumbs or panko
    Salt and black pepper
2   Tbsp. chopped fresh thyme, oregano, or marjoram
½   cup thinly sliced yellow onion
1   2- to 2½-lb. head cauliflower, cored and coarsely chopped
1   cup heavy cream
1   clove garlic, minced
¼   tsp. grated fresh nutmeg (optional)
1   8-oz. bunch fresh kale, Swiss chard, or mustard greens, thick stems removed and coarsely torn
½   cup finely shredded Parmesan cheese (optional)

1. In a 5- to 6-qt. pot heat 3 Tbsp. olive oil over medium-high heat. Add bread crumbs; season lightly with salt and pepper. Cook 4 to 5 minutes, stirring occasionally, until golden brown and crisped. Transfer to a small bowl; stir in thyme.
2. Wipe out pot. Heat remaining 3 Tbsp. olive oil over medium. Add onion. Season with salt and pepper. Cook, stirring occasionally, 10 to 12 minutes or until onion is softened and beginning to brown and caramelize around edges.
3. Add cauliflower to pot. Season with salt and pepper. Cook, stirring occasionally, 8 to 10 minutes or until cauliflower is tender but not browned. Add cream, garlic, and, if desired, nutmeg. Bring to boiling; reduce heat. Simmer, uncovered, 5 to 7 minutes or until reduced by about half and slightly thickened.
4. Add kale to pot. Toss with tongs and cook 4 minutes or until kale is wilted and incorporated in cauliflower mixture. Add Parmesan, if desired, and season with salt and pepper. Transfer to a serving dish. Top with bread crumb mixture. Makes 6 servings.
PER SERVING *355 cal, 29 g fat, 45 mg chol, 228 mg sodium, 20 g carb, 6 g fiber, 7 g sugars, 8 g pro.*

PIES "I want people to make pies. And to realize they can make good pies," says Erin Jeanne McDowell, cookbook author and dessert evangelist. For Erin, planning her next Thanksgiving dessert spread begins immediately after the dishes are done. These recipes all have the same pastry recipe but quickly diverge into unexpected riffs on classic pie flavors. Leave your pies sans frills or try one of Erin's tricks to finish them with a bit of flair.

ERIN'S ALL-BUTTAH PIECRUST

HANDS-ON TIME 15 min.
TOTAL TIME 30 min., plus chilling

1¼ cups all-purpose flour
¼ tsp. fine sea salt
½ cup cold unsalted butter, cut into ½-inch cubes
¼ cup ice water, plus more as needed

1. In a medium bowl whisk together flour and salt. Using your hands, toss butter through flour until each piece is well-coated. Cut butter into flour by pressing butter between your fingers and thumbs, flattening the cubes into big shards. For a flaky crust, mix until butter pieces are about the width of walnut halves. For a sturdier crust (for custard pies and for decorative techniques), mix until the butter is about the size of peas.
2. Make a well in center of flour mixture. Add ¼ cup ice water and toss the flour mixture gently (rather than stirring) to moisten and incorporate the water without overworking the flour. Continue adding water, 1 to 2 Tbsp. at a time, and tossing until dough comes together. (Dough should hold together easily without feeling wet or sticky.)
3. Form dough into a disk and wrap tightly in plastic wrap. Refrigerate at least 30 minutes and up to overnight.
4. Once well chilled, roll out dough on a lightly floured surface to about ⅛-inch thickness. Press firmly and evenly, rotating dough as you work to prevent sticking without adding too much flour. (Ideally, roll dough about 2 inches larger than pie plate diameter.)

5. To transfer dough to pie plate, wrap one end of dough around rolling pin. Lift rolling pin to edge of pie plate and unroll dough. Press dough into base of pie plate then trim excess dough to ½ inch around edge of plate. Tuck dough under flush with rim of pie plate. Crimp edges as desired, then refrigerate at least 30 minutes.
6. To parbake: Preheat oven to 425°F. Prick chilled crust with a fork all over base and sides. Cut a square of parchment paper slightly larger than pie plate; press it into base of chilled crust. Fill crust with pie weights (such as dried beans) to brim, making sure weights are flush against sides. Place pie plate on a parchment paper-lined baking sheet. Bake on bottom rack (preferably on a preheated baking stone) 12 to 15 minutes or until edges begin to brown. Remove parchment and pie weights; bake 2 to 3 minutes more or until bottom crust appears set. If crust puffs at any point, prick air bubble with a fork to deflate. Cool completely before filling. Makes one single crust (8 servings).
Make Ahead Make dough, wrap tightly, and refrigerate up to 2 days. For longer storage, wrap in plastic wrap then heavy foil and freeze up to 3 months. Thaw overnight in refrigerator and let stand at room temperature to soften slightly.
PER SERVING *173 cal, 12 g fat, 31 mg chol, 72 mg sodium, 15 g carb, 1 g fiber, 2 g pro.*

Cinnamon Crust Add 1 Tbsp. ground cinnamon and ½ tsp. freshly grated nutmeg to the flour.

Gingerbread Crust Add 1 tsp. ground cinnamon, ¾ tsp. ground ginger, ½ tsp. ground allspice, and ¼ tsp. ground cloves to the flour.

CRANBERRY PIE WITH HONEY MERINGUE

A cloud of honey-sweetened meringue delivers drama and tames the pucker of the filling.

HANDS-ON TIME 30 min.
TOTAL TIME 3 hr. 45 min.

20 oz. fresh or frozen cranberries
1 cup sugar
1 cup orange juice

2 tsp. ground cinnamon
1 tsp. ground ginger
¼ to ½ tsp. ground cloves
Pinch sea salt
¼ cup unsalted butter, at room temperature
Erin's Gingerbread All-Buttah Piecrust, parbaked and cooled (left)
½ cup honey
⅓ cup sugar
4 large egg whites
Pinch ground cinnamon
Generous pinch fine sea salt
1½ tsp. vanilla

1. In a 4- to 5-qt. pot combine cranberries, the 1 cup sugar, orange juice, cinnamon, ginger, cloves, and salt. Cook over medium-high until mixture comes to a simmer, stirring constantly.
2. Reduce heat to medium-low and continue to cook 15 to 17 minutes or until cranberries burst and mixture thickens slightly, stirring occasionally. Stir in butter. Let cool completely.
3. Place oven rack in lower third of oven. Preheat oven to 375°F. Spoon cooled filling into piecrust. Bake 30 to 35 minutes or until crust is golden brown and filling is bubbly. Let cool completely.
4. For meringue: In a large heatproof bowl whisk together honey, the ⅓ cup sugar, egg whites, cinnamon, salt, and vanilla. Set bowl over a large saucepan of simmering water (being careful that bowl doesn't touch water).
5. Cook, whisking constantly, 8 to 10 minutes or until meringue reaches 160°F (or 145°F for at least 3 minutes). Using a mixer with a whisk attachment, whip to medium-stiff peaks.
6. Pile meringue on filling. If desired, toast meringue with a kitchen torch. Makes 8 servings.
PER SERVING *577 cal, 18 g fat, 46 mg chol, 145 mg sodium, 101 g carb, 4 g fiber, 75 g sugars, 6 g pro.*

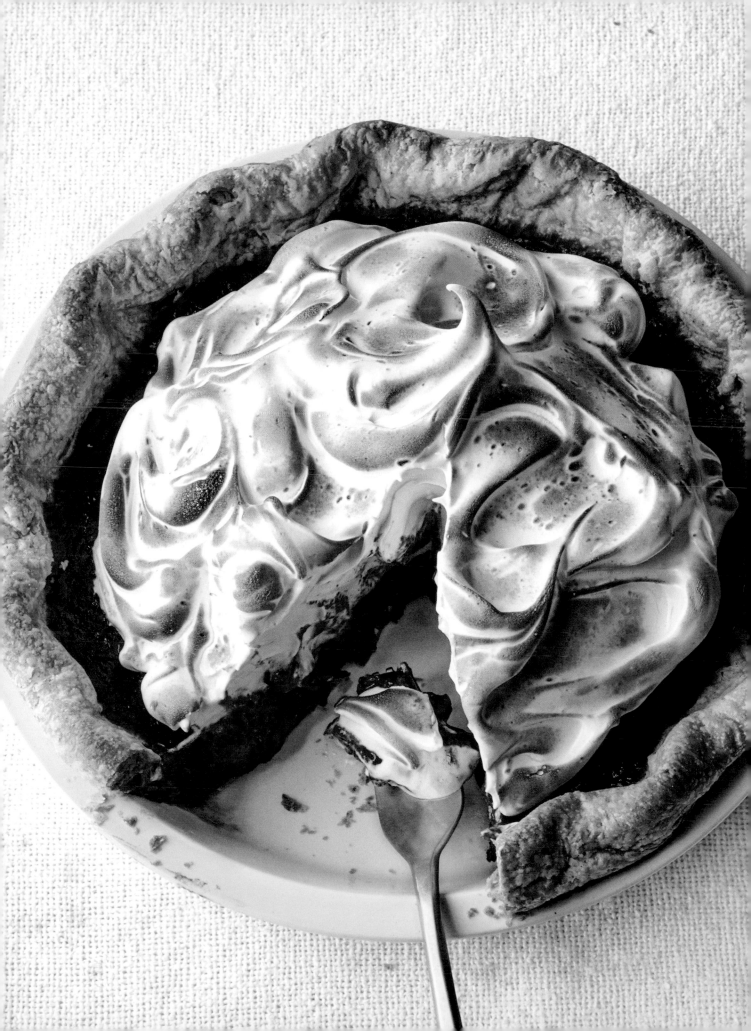

SPICED CIDER
CUSTARD PIE

PUMPKIN-
PECAN PIE

BROWNIE
PIE

CRANBERRY PIE
WITH HONEY
MERINGUE

SPICED CIDER CUSTARD PIE

Even apple pie purists will fall for this one. "I pipe on lots of different-size dots of whipped cream for a graphic look," Erin says. "Don't bother to make them identical."

HANDS-ON TIME 20 min.
TOTAL TIME 3 hr. 15 min.

4	cups apple cider
1	cup whole milk
¾	cup heavy cream
¾	cup packed light brown sugar
½	cup all-purpose flour
1	tsp. ground cinnamon
½	tsp. fine sea salt
	Erin's Cinnamon All-Buttah Piecrust, parbaked and cooled (page 262)
1	cup heavy cream
⅓	cup powdered sugar
1½	tsp. vanilla
1	tsp. ground cinnamon

1. For cider syrup: In a large saucepan bring cider to a simmer over medium. Reduce heat to medium-low. Simmer 1 to 2 hours (depends on pot size), uncovered, until cider is reduced to ½ cup. Let cool completely.
2. In a large liquid measuring cup whisk together cider syrup, milk, and ¾ cup cream.
3. For custard: In a medium bowl whisk together brown sugar, flour, 1 tsp. cinnamon, and the salt. Add cider mixture. Stir until combined.
4. Place a baking sheet on bottom oven rack. Preheat oven to 375°F. Place pie plate on center oven rack. Pour custard into piecrust. Bake 35 to 40 minutes or until custard appears set at edges but is still slightly jiggly in center. Let cool completely.
5. For topping: In a medium bowl whisk together 1 cup cream, the powdered sugar, vanilla, and 1 tsp. cinnamon to medium-stiff peaks. Spread or pipe onto pie. Chill until ready to serve. If desired, sprinkle with additional ground cinnamon. Makes 8 servings.
PER SERVING *580 cal, 32 g fat, 78 mg chol, 378 mg sodium, 67 g carb, 1 g fiber, 41 g sugars, 6 g pro.*

PUMPKIN-PECAN PIE

The pumpkin layer of this double-decker stays soft and spoonable. For extra flavor, add 1½ Tbsp. pumpkin pie spice to the flour in the crust.

HANDS-ON TIME 30 min.
TOTAL TIME 1 hr. 50 min., plus chilling

4	large eggs
½	cup granulated sugar
1	tsp. ground cinnamon
¾	tsp. ground ginger
¼	to ½ tsp. ground cloves
¼	tsp. freshly grated nutmeg
1	15-oz. can pumpkin puree
⅓	cup heavy cream
	Erin's All-Buttah Piecrust, parbaked and cooled (page 262)
⅓	cup packed dark brown sugar
2	Tbsp. maple syrup
1	large egg yolk
1	Tbsp. unsalted butter, melted
1	tsp. vanilla
½	tsp. fine sea salt
1½	cups pecan halves and/or pieces

1. Place oven rack in lower third of oven. Preheat oven to 350°F.
2. For pumpkin filling: In a medium bowl whisk together 2 eggs, granulated sugar, cinnamon, ginger, cloves, and nutmeg until well combined. Whisk in pumpkin and cream until well combined.
3. Pour filling into piecrust. Bake about 30 minutes or until filling is set at edges but still slightly jiggly in center. Let cool completely at room temperature then transfer to freezer while you prepare pecan filling. (Do not place in freezer while warm.)
4. For pecan filling: In a medium bowl whisk together brown sugar, maple syrup, remaining 2 eggs, egg yolk, melted butter, vanilla, and salt.
5. Arrange pecans in an even layer on pumpkin filling. Pour brown sugar mixture over pecans. Transfer pie to oven. Place a foil-lined baking sheet on rack below pie. Bake 40 minutes or until crust is golden brown and custard appears set. Let pie cool completely before serving. Makes 8 servings.
PER SERVING *506 cal, 33 g fat, 162 mg chol, 256 mg sodium, 47 g carb, 4 g fiber, 27 g sugars, 8 g pro.*

BROWNIE PIE

Chocolate fans, rejoice—and make room on the table for this fudgy, almond-studded number. Top with ice cream, whipped cream, chocolate sauce, caramel sauce, or all of the above.

HANDS-ON TIME 20 min.
TOTAL TIME 3 hr.

4	Tbsp. unsalted butter
¼	cup vegetable, canola, or peanut oil
8	oz. bittersweet chocolate, chopped
½	cup granulated sugar
½	cup packed light brown sugar
3	large eggs
2	tsp. vanilla
⅔	cup all-purpose flour
½	tsp. fine sea salt
6	oz. semisweet chocolate, chopped
⅔	cup chopped almonds
	Erin's All-Buttah Piecrust, parbaked and cooled (page 262)
	Ice cream, whipped cream, chocolate sauce, and/or caramel sauce (optional)

1. Preheat oven to 350°F, preferably with a baking stone on bottom rack.
2. In a medium heatproof bowl combine butter, oil, and bittersweet chocolate. Set bowl over a medium saucepan of simmering water (being careful that bowl doesn't touch water) and heat, stirring occasionally, until chocolate and butter are fully melted and combined. Let cool.
3. Add both sugars to the chocolate mixture and mix well with a spatula. Add eggs, one at a time, whisking to fully incorporate. Whisk in vanilla. Mix in flour and salt. Fold in semisweet chocolate and almonds.
4. Pour batter into piecrust. Bake 40 to 45 minutes or until a toothpick inserted into center of pie comes out with moist crumbs. (Avoid overbaking.) Let pie cool at least 20 minutes before serving. If desired, serve with ice cream, whipped cream, chocolate sauce, and/or caramel sauce. Makes 8 servings.
PER SERVING *748 cal, 49 g fat, 116 mg chol, 251 mg sodium, 77 g carb, 6 g fiber, 46 g sugars, 12 g pro.*

great starts
ONE-DISH WONDER

This ham and cheese spin on shirred eggs is everything we want brunch to be: satisfying, indulgent, and practically effortless. Please pass the toast.

SKILLET-BAKED EGGS AND HAM

Traditionally, shirred eggs are baked in a flat-bottom dish with a splash of cream until the whites are firm and yolks are runny. After baking, the mixture may appear loose. It continues to firm up while standing.

TOTAL TIME 25 min.

1   Tbsp. butter
½   cup chopped cooked ham
¼   cup sliced leek
6   eggs
½   cup heavy cream
¼   cup shredded Gruyère cheese (1 oz.)
2   Tbsp. chopped fresh basil
     Kosher salt and black pepper

1. Preheat oven to 400°F. In a 9- or 10-inch cast-iron or oven-going skillet melt butter over medium heat.* Add ham and leek; cook and stir 2 to 3 minutes or until leek is softened.
2. Break eggs, one at a time, into a custard cup and gently pour into skillet, evenly spacing yolks. Drizzle cream around eggs. Sprinkle with cheese and basil.
3. Transfer to oven. Bake 5 to 7 minutes or until whites are set and yolks are just starting to thicken. Remove from oven. Let stand 5 minutes. Season with salt and pepper. Top with additional fresh basil. Makes 4 to 6 servings.
*Tip To serve a crowd, double the recipe. Cook in a 12-inch skillet and bake 8 to 10 minutes.
PER SERVING *378 cal, 26 g fat, 340 mg chol, 693 mg sodium, 17 g carb, 1 g fiber, 2 g sugars, 19 g pro.*

from our test kitchen

PREP SQUASH LIKE A PRO

If peeling and cutting up a butternut squash seems daunting, we can help.

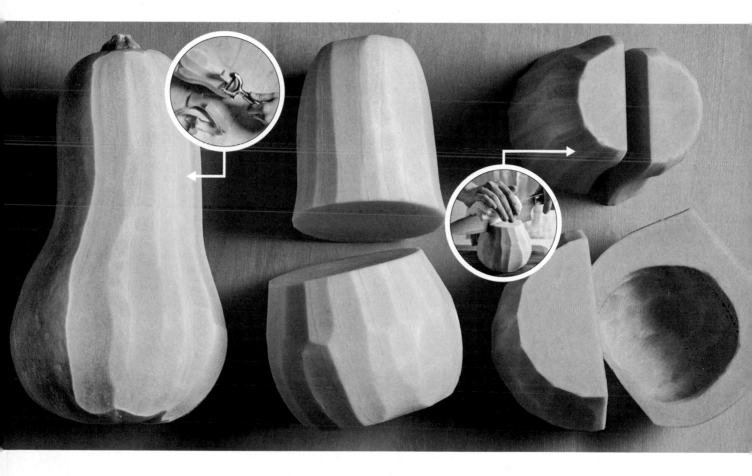

1 PEEL THE SKIN With top of the squash (neck) toward you, start in the middle and peel in firm strokes to the stem. Rotate and repeat with the opposite half (bell shape).

PEELER SMARTS A sharp Y-peeler works best for easily slicing over curves and through thick skin.

2 CUT CROSSWISE Lay the squash on its side. Using a large sharp chef's knife, trim off the top and bottom, then cut through the center.

SAFETY FIRST Stabilize the squash with your nondominant hand. Make an initial cut using light pressure to penetrate the squash flesh, then firmly slice all the way through. That first cut ensures the squash stays put.

3 REMOVE SEEDS Cut each section in half lengthwise. Using a large spoon, scrape out seeds and any pulp or stringy bits. Place each half cut side down and slice or chop as desired.

BONUS SNACK To roast the seeds: Rinse, drain, and dry with paper towels. Toss with salt and olive oil; roast on a baking sheet at 300°F, 50 to 60 minutes until crisp, stirring every 15 minutes.

PETITE BEEF
WELLINGTONS
Recipe on page 290

december

Stir up magical moments with this slate of revitalized holiday recipes. Discover how a tweak, added ingredient, or presentation can renew attraction to long-ago favorites.

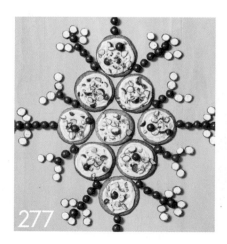

277

284

294

EGGNOG
DREAM
BARS

holiday baking
RETRO REDO

"A tried-and-true cookie recipe is a springboard for twisting and tweaking," says Jessie Sheehan, who, as author of *The Vintage Bake,* has a knack for reimagining old-fashioned treats. This holiday, she nudges a few Christmas cookie Hall of Famers toward modern with spices, nuts, and sprinkles. It's a collection that will remind you of treats you grew up with—only better.

Jessie Sheehan derives much of her baking inspiration from vintage recipe booklets collected during more than a decade while working at Baked, a Brooklyn bakery known for classic American desserts, she was drawn to the timeless nature of these old-school recipes. "They were simple and reliable—ideal for experimentation," she says. "By playing with an unexpected spice or extract, I can appeal to the adventurous palates of today's bakers."

EGGNOG DREAM BARS

You might know this crisp, gooey, layered bar of chocolate chips, walnuts, and coconut by magic bar, seven-layer bar, or Hello Dolly bar. Jessie updates her holiday version with cinnamon, nutmeg, cloves, and rum to play off eggnog. "As flavors intensify, they taste even better the next day—if you can wait," she says.

HANDS-ON TIME 20 min.
TOTAL TIME 2 hr. 20 min., includes cooling

	Nonstick cooking spray
10	Tbsp. unsalted butter, melted
5	Tbsp. rum (optional)
4	tsp. ground cinnamon
2	cups finely crushed graham cracker crumbs (12 rectangle crackers)
2	cups shredded sweetened coconut
1	14-oz. can sweetened condensed milk
2	tsp. vanilla
1	tsp. freshly grated nutmeg or ½ tsp. ground nutmeg
⅛	tsp. ground cloves
1¼	cups chopped walnuts, toasted (tip, page 37)
1	cup bittersweet chocolate chips
½	cup milk chocolate chips
½	cup white baking chips

1. Preheat oven to 350°F. Line a 13×9-inch baking pan with foil. Coat with nonstick cooking spray.
2. For crust: In a large bowl combine butter, 2 Tbsp. rum (if using), and 2 tsp. cinnamon. Stir in cracker crumbs and 1 cup coconut to combine. Transfer to prepared pan. Press firmly and evenly into bottom of pan. Freeze 20 minutes. Bake crust 10 minutes or until lightly browned. Place on a wire rack.
3. In a medium bowl whisk together sweetened condensed milk, 3 Tbsp. rum (if using), vanilla, remaining 2 tsp. cinnamon, the nutmeg, and cloves. Set aside. Sprinkle walnuts, bittersweet and milk chocolate chips, and white baking chips over crust. Top with remaining 1 cup coconut. Drizzle with sweetened condensed milk mixture.
4. Bake 25 to 30 minutes or until filling is set and lightly browned, rotating pan once halfway through. Cool completely on a wire rack. Using edges of foil, lift out uncut bars. Cut into bars. Store in an airtight container in the refrigerator up to 3 days. Makes 24 bars.
PER BAR *302 cal, 19 g fat, 20 mg chol, 103 mg sodium, 31 g carb, 2 g fiber, 23 g sugars, 4 g pro.*

PB&M FUDGE

Photo on page 272.

Jessie turns a childhood favorite— peanut butter and marshmallow creme on white bread—into a confection that hits the same salty-sweet notes.

HANDS-ON TIME 20 min.
TOTAL TIME 2 hr. 20 min., includes chilling

1	lb. white baking chocolate, chopped
¾	cup creamy peanut butter
1	14-oz. can sweetened condensed milk
1	Tbsp. vanilla
1	tsp. kosher salt
3	cups tiny marshmallows
2	cups salted, roasted peanuts, chopped
	Sea salt flakes
	Turbinado sugar

1. Grease a 9×9-inch baking pan. Line with parchment paper, allowing edges to extending paper beyond edges of pan. Grease paper.
2. Place chocolate and peanut butter in a large heatproof bowl. Set bowl over a pan of simmering water (water should not touch bottom of bowl). Stir occasionally until melted and smooth. Stir in sweetened condensed milk, vanilla, and kosher salt until combined. Remove from heat.
3. Stir in marshmallows and peanuts. Transfer to prepared pan. Cover with plastic wrap; flatten fudge evenly. Remove plastic wrap. Sprinkle with sea salt and sugar.
4. Chill, covered, 2 hours or until firm. Cut into 1-inch pieces. Store in an airtight container in the refrigerator up to 1 month or freeze up to 2 months. Makes 81 pieces.
PER PIECE *88 cal, 5 g fat, 3 mg chol, 65 mg sodium, 9 g carb, 8 g sugars, 2 g pro.*

PB&M FUDGE
Recipe on page 271

TAHINI BLOSSOMS
Recipe on page 274

TAHINI BLOSSOMS

Photo on page 273.

If peanut butter blossoms are a must-have in your cookie tin, consider this version. Jessie swaps in tahini, the Middle Eastern sesame seed paste commonly used in hummus. It gives the chocolate-topped cookie complex nuttiness.

HANDS-ON TIME 30 min.
TOTAL TIME 3 hr., includes freezing

- 2¼ cups all-purpose flour
- 1¼ tsp. kosher salt
- 1 tsp. baking soda
- ¼ tsp. baking powder
- 1¼ cups packed light brown sugar
- ¾ cup unsalted butter, melted and slightly cooled
- ¼ cup shortening
- ¾ cup granulated sugar
- 1 Tbsp. vanilla
- 1 egg
- 2 egg yolks
- ¾ cup tahini (sesame seed paste)
  Sea salt flakes
- 60 milk chocolate Kisses

1. Line two cookie sheets with parchment paper. In a medium bowl whisk together flour, kosher salt, baking soda, and baking powder.
2. In a large bowl beat brown sugar, butter, shortening, ¼ cup granulated sugar, and the vanilla with a mixer on medium until combined. Beat in egg and egg yolks. Beat in tahini. Add flour mixture; beat on low until combined.
3. Chill, covered, 30 minutes or until firm enough to handle. Roll into sixty 2-tsp.-size balls. Place remaining ½ cup granulated sugar in a small bowl. Roll balls in sugar to coat. Arrange on one prepared cookie sheet. Sprinkle with sea salt. Cover with plastic wrap. Freeze 2 hours or until firm.
4. Preheat oven to 350°F. Transfer 16 dough balls at a time to second cookie sheet. Bake 10 to 12 minutes or until light brown, rotating sheet halfway through. Immediately after removing from oven, gently press a Kiss in center of cookies. Cool on a wire rack. Store in an airtight container at room temperature up to 3 days. Makes 60 cookies.
PER COOKIE *119 cal, 7 g fat, 17 mg chol, 74 mg sodium, 15 g carb, 10 g sugars, 2 g pro.*

CHOCOLATE-PISTACHIO WHIRLIGIGS

"I love the old-timey name for a slice-and-bake pinwheel or spiral cookie," Jessie says. For this iteration, she mixes Dutch-process cocoa into the dough for deep chocolate flavor and makes homemade pistachio paste for the swirl.

HANDS-ON TIME 40 min.
TOTAL TIME 3 hr. 40 min., includes chilling

- 1½ cups all-purpose flour
- ¾ cup Dutch-process cocoa powder
- 1⅛ tsp. salt
- ¾ tsp. baking powder
- ½ tsp. baking soda
- 1¼ cups packed light brown sugar
- ¾ cup plus 1 Tbsp. unsalted butter, softened
- ½ cup granulated sugar
- 3 Tbsp. vegetable oil
- 2 tsp. vanilla
- 2 eggs
- 1 egg yolk
- 1½ cups shelled roasted pistachios
- ⅛ tsp. almond extract
  Green food coloring
- 2 Tbsp. milk

1. In a medium bowl whisk together flour, cocoa powder, 1 tsp. salt, the baking powder, and baking soda.
2. In a large bowl beat brown sugar, ¾ cup butter, ¼ cup granulated sugar, the oil, and vanilla 2 minutes on medium or until well combined. Add one egg and yolk; beat on low until combined.
3. Add flour mixture. Beat on low until some streaks of flour remain. Stir until combined. (Dough will be sticky.) Chill, covered, 2 to 24 hours.

4. For pistachio paste: In a food processor combine 1 cup pistachios and remaining ¼ cup granulated sugar. Pulse until finely chopped. Add 2 Tbsp. water, remaining 1 Tbsp. butter and egg, the almond extract, and remaining ⅛ tsp. salt. Pulse until a thick paste forms. Add a few drops of green food coloring. Pulse to combine. Transfer to a bowl. Chill, covered, 30 minutes.
5. Between two sheets of parchment paper sprinkled with cocoa powder roll out half the chilled dough to a 10×8-inch rectangle; repeat with the second half of dough. Chill 15 to 30 minutes or just until firm.
6. Remove top sheet of parchment from one sheet of dough. Spread with half the pistachio paste, leaving a ½-inch border. From a long side, tightly roll up dough, using parchment paper to help. (If dough sticks, use a thin metal spatula to scrape dough from paper.) Repeat with remaining dough and pistachio paste. Chill, covered, overnight. (Roll the logs occasionally to keep their shape.)
7. Preheat oven to 350°F. Line a cookie sheet with parchment paper. Finely chop remaining pistachios; place in a small bowl. Place milk in a second small bowl. Using a sharp knife, cut logs into ½-inch slices. Roll edge of each slice in milk then pistachios. Place slices 2 inches apart on prepared cookie sheet. Bake 11 to 13 minutes or until edges are firm. Let cool on a wire rack. Store in an airtight container at room temperature up to 3 days. Makes 38 cookies.
PER COOKIE *141 cal, 8 g fat, 25 mg chol, 137 mg sodium, 16 g carb, 1 g fiber, 10 g sugars, 2 g pro.*

"I LOVE TAKING AN AIRTIGHT RECIPE AND GIVING IT A NEW PERSONALITY." — JESSIE SHEEHAN

CHOCOLATE-PISTACHIO
WHIRLIGIGS

MALTED BUTTER
RICHES

MALTED BUTTER RICHES

Jessie discovered the butter rich—a thin, tender brown sugar cookie with brown butter frosting—in a vintage recipe pamphlet then rejiggered it to incorporate malted milk powder, a favorite ingredient. "I'm unapologetically generous with the frosting. Brown butter highlights the toasted nuttiness of the malt."

HANDS-ON TIME 45 min.
TOTAL TIME 2 hr. 30 min., includes chilling

COOKIES

2   cups all-purpose flour
⅔   cup malted milk powder
1   tsp. baking soda
1   tsp. salt
¾   cup unsalted butter, softened
¼   cup shortening
¾   cup packed light brown sugar
1   Tbsp. vanilla
1   egg
1   egg yolk

MALTED BROWN BUTTER FROSTING

¾   cup unsalted butter
4   cups powdered sugar
1   cup malted milk powder
½   tsp. salt
2   tsp. vanilla
½   to ⅔ cup heavy cream

1. For Cookies: Line two cookie sheets with parchment paper. In a medium bowl whisk together flour, malted milk powder, baking soda, and salt.
2. In a large mixing bowl beat softened butter, shortening, brown sugar, and vanilla on medium 2 minutes or until fluffy. Add egg and egg yolk. Beat on low until combined. Add dry ingredients. Beat on low until some streaks of flour remain. Use a wooden spoon to stir until combined.
3. Using a small cookie scoop or 1 Tbsp. measure, scoop dough and roll into 1¼-inch balls. Place 2 inches apart on prepared cookie sheets. Cover with plastic wrap. Chill 1 hour or up to 2 days.
4. Preheat oven to 350°F. Bake cookies 9 to 11 minutes or until light brown. Cool on a wire rack.
5. Meanwhile, for Malted Brown Butter Frosting: In a medium saucepan heat butter over medium-high heat 5 minutes or until butter smells nutty and browned bits begin to form on bottom of pan. Remove from heat. Cool slightly. In a

JUMBO SPRINKLE COOKIES

large bowl combine powdered sugar, malted milk powder, and salt. Add brown butter (and the browned bits) and vanilla. Stir in enough heavy cream to reach spreadable consistency. Spread frosting over cooled cookies. If desired, top with crushed malted milk balls. Store in an airtight container in the refrigerator up to 3 days. Makes 36 cookies.
PER COOKIE *214 cal, 11 g fat, 36 mg chol, 163 mg sodium, 27 g carb, 20 g sugars, 2 g pro.*

JUMBO SPRINKLE COOKIES

"Bigger is better when it comes to a sugar cookie," says Jessie, who uses a ¼-cup ice cream scoop for oversize portions of the rainbow-flecked dough. "The key is not to overbake. Pull them from the oven a minute or two early to ensure the centers are super chewy."

HANDS-ON TIME 15 min.
TOTAL TIME 24 hr. 30 min., includes chilling

2½   cups all-purpose flour
1   tsp. baking soda
¾   tsp. salt
½   cup unsalted butter, melted
6   Tbsp. vegetable oil
1   cup sugar
1   egg
1   egg yolk
⅓   cup light-color corn syrup
1   Tbsp. vanilla
½   cup multicolor sprinkles

1. Line a large cookie sheet with parchment paper. In a medium bowl whisk together flour, soda, and salt.
2. In a large bowl beat butter, oil, and sugar on medium 1 minute or until smooth. Add egg, egg yolk, corn syrup, and vanilla. Beat until combined. Add flour mixture and sprinkles. Beat on low until combined.
3. Using a ¼-cup measure cup, place dough mounds on prepared sheet. Cover with plastic wrap. Chill 24 hours or up to 3 days.
4. Preheat oven to 350°F. Divide dough between two parchment-lined cookie sheets, placing each 3 inches apart. Top each with additional sprinkles. Bake 14 to 16 minutes or until edges are light brown and centers appear slightly underdone, rotating halfway through. Remove to a wire rack. Gently press with spatula to flatten cookies. Cool completely. Store in an airtight container at room temperature up to 3 days. Makes 12 cookies.
PER COOKIE *369 cal, 18 g fat, 51 mg chol, 265 mg sodium, 44 g carb, 1 g fiber, 28 g sugars, 4 g pro.*

TRADITION REDEFINED

A writer and lifestyle expert embraces her Japanese-American heritage and blended family by reimagining two Hanukkah favorites.

"I wholeheartedly believe that when we adapt rituals to fit our modern lifestyles, we ensure they continue for years to come," says Kristin Eriko Posner, founder of *Nourish Co.,* a website that helps ethnically blended families develop modern traditions. When Kristin converted to Judaism before marrying husband Bryan, she wanted to find ways to embrace and celebrate both their cultural backgrounds. "Too often we think of rituals in black-and-white. But there's beauty in the shades between," she says. "If it helps you connect, break the rules." For Kristin, that means incorporating Japanese ingredients in Hanukkah dishes, like adding mochi (sweet rice) flour to latkes and yuzu zest to doughnut filling. "I want to help give people permission to play."

MOCHI LATKES

Mochi flour (also called sweet rice flour or mochiko) is ground from the sweet starchy rice used to make sticky rice. Here, it gives fried potato fritters crisp edges with a slightly chewy interior. "I set out a latke bar with an array of toppings," she says. "Some options are classics like lox and crème fraîche. Others, like matcha salt, have a Japanese tilt."

TOTAL TIME 45 min.

1   russet potato (1 lb.), peeled
1   medium yellow onion
⅓   cup plus 2 Tbsp. mochi flour
2   eggs, lightly beaten
½   tsp. salt
3   cups vegetable oil for frying
    Toppings, such as Asian Pear Sauce, Matcha Salt, lox, crème fraîche, and/or fresh dill weed

1. Using a box grater, grate potato and onion. Place on a double thickness of 100%-cotton cheesecloth; squeeze to remove liquid. Transfer potato and onion to a large mixing bowl. Add mochi flour, eggs, and salt. Stir to combine.

2. In a heavy 12-inch skillet heat oil to 325°F over medium-low heat. Place a wire rack on a cookie sheet. Pat potato mixture into 2½-inch rounds. Cook a few at a time in hot oil 5 to 7 minutes or until golden brown, turning once. Transfer to a wire rack to cool slightly. Serve with toppings. Makes 20 latkes.

PER LATKE 85 cal, 6 g fat, 19 mg chol, 36 mg sodium, 7 g carb, 1 g pro.

Asian Pear Sauce In a large saucepan combine 1 lb. cored Asian pears, 1 small cored Fuji apple, 2 Tbsp. water, 1½ tsp. lemon juice, ½ tsp. vanilla, ¼ tsp. ground cinnamon, and ⅛ tsp. salt. Bring to boiling; reduce heat to low. Simmer, covered, 30 to 40 minutes or until fruit is very soft, stirring every 10 minutes. Uncover; cool. Transfer to a blender. Blend until smooth.

Matcha Salt Sift 1 tsp. culinary matcha powder into a small bowl; stir in 1 Tbsp. kosher salt. Sprinkle over latkes just before serving.

"THERE'S MAGIC TO LETTING A TRADITION EVOLVE SO IT CAN PICK UP A PIECE OF EACH GENERATION ALONG THE WAY."
— KRISTIN ERIKO POSNER

YUZU (A TART ASIAN CITRUS FRUIT) IS IN SEASON DURING EARLY WINTER. "AT THE DARKEST TIME OF YEAR, IT'S REFRESHING TO HAVE A FLAVOR THAT'S SO BRIGHT," KRISTIN SAYS.

YUZU DOUGHNUTS

If you can't find fresh yuzu, substitute Meyer lemon. Or reduce milk in filling to ½ cup and use 2 Tbsp. bottled yuzu juice, available at Asian markets.

HANDS-ON TIME 25 min.
TOTAL TIME 3 hr. 20 min., includes chilling and rising

- ¾ cup plus 2 Tbsp. sugar
- ½ cup warm milk (105°F to 115°F)
- 1 tsp. active dry yeast
- 1¼ cups bread flour
- ¼ cup all-purpose flour
- 1 tsp. salt
- 1 Tbsp. butter, cubed and softened
- 2 egg yolks
- 2 Tbsp. cornstarch
- ⅔ cup milk
- 2 yuzu, zested (2 tsp.)
  Vegetable oil for deep-frying

1. For dough: In a small bowl combine 2 Tbsp. sugar, the warm milk, and yeast. Let stand 10 minutes. Meanwhile, in a medium bowl combine flours and 1 tsp. salt. Add milk mixture and butter. Stir until a soft dough forms. Transfer to a lightly floured surface. Knead 2 minutes or until dough feels elastic and comes together into a ball. Cover; let rise 1 to 1½ hours or until doubled in size.

2. Meanwhile, for filling: In a medium bowl beat egg yolks with a mixer on medium, slowly adding ¼ cup sugar. Beat 1 to 2 minutes more until color lightens. Sift cornstarch into egg mixture. Beat on low just until combined.

3. In a small saucepan heat milk until steam forms (do not boil). Remove from heat. Gradually whisk half the hot milk into egg mixture. Return egg and milk mixture to saucepan. Turn heat to medium-low. Whisk 1 minute more or until thickened and bubbly. Remove from heat. Stir in zest. Transfer to a medium bowl. Lay plastic wrap on filling to cover. Chill 1 hour.

4. On the floured surface, divide dough into eight equal pieces. Shape each into a ball. Cover. Let rest 15 minutes.

5. Line a baking sheet with parchment paper. Using a rolling pin, roll each ball into a 5-inch circle. For each doughnut: Add 1 Tbsp. filling to center of dough. Moisten dough edges with water; bring edges up and over filling, pinching and folding to seal. Place on prepared baking sheet. Cover; let rise 45 to 60 minutes or until nearly double in size.

6. Meanwhile, in a large saucepan heat 2 inches oil to 365°F. Place remaining ½ cup sugar in a shallow dish. Cook doughnuts, two at a time, in hot oil 2 minutes or until golden, turning once. Using a slotted spoon, transfer to a paper-towel-lined baking sheet. While warm, roll in sugar to coat. Makes 8 doughnuts.

PER DOUGHNUT *291 cal, 11 g fat, 53 mg chol, 171 mg sodium, 45 g carb, 1 g fiber, 24 g sugars, 5 g pro.*

WINTER BEAUTIES

Celebrate the distinctively winter crop of sweet and satisfying produce. Fuyu persimmons, pomelos, and quince are three cold-weather fruits to watch for this season.

ESCAROLE, RADICCHIO, AND FUYU PERSIMMON SALAD

TOTAL TIME 20 min.

2   Tbsp. apple cider
1   Tbsp. cider vinegar
1   Tbsp. minced shallot
¼   tsp. salt
⅛   tsp. black pepper
1   Tbsp. extra virgin olive oil
1½   tsp. walnut or olive oil
½   tsp. Dijon mustard
½   head radicchio, leaves torn into bite-size pieces
½   head escarole, leaves torn into bite-size pieces
2   medium Fuyu persimmons, cap removed, halved, and thinly sliced
⅓   cup toasted walnuts, chopped (tip, page 37)
3   oz. Manchego cheese, thinly sliced

1. In a screw-top jar combine cider, vinegar, shallot, salt, and pepper. Let stand 5 minutes. Add oils and mustard. Cover; shake to combine. Season to taste.
2. In a large bowl combine radicchio, escarole, persimmons, and walnuts. Drizzle with vinaigrette; toss to coat. Serve with cheese. Makes 4 servings.
PER SERVING *332 cal, 20 g fat, 21 mg chol, 271 mg sodium, 33 g carb, 2 g fiber, 2 g sugars, 8 g pro.*

POMEGRANATE POT ROAST

To deseed a pomegranate, trim the top and bottom to expose the seeds. Score an X across top to loosen the fruit. Working in a bowl of water, split the pomegranate in half and separate the seeds from the peel and white membranes.

HANDS-ON TIME 25 min.
TOTAL TIME 2 hr. 40 min.

2½   lb. boneless beef chuck roast
1   Tbsp. olive oil
1½   cups chopped yellow onions
     Salt and black pepper
¼   cup tomato paste
6   large cloves garlic, minced
2½   cups pomegranate juice
1   cup reduced-sodium beef broth
6   sprigs fresh thyme
3   sprigs fresh rosemary
3   bay leaves
1   lb. carrots, peeled and cut into 1½-inch pieces
2   medium Fuyu persimmons, caps removed, halved, and cut into wedges
¼   cup honey
1   Tbsp. lemon juice
¼   cup pomegranate seeds

1. Preheat oven to 350°F. Sprinkle meat with 1 tsp. salt and ½ tsp. black pepper. In a 5- to 6-qt. Dutch oven heat oil over medium-high. Add meat. Cook on all sides until browned, about 4 minutes per side. Transfer to a plate.
2. Reduce heat to medium. Add onions to pot. Season with salt and pepper. Cook 4 minutes or until tender, stirring to scrape up browned bits. Push onions to one side; add tomato paste to center of pot. Cook and stir 2 minutes. Add garlic. Cook 1 minute more, stirring to combine all.
3. Add 1 cup pomegranate juice and the beef broth, stirring to scrape up any bits. Tie thyme and rosemary together with 100%-cotton kitchen string. Add to pot with bay leaves. Bring to boiling. Return meat to pot. Add carrots.
4. Transfer to oven. Cook, covered, 1½ hours. Add persimmons. Cook, covered, 30 minutes more or until beef is very tender. Remove from oven. Discard bay leaves and herb stems. Let stand 15 minutes.
5. Meanwhile, for pomegranate syrup: In a medium saucepan combine remaining 1½ cups pomegranate juice, the honey, and lemon juice. Bring to boiling over medium heat, stirring to dissolve honey; reduce heat. Simmer, uncovered, 30 minutes or until reduced to ½ cup. Cool (syrup will thicken slightly as it cools).
6. To serve: Drizzle meat with pomegranate syrup. Top with pomegranate seeds and, if desired, additional fresh thyme and rosemary. Makes 6 servings.
PER SERVING *412 cal, 12 g fat, 107 mg chol, 849 mg sodium, 44 g carb, 4 g fiber, 33 g sugars, 35 g pro.*

ESCAROLE, RADICCHIO, AND FUYU PERSIMMON SALAD

POMEGRANATE
POT ROAST

POMELO MARGARITA BARS

One aspect of margarita flavor in these bars is a hint of natural bitterness from tequila. For milder flavor reduce tequila to 1 tablespoon.

HANDS-ON TIME 20 min.
TOTAL TIME 4 hr., includes chilling

1   cup all-purpose flour
⅓   cup packed brown sugar
1   tsp. kosher salt
½   cup unsalted butter, cut into small pieces
2   pomelos or pink grapefruit
6   egg yolks
⅔   cup granulated sugar
2   Tbsp. cornstarch
2   Tbsp. unsalted butter
2   Tbsp. tequila (optional)
½   tsp. vanilla
2   Tbsp. granulated sugar
½   tsp. sea salt flakes

1. Preheat oven to 350°F. Grease an 8×8-inch baking pan. Line the pan with parchment paper, extending paper to beyond pan edges; grease paper.

POMELO MARGARITA BARS

2. In a food processor combine flour, brown sugar, and ½ tsp. salt; pulse to combine. Add ½ cup butter. Process until dough resembles fine crumbs. Press firmly and evenly into bottom of prepared pan. Bake 25 minutes or until lightly browned. Reduce oven to 300°F.
3. While crust is baking, remove 1 tsp. zest from one pomelo; wrap zest in plastic wrap and chill. Using a sharp knife, remove peel and white pith from both pomelos. Working over a bowl to catch juices, carefully cut between membrane and flesh to remove fruit segments. Add segments and any juice to a blender. Blend until pureed. Strain through a fine-mesh sieve; discard solids (about 1 cup foamy juice).
4. In a medium saucepan stir together juice, egg yolks, ⅔ cup granulated sugar, the cornstarch, and remaining ½ tsp. salt. Cook and stir over medium heat until thickened and bubbly. Reduce heat to medium-low. Cook and stir 1 minute more. Remove from heat. Stir in 2 Tbsp. butter until melted. Stir in tequila, if using, and vanilla.
5. Pour filling over hot crust. Bake 15 minutes. Cool in pan on wire rack 1 hour. Chill 2 hours or overnight.
6. In a small bowl mix together 2 Tbsp. granulated sugar and chilled zest. Stir in sea salt. Sprinkle evenly over uncut bars. Lift uncut bars from pan using parchment. Remove paper. Cut into bars. Store in a single layer in an airtight container in refrigerator up to 2 days or freeze up to 3 months. Makes 16 bars.
PER BAR *186 cal, 9 g fat, 88 mg chol, 148 mg sodium, 25 g carb, 1 g fiber, 17 g sugars, 2 g pro.*

SPICED RICE WITH PICKLED QUINCE AND POMEGRANATE

Pickled quince can be made up to a week ahead. Store in the pickling brine in the refrigerator then drain just before serving.

HANDS-ON TIME 25 min.
TOTAL TIME 2 hr.

PICKLED QUINCE
1   cup apple cider vinegar
½   cup sugar
1   2- to 3-inch stick cinnamon
1   tsp. allspice berries

⅛   tsp. ground cardamom
3   fresh quince, peeled, cored, and cut into ½-inch wedges (1½ lb.)

RICE
1   Tbsp. unsalted butter
½   cup chopped yellow onion
2   large cloves garlic, minced
1½   tsp. salt
¾   tsp. ground cumin
½   tsp. ground coriander
½   tsp. ground cinnamon
¼   tsp. ground cardamom
¼   tsp. ground turmeric
⅛   tsp. ground cloves
¼   tsp. black pepper
1   cup basmati rice, rinsed and well drained
1¾   cups reduced-sodium chicken or vegetable broth
½   cup pomegranate seeds
⅓   cup chopped toasted pistachios (tip, page 37)
2   Tbsp. chopped fresh mint
2   Tbsp. chopped fresh cilantro

1. For pickled quince: In a medium saucepan combine vinegar, ½ cup water, the sugar, cinnamon, allspice, and cardamom. Bring to boiling; reduce heat. Simmer over medium heat, stirring to dissolve sugar. Add quince. Cover. Bring to boiling over medium-high heat; reduce heat to medium-low. Simmer 15 to 20 minutes or until tender. Cool.
2. For rice: In a 3-qt. saucepan melt butter over medium. Add onion. Cook and stir 5 minutes or until tender. Add garlic; cook 1 minute more. Add salt, cumin, coriander, cinnamon, cardamom, turmeric, cloves, and pepper. Add rice. Cook and stir 2 minutes or until rice begins to smell toasted. Add broth. Bring to boiling over high; reduce heat to medium-low. Simmer, covered, 15 minutes or until rice is tender and liquid is absorbed. Remove from heat. Fluff with a fork. Let stand, covered, 10 minutes.
3. Drain pickled quince, discarding whole spices. Stir quince into rice. Top with pomegranate seeds, nuts, mint, and cilantro. Makes 8 servings.
PER SERVING *177 cal, 4 g fat, 4 mg chol, 335 mg sodium, 33 g carb, 2 g fiber, 4 g sugars, 4 g pro.*

SPICED RICE
WITH PICKLED
QUINCE AND
POMEGRANATE

MINI GREENS-AND-
CHEESE SOUFFLÉS

good things come in
SMALL PACKAGES

Elegantly individual, petite dishes of traditional holiday fare are easy to serve on a buffet or around the table. Guests will appreciate the host's attention to detail.

MINI GREENS-AND-CHEESE SOUFFLÉS

For a large soufflé to serve 8, use a 1½-quart soufflé dish. Top with sage leaves then bake 45 minutes or until a knife inserted in center comes out clean.

HANDS-ON TIME 20 min.
TOTAL TIME 1 hr. 5 min.

4	eggs, separated
2	Tbsp. butter
2	Tbsp. olive oil
½	cup finely chopped onion
2	cloves garlic, minced
4	cups chopped, stemmed Swiss chard
¼	cup all-purpose flour
¼	tsp. dry mustard
½	tsp. salt
¼	tsp. black pepper
1	cup milk
2	cups shredded Fontina cheese (8 oz.)
1	Tbsp. chopped fresh sage
16	sage leaves

1. Let egg whites and yolks stand at room temperature 30 minutes. Meanwhile, arrange eight 4- to 6-oz. ramekins in a 15×10-inch baking pan.
2. In a medium saucepan heat butter and oil over medium-high heat until butter is melted. Add onion and garlic. Cook and stir 3 minutes. Gradually add chard, tossing until wilted. Stir in flour, mustard, salt, and pepper. Cook and stir until coated with flour. Add milk. Cook and stir until thickened and bubbly. Reduce heat to low. Add cheese, a little at a time, stirring until melted. Stir in chopped sage. In a small bowl beat egg yolks with a fork until combined. Add 1 cup chard mixture to yolks, stirring constantly. Pour yolk mixture into saucepan. Cook and stir over medium heat just until boiling. Transfer to a large bowl; cover surface with plastic wrap. Cool at least 15 minutes or up to 1 hour.
3. Preheat oven to 350°F. In a medium bowl beat egg whites on medium to high until stiff peaks form. Gently fold about half the egg whites into chard mixture. Repeat with remaining egg whites.
4. Spoon mixture into ramekins, filling each nearly full. Lay two sage leaves on each. Bake 35 to 40 minutes or until puffed and golden and a knife inserted near centers comes out clean. Serve immediately. Makes 8 servings.
PER SERVING *241 cal, 18 g fat, 136 mg chol, 411 mg sodium, 7 g carb, 1 g fiber, 3 g sugars, 12 g pro.*

SAUSAGE-STUFFED HONEYNUT SQUASH

Photo on page 288.
HANDS-ON TIME 20 min.
TOTAL TIME 1 hr. 5 min.

4	honeynut squash (about 13 oz. each), halved lengthwise, or 4 very small (about 1 lb.) butternut squash, halved lengthwise
2	Tbsp. olive oil
4	oz. bulk pork sausage
1	small onion, halved and thinly sliced (½ cup)
2	cloves garlic, minced
1½	cups cauliflower florets, finely chopped
1	cup chopped fresh baby spinach
¼	cup dried tart red cherries, chopped
¼	cup salted, roasted pistachios, chopped
¼	tsp. salt
¼	tsp. black pepper
	Chopped flat-leaf parsley
	Lemon zest
	Balsamic Reduction

1. Preheat oven to 400°F. Line a large baking sheet with foil. Coat with nonstick cooking spray. Scoop out seeds from squash. Place cut sides down on prepared baking sheet. Bake 20 minutes for honeynut squash (35 to 40 minutes for butternut halves) or until tender and starting to brown.
2. In a large skillet heat 1 Tbsp. oil over medium heat. Add sausage, onion, and garlic; cook and stir until sausage is cooked through, breaking up sausage as it cooks. Stir in cauliflower; spread in an even layer in skillet. Cook 4 minutes or until tender and just starting to brown. Stir occasionally, then return cauliflower to an even layer for best browning.
3. Remove from heat. Stir in spinach until wilted. Stir in cherries, pistachios, salt, and pepper.
4. Turn squash halves cut sides up. Season with additional salt and pepper. Fill cavities with sausage mixture. Bake 10 minutes more. Top with parsley and lemon zest. Drizzle with Balsamic Reduction just before serving. Makes 8 servings.
Balsamic Reduction In a small saucepan stir together 1 cup balsamic vinegar and 2 Tbsp. honey. Bring to boiling; reduce heat. Simmer, uncovered, 25 to 30 minutes or until syrupy and reduced to ⅓ cup. Let cool. Store in an airtight container at room temperature up to 1 day.
PER SERVING *230 cal, 8 g fat, 9 mg chol, 265 mg sodium, 36 g carb, 4 g fiber, 17 g sugars, 5 g pro.*

**SAUSAGE-STUFFED
HONEYNUT SQUASH**
Recipe on page 287

PETITE BEEF
WELLINGTONS
Recipe on page 290

SIX PANTRY STAPLES AND A MANDOLINE TRANSFORM VERSATILE SPUDS INTO ONE EXCEPTIONAL SIDE DISH. EACH BUTTERY, ROSEMARY-SALT-DUSTED LAYER IS CRISPY ON THE TOP, TENDER ON THE BOTTOM.

PETITE BEEF WELLINGTONS

Photo on page 289.

Swap wrapping paper for pastry. Top slices of beef tenderloin with a mushroom-herb sauté, then wrap it in paper-thin prosciutto then in puff pastry.

HANDS-ON TIME 45 min.
TOTAL TIME 1 hr. 15 min.

1   2- to 2½-lb. center cut beef tenderloin roast, cut into eight 1-inch-thick slices
    Salt and black pepper
3   Tbsp. olive oil
2   Tbsp. butter
½   cup finely chopped shallots
3   portobello mushroom caps, stemmed and sliced (3½ cups)
½   cup chopped fresh thyme, oregano, basil, and/or flat-leaf parsley
1   17.3-oz. pkg. puff pastry sheets (2 sheets), thawed
¼   cup Dijon mustard
½   cup crumbled goat cheese (chèvre) or shredded sharp white cheddar cheese (2 oz.)
2   2-oz. pkg. very thinly sliced prosciutto (about 16 slices)
3   egg yolks
1   Tbsp. white balsamic vinegar
4   cups baby arugula

1. Preheat oven to 450°F. Line an extra-large baking sheet with foil. Season both sides of beef with salt and black pepper. In an extra-large skillet heat 1 Tbsp. oil over medium-high. Add half the fillets. Cook each side 1 minute or until browned (fillets will not be cooked through). Remove. Repeat with 1 Tbsp. oil and remaining four fillets.

2. In same skillet heat butter over medium. Add shallots; cook and stir 3 minutes. Add mushrooms; cook and stir 8 to 10 minutes or until tender and browned and liquid has evaporated. Remove from heat. Stir in herbs. Season with ¼ tsp. each salt and pepper. Cool slightly.

3. Cut each pastry sheet into quarters. On a lightly floured surface, roll each quarter to an 8-inch square. Cut ¼-inch-wide strips from each side of each square; set aside. Spread a 3-inch area in the center of each pastry square with mustard. Evenly divide mushroom mixture then cheese among squares, on mustard. Wrap each fillet with two slices prosciutto. Place a fillet on cheese. Beat together egg yolks and 1 Tbsp. water. Brush edges of pastry with egg mixture. Bring corners of pastry up and over fillet, pinching edges to seal. Place seam sides down on prepared baking sheet. Brush egg mixture over pastry. Use trimmed pastry strips to make bows. Attach pastry bows; brush bows with egg mixture.

4. Bake 14 minutes or until pastry is golden and an instant-read thermometer inserted into fillet registers 135°F. Let stand 5 minutes before serving. (Temperature will rise to 145°F.)

5. For salad: In a large bowl whisk together remaining 1 Tbsp. oil, the vinegar, and ¼ tsp. each salt and pepper. Toss in arugula; serve with beef Wellingtons. Makes 8 servings.

PER SERVING *576 cal, 37 g fat, 148 mg chol, 703 mg sodium, 29 g carb, 3 g fiber, 4 g sugars, 36 g pro.*

CRISPY POTATOES WITH ROSEMARY-SALT

To make one large casserole, arrange all the potatoes in a 2-quart baking dish and bake 1 hour 15 minutes or until potatoes are tender and golden.

HANDS-ON TIME 25 min.
TOTAL TIME 1 hr. 45 min.

2   Tbsp. sea salt flakes
2   Tbsp. fresh rosemary leaves
5   lb. russet potatoes, peeled
½   cup butter, melted
¼   cup olive oil
1   tsp. cracked black pepper

1. Preheat oven to 400°F. Grease eight 4- to 5-inch miniature loaf pans; arrange pans in a shallow baking pan.

2. In a small food processor combine salt and rosemary; process until rosemary is finely chopped.

3. Use a mandoline to thinly slice potatoes into a large bowl. Add butter, oil, 1 Tbsp. rosemary-salt, and the pepper. Toss to coat potato slices well.

4. Arrange potato slices upright to tightly fill pans. Drizzle any butter-oil mixture remaining in bowl over potatoes. Bake 70 to 75 minutes or until tender and golden with crisp edges. Let stand 10 minutes before serving. Serve with remaining rosemary-salt. Makes 8 servings.

PER SERVING *277 cal, 18 g fat, 31 mg chol, 971 mg sodium, 27 g carb, 2 g fiber, 1 g sugars, 3 g pro.*

CRISPY POTATOES
WITH ROSEMARY-SALT

SPARKLING CRANBERRY-
GINGER PANNA COTTA
Recipe on page 294

**APRICOT-CRANBERRY
PANETTONES**
Recipe on page 294

APRICOT-CRANBERRY PANETTONES

Photo on page 293.

To avoid any risk of a dry panettone, we made miniatures to decrease the chance of overbaking and brushed the tops with rum after baking.

HANDS-ON TIME 20 min.
TOTAL TIME 2 hr. 35 min.

⅔ cup warm milk (105°F to 115°F)
1 Tbsp. active dry yeast
2¾ cups all-purpose flour
½ cup butter, cut up and softened
½ cup granulated sugar
1 tsp. salt
2 eggs
2 egg yolks
1 orange (2 tsp. zest, 4 Tbsp. juice)
1½ tsp. vanilla
½ cup dried cranberries
½ cup dried apricots, chopped
½ cup chopped toasted almonds
2 Tbsp. chopped candied ginger
1 Tbsp. melted butter
3 Tbsp. rum, bourbon, or orange juice
2 cups powdered sugar

1. In a small bowl stir together milk and yeast until yeast is dissolved. Stir in 1 cup flour. Cover; let stand 20 minutes until foamy. Butter eight or nine popover pan cups or 6-oz. custard cups or ramekins.
2. In a food processor combine softened butter, sugar, salt, eggs, egg yolks, orange zest, 1 Tbsp. orange juice, and the vanilla. Pulse just until combined. Add yeast mixture; pulse until combined. Add 1½ cups flour. Pulse just until dough comes together. (Dough will be sticky.)
3. Flour work surface with remaining ¼ cup flour. Turn dough out onto flour. Sprinkle with dried fruits, nuts, and ginger. Using a pastry scraper or spatula, fold fruits, nuts, ginger, and flour into dough. If necessary, sprinkle lightly with additional flour. (Dough should remain sticky and will not yet hold a shape. Do not add too much flour or panettones will be dry.) Divide dough into eight or nine equal portions. Spoon into prepared popover cups. Cover with waxed paper. Let rise in a warm place until dough is almost at the rims (about 1 hour).

4. Preheat oven to 350°F. Brush dough with melted butter. Bake 20 minutes or until golden. (An instant-read thermometer inserted in centers should register 190°F.) Cool in cups 5 minutes. Transfer from cups to wire racks. Brush tops with rum while warm. Cool.
5. In a small bowl stir together powdered sugar and remaining 3 Tbsp. orange juice to spreading consistency. Spread each panettone with icing. If desired, sprinkle with additional dried fruit and/or candied ginger. Makes 8 or 9 servings.

PER SERVING *589 cal, 20 g fat, 129 mg chol, 426 mg sodium, 93 g carb, 3 g fiber, 55 g sugars, 10 g pro.*

SPARKLING CRANBERRY-GINGER PANNA COTTA

Photo on page 292.

Ginger beer originated in England as a fermented beverage, thus the word beer in its name. The beer has stronger ginger flavor than ginger ale, but you can substitute ginger ale if you like. Although most ginger beers are nonalcoholic, check the label for alcohol.

HANDS-ON TIME 20 min.
TOTAL TIME 2 hr. 15 min.

1¾ cups ginger beer
3 envelopes unflavored gelatin
⅓ cup water
⅓ cup sugar
1 cup fresh or frozen cranberries
1 Tbsp. grated fresh ginger
1 Tbsp. lime zest
¼ cup cold water
1¾ cups heavy cream
¼ cup sugar
1 cup plain Greek yogurt
1 vanilla bean, halved lengthwise and seeds scraped out; 1 tsp. vanilla bean paste; or 1 tsp. vanilla extract
 Sugared Cranberries and/or mint leaves (optional)

1. Place ¼ cup ginger beer in a medium bowl; sprinkle 1½ envelopes (about 1 Tbsp.) gelatin over ginger beer; let stand without stirring.
2. In a small saucepan combine ⅓ cup water and ⅓ cup sugar. Bring to boiling, stirring constantly to dissolve sugar. Stir in cranberries and fresh ginger. Return to boiling; reduce heat. Simmer gently,

uncovered, 2 to 3 minutes or until mixture is thickened and cranberries pop, stirring occasionally. Remove from heat. Stir in lime zest. Pour cranberry mixture over gelatin mixture. Stir until gelatin is completely dissolved. Stir in remaining ginger beer. Cool completely (about 30 minutes).
3. In another medium bowl place the ¼ cup cold water. Sprinkle 1½ envelopes (about 1 Tbsp.) gelatin over water.
4. In a small saucepan stir together heavy cream and ¼ cup sugar. Cook over medium heat until sugar is dissolved and mixture is steaming. Pour over water-gelatin mixture. Stir until gelatin is dissolved. Whisk in yogurt and vanilla seeds; set aside to cool.
5. Set eight 4- to 5-oz. glasses on a tray. Carefully spoon about 2 Tbsp. cranberry-gelatin mixture* into each glass. Chill 30 minutes or until set. Spoon about 2 Tbsp. yogurt mixture* over cranberry mixture in each glass. Chill 10 to 20 minutes or until set. Continue layering and chilling to use remaining cranberry and vanilla mixtures. Chill, covered, up to 24 hours. If desired, garnish with Sugared Cranberries and mint leaves. Makes 8 servings.

*Tip Keep unused portions of both cranberry and yogurt mixtures covered and at room temperature while pouring and chilling layers in the glasses.

PER SERVING *328 cal, 20 g fat, 63 mg chol, 27 mg sodium, 32 g carb, 1 g fiber, 30 g sugars, 7 g pro.*

Sugared Cranberries Toss ½ cup frozen cranberries with 2 Tbsp. sugar. Spread on a paper towel-lined tray to thaw. As cranberries thaw, add additional sugar to coat (1 to 2 Tbsp. additional).

BRUNCH *for a* CROWD

The best thing since sliced bread? This update on a classic egg bake—cooked in a hollowed-out loaf of bread. Simply slice and serve.

EGG AND SAUSAGE BREAD BAKES

Save the bread removed from each loaf for croutons, an egg strata, or stuffing. For a vegetarian version, replace the sausage with 1 cup cooked veggies, such as sliced mushrooms and/or broccoli florets.

HANDS-ON TIME 30 min.
TOTAL TIME 1 hr. 10 min.

- 2   14×4-inch unsliced loaves Italian or French bread
- 8   oz. uncooked sweet or mild Italian sausage, casings removed
- ¾   cup chopped bell pepper
- ½   cup sliced green onions
- 10   eggs, lightly beaten
- ⅔   cup heavy cream or half-and-half
- ¼   cup chopped fresh basil
- ½   tsp. salt
- 1½   cups shredded Fontina, mozzarella, or provolone cheese (6 oz.)

1. Preheat oven to 350°F. Line a large baking sheet with parchment paper. With a serrated knife, cut a wedge into tops of loaves. With a spoon or fingers, hollow out the center of each loaf. Place bread shells on prepared baking sheet.
2. For filling, in a 10-inch skillet cook sausage and bell pepper over medium heat 8 minutes or until sausage is browned and pepper is just tender, stirring in green onions the last 1 minute. Drain off fat.
3. In a large bowl combine eggs, cream, basil, and salt. Stir in sausage mixture and 1 cup cheese.
4. Pour filling into bread shells. Sprinkle with remaining cheese. Bake 35 to 40 minutes or until eggs are set (at least 160°F). Let stand 5 minutes before slicing. If desired, sprinkle with additional basil. Makes 10 servings.
PER SERVING *490 cal, 23 g fat, 245 mg chol, 977 mg sodium, 45 g carb, 1 g sugars, 20 g pro.*

RECIPE INDEX

METRIC INFORMATION

PRODUCT DIFFERENCES

Most of the ingredients called for in the recipes in this book are available in most countries. However, some are known by different names. Here are some common American ingredients and their possible counterparts:

SUGAR (white) is granulated, fine granulated, or castor sugar.

POWDERED SUGAR is icing sugar.

ALL-PURPOSE FLOUR is enriched, bleached or unbleached white household flour. When self-rising flour is used in place of all-purpose flour in a recipe that calls for leavening, omit the leavening agent (baking soda or baking powder) and salt.

LIGHT-COLOR CORN SYRUP is golden syrup.

CORNSTARCH is cornflour.

BAKING SODA is bicarbonate of soda.

VANILLA OR VANILLA EXTRACT is vanilla essence.

GREEN, RED, OR YELLOW SWEET PEPPERS are capsicums or bell peppers.

GOLDEN RAISINS are sultanas.

SHORTENING is solid vegetable oil (substitute Copha or lard).

MEASUREMENT ABBREVIATIONS

MEASUREMENT	ABBREVIATIONS
fluid ounce	fl. oz.
gallon	gal.
gram	g
liter	L
milliliter	ml
ounce	oz.
package	pkg.
pint	pt.

COMMON WEIGHT EQUIVALENTS

IMPERIAL / U.S.	METRIC
½ ounce	14.18 g
1 ounce	28.35 g
4 ounces (¼ pound)	113.4 g
8 ounces (½ pound)	226.8 g
16 ounces (1 pound)	453.6 g
1¼ pounds	567 g
1½ pounds	680.4 g
2 pounds	907.2 g

OVEN TEMPERATURE EQUIVALENTS*

FAHRENHEIT SETTING	CELSIUS SETTING
300°F	150°C
325°F	160°C
350°F	180°C
375°F	190°C
400°F	200°C
425°F	220°C
450°F	230°C
475°F	240°C
500°F	260°C
Broil	Broil

*For convection or forced air ovens (gas or electric), lower the temperature setting 25°F/10°C when cooking at all heat levels.

APPROXIMATE STANDARD METRIC EQUIVALENTS

MEASUREMENT	OUNCES	METRIC
⅛ tsp.		0.5 ml
¼ tsp.		1 ml
½ tsp.		2.5 ml
1 tsp.		5 ml
1 Tbsp.		15 ml
2 Tbsp.	1 fl. oz.	30 ml
¼ cup	2 fl. oz.	60 ml
⅓ cup	3 fl. oz.	80 ml
½ cup	4 fl. oz.	120 ml
⅔ cup	5 fl. oz.	160 ml
¾ cup	6 fl. oz.	180 ml
1 cup	8 fl. oz.	240 ml
2 cups	16 fl. oz. (1 pt.)	480 ml
1 qt.	64 fl. oz. (2 pt.)	0.95 L

CONVERTING TO METRIC

centimeters to inches	divide centimeters by 2.54
cups to liters	multiply cups by 0.236
cups to milliliters	multiply cups by 236.59
gallons to liters	multiply gallons by 3.785
grams to ounces	divide grams by 28.35
inches to centimeters	multiply inches by 2.54
kilograms to pounds	divide kilograms by 0.454
liters to cups	divide liters by 0.236
liters to gallons	divide liters by 3.785
liters to pints	divide liters by 0.473
liters to quarts	divide liters by 0.946
milliliters to cups	divide milliliters by 236.59
milliliters to fluid ounces	divide milliliters by 29.57
milliliters to tablespoons	divide milliliters by 14.79
milliliters to teaspoons	divide milliliters by 4.93
ounces to grams	multiply ounces by 28.35
ounces to milliliters	multiply ounces by 29.57
pints to liters	multiply pints by 0.473
pounds to kilograms	multiply pounds by 0.454
quarts to liters	multiply quarts by 0.946
tablespoons to milliliters	multiply tablespoons by 14.79
teaspoons to milliliters	multiply teaspoons by 4.93